Experiencing Choral Music

MIXED

Developed by

New York, New York Columbus, Ohio Chicago, Illinois Peoria, Illinois Woodland Hills, California

A portion of the sales of this material goes to support music education programs through programs of MENC–The National Association for Music Education.

The McGraw·Hill Companies

Printed in the United States of America.

Send all inquiries to:
Glencoe/McGraw-Hill
21600 Oxnard Street, Suite 500
Woodland Hills, CA 91367

ISBN 0-07-861108-3 (Student Edition)
ISBN 0-07-861109-1 (Teacher Wraparound Edition)

1 2 3 4 5 6 7 8 9 045 09 08 07 06 05 04

Table of Contents

SECTION		National Standards								
Selection	**Concepts and Skills**	**1**	**2**	**3**	**4**	**5**	**6**	**7**	**8**	**9**
LESSONS										
Rise Up This Day To Celebrate	Describe and perform music from the Classical period; sing phrases using repetition and contrast; identify cadences.	a, b, c, d	a			c, e	a, b	a, b		b
Down In The Valley	Read 3/4 meter; demonstrate accurate intonation; read and write in key of E♭ major.	a, b, c, d, e	a, c	a	b	a, b, c, d, e	a, b, c	a, b, c		
Elijah Rock!	Perform syncopated rhythms; African American spiritual.	c, d, e	c, d			a, c	a, b	a, b	b	a, c
Spotlight On Diction	Performance techniques—diction.	b							b	
America The Beautiful	Demonstrate musical artistry; describe suspension; relationship of other fine arts and music.	b, d, e		a			a, b, c	b	a, b	
Spotlight On Posture	Performance techniques—posture.	b								
Cantemos Alleluia	ABA form; parallel sixths; interpret text expressively.	a, b, c	b		b	a	a, b, c	a, b		a
Winter Storm	Relate music to other subjects; describe chords; syncopated rhythmic patterns.	a, d, e			a	a, c	a, c	a, b, c	a	a, b
Spotlight On Vowels	Performance techniques—vowels.	b								
Shalom Aleichem	Articulation styles; key of A minor; music of the Jewish culture.	a, b, c d, e				a, b, c, d, e	a, b, c	a, b	a	a, b
Spotlight On Arranging	Arrange melodic and rhythmic phrases.				b					
Calypso Gloria	Sing in Latin using tall, pure vowels; calypso rhythms; create rhythmic phrases.	a, b, c, d			a		a	b	a, b	a, d
Spotlight On Pitch Matching	Accurate intonation.	b								
Innsbruck, ich muss dich lassen	Describe and perform music of the Renaissance period; read and write music in 3/2 and 2/2 meter.	b, c	a		a	b	b		b	a, b
Spotlight On Breath Management	Sing accurately with good breath control.	b								
Come Joyfully Sing	Describe and perform music of the Baroque period; dynamics; read and conduct in 3/4.	b				a	b		a	b
Bless The Lord, O My Soul	Read and write syncopated patterns; read music in key of E♭ major; describe and perform music of the Romantic period.	a, b, c			a	a		b		
Spotlight On Concert Etiquette	Apply concert etiquette in a variety of settings.							a, b		
Sing To The Lord	Mixed meter; identify musical symbols; describe and perform music of the Contemporary period.	b, c			b	a, b		a		

SECTION		National Standards								
Selection	**Concepts and Skills**	**1**	**2**	**3**	**4**	**5**	**6**	**7**	**8**	**9**
MUSIC & HISTORY										
Renaissance, Baroque, Classical, Romantic and Contemporary periods.	Describe, listen to and analyze music from the five main historical periods.						a, b, c, d, e, f		a, b, c, d, e	a, c, d, e
CHORAL LIBRARY										
Spotlight On Careers in Music	Describe music-related vocations and avocations.									b
¡Aleluya, Amén!	Mixed meter; music from the Dominican Republic.	a, b, c, d, e			b		a, b, c	b	a	a, b
Bound For The Rio Grande	Identify melody line; read music in 6/8; music from American heritage.	a, b, c, d, e				a, b, c	a, c	a, b	a, b	a, b, c
Spotlight On Gospel Music	Classify aurally-presented music representing diverse styles.	a, b, c						a, b		
City Called Heaven	Read music in 9/8; identify tenuto markings; gospel style music.	a, b, c, d		b, c		a, c		b		a, c
Duond Akuru	Syncopation; diction in a foreign language; African style music.	a, b, c, d				a, c	b, c	a, b		a
I Know Where I'm Goin'	Perform two-part music; sing phrases expressively; music from Irish culture.	a, b, c, d				a, c		a	a	a, c
Spotlight On Improvisation	Create rhythmic and melodic phrases. Improvise melodic embellishments.	a, b, c		a, b, c						
Kyrie	Accurate pitch matching; ABA form and coda; music from the Contemporary period.	a, b, c, d				a	c	a, b		b
Lakota Wiyanki	Sing with proper vowel sounds; Native American music.	a, b, c			a			a, b	b	a, b, c
Miserere Nobis	Sing with pure Latin vowels; understanding the Latin text.	a, b, d			a		c	a, b	b	
Spotlight On Musical Theater	Relate music to history; relationship between other fine arts and music; evaluate musical performances.							b	a	b
The River Sleeps Beneath The Sky	Dotted rhythms; relate music to poetry.	a, b, d			a	a, c, d		b	b	
Set Me As A Seal	Identify compositional techniques; read and write music in 4/4 meter; breath management.	a, b, c, d			a	a, b, c, d	c			
Sing Out This Maytime	ABA form; perform independently with accurate rhythm; varying dynamics.	b			a	c, d	a, b	a, b		b
The Wells Fargo Wagon	Proper diction; syncopated rhythmic patterns; musical theater genre.	a, b, c, d			a	a, d	c	b	b	

National Standards Middle School Grades 5–8

The National Standards for Music Education were developed by the Music Educators National Conference. Reprinted by permission.

MUSIC

The period represented by grades 5–8 is especially critical in students' musical development. The music they perform or study often becomes an integral part of their personal musical repertoire. Composing and improvising provide students with unique insight into the form and structure of music and at the same time help them develop their creativity. Broad experience with a variety of music is necessary if students are to make informed musical judgments. Similarly, this breadth of background enables them to begin to understand the connections and relationships between music and other disciplines. By understanding the cultural and historical forces that shape social attitudes and behaviors, students are better prepared to live and work in communities that are increasingly multicultural. The role that music will play in students' lives depends in large measure on the level of skills they achieve in creating, performing and listening to music.

Every course in music, including performance courses, should provide instruction in creating, performing, listening to and analyzing music, in addition to focusing on its specific subject matter.

1. **Content Standard:** Singing, alone and with others, a varied repertoire of music
Achievement Standard:
Students
    a. sing accurately and with good breath control throughout their singing ranges, alone and in small and large ensembles.
    b. sing with *expression and *technical accuracy a repertoire of vocal literature with a *level of difficulty of 2, on a scale of 1 to 6, including some songs performed from memory.
    c. sing music representing diverse *genres and cultures, with expression appropriate for the work being performed.
    d. sing music written in two and three parts.

Students who participate in a choral ensemble
    e. sing with expression and technical accuracy a varied repertoire of vocal literature with a level of difficulty of 3, on a scale of 1 to 6, including some songs performed from memory.

2. **Content Standard:** Performing on instruments, alone and with others, a varied repertoire of music
Achievement Standard:
Students
    a. perform on at least one instrument[1] accurately and independently, alone and in small and large ensembles, with good posture, good playing position and good breath, bow or stick control.
    b. perform with expression and technical accuracy on at least one string, wind, percussion or *classroom instrument a repertoire of instrumental literature with a level of difficulty of 2, on a scale of 1 to 6.
    c. perform music representing diverse genres and cultures, with expression appropriate for the work being performed.
    d. play by ear simple melodies on a melodic instrument and simple accompaniments on a harmonic instrument.

Students who participate in an instrumental ensemble or class
    e. perform with expression and technical accuracy a varied repertoire of instrumental literature with a level of difficulty of 3, on a scale of 1 to 6, including some solos performed from memory.

3. **Content Standard:** Improvising melodies, variations and accompaniments
Achievement Standard:
Students
    a. improvise simple harmonic accompaniments.
    b. improvise melodic embellishments and simple rhythmic and melodic variations on given pentatonic melodies and melodies in major keys.
    c. improvise short melodies, unaccompanied and over given rhythmic accompaniments, each in a consistent *style, *meter and *tonality.

4. **Content Standard:** Composing and arranging music within specified guidelines
Achievement Standard:
Students
    a. compose short pieces within specified guidelines,[2] demonstrating how the elements of music are used to achieve unity and variety, tension and release, and balance.
    b. arrange simple pieces for voices or instruments other than those for which the pieces were written.

c. use a variety of traditional and nontraditional sound sources and electronic media when composing and arranging.

5. **Content Standard:** Reading and notating music
Achievement Standard:
Students
a. read whole, half, quarter, eighth, sixteenth and dotted notes and rests in 2/4, 3/4, 4/4, 6/8, 3/8 and *alla breve meter signatures.
b. read at sight simple melodies in both the treble and bass clefs.
c. identify and define standard notation symbols for pitch, rhythm, *dynamics, tempo, *articulation and expression.
d. use standard notation to record their musical ideas and the musical ideas of others.

6. **Content Standard:** Listening to, analyzing and describing music
Achievement Standard:
Students
a. describe specific music events[3] in a given aural example, using appropriate terminology.
b. analyze the uses of *elements of music in aural examples representing diverse genres and cultures.
c. demonstrate knowledge of the basic principles of meter, rhythm, tonality, intervals, chords and harmonic progressions in the analyses of music.

7. **Content Standard:** Evaluating music and music performances
Achievement Standard:
Students
a. develop criteria for evaluating the quality and effectiveness of music performances and compositions and apply criteria in their personal listening and performing.
b. evaluate the quality and effectiveness of their own and others' performances, compositions, arrangements and improvisations by applying specific criteria appropriate for the style of the music and offer constructive suggestions for improvement.

8. **Content Standard:** Understanding relationships between music, the other arts and disciplines outside the arts
Achievement Standard:
Students
a. compare in two or more arts how the characteristic materials of each art (that is, sound in music, visual stimuli in visual arts, movement in dance, human interrelationships in theatre) can be used to transform similar events, scenes, emotions or ideas into works of art.
b. describe ways in which the principles and subject matter of other disciplines taught in the school are interrelated with those of music.[4]

9. **Content Standard:** Understanding music in relation to history and culture
Achievement Standard:
Students
a. describe distinguishing characteristics of representative music genres and styles from a variety of cultures.
b. classify by genre and style (and, if applicable, by historical period, composer and title) a varied body of exemplary (that is, high-quality and characteristic) musical works and explain the characteristics that cause each work to be considered exemplary.
c. compare, in several cultures of the world, functions music serves, roles of musicians[5] and conditions under which music is typically performed.

Terms identified by an asterisk (*) are explained further in the glossary of *National Standards for Arts Education,* published by Music Educators National Conference, © 1994.

1. E.g., band or orchestra instrument, *fretted instrument, electronic instrument
2. E.g., a particular style, form, instrumentation, compositional technique
3. E.g., entry of oboe, change of meter, return of refrain
4. E.g., language arts: issues to be considered in setting texts to music; mathematics: frequency ratios of intervals; sciences: the human hearing process and hazards to hearing; social studies: historical and social events and movements chronicled in or influenced by musical works
5. E.g., lead guitarist in a rock band, composer of jingles for commercials, singer in Peking opera

INTRODUCTION

Experiencing Choral Music is a four-level series designed to build music literacy and promote vocal development for all students and voice categories in grades 6–12. The series is a multitextbook program supported with print materials and audio listening components that enable students to develop music skills and conceptual understanding, and provides teachers with a flexible, integrated program.

Experiencing Choral Music presents beginning, intermediate, proficient and advanced literature for various voice groupings: unison, 2-part/3-part, mixed, treble, and tenor/bass. All selections in *Experiencing Choral Music* are recorded three ways: full performance with voices, accompaniment only, and individual part-dominant recordings. The program also includes companion *Sight-Singing* textbooks that present a sequential approach to musical literacy and is directly correlated to the literature books. This comprehensive choral music program includes student texts, teacher wraparound editions, teacher resource binders, and rehearsal and performance audio recordings designed to enhance student learning while reducing teacher preparation time.

Experiencing Choral Music is a curriculum that provides your students with a meaningful, motivating choral music experience, and will help you and your students build choral music knowledge and skills. For example:

Experiencing Choral Music connects to . . . the National Standards

The National Standards are correlated to each lesson for quick-and-easy identification and reference. The performance standards related to singing and reading notations are explicit in each lesson, and by using the extension activities, teachers can connect the musical elements through improvisation and composition. Analysis and evaluation are an active and consistent component of lessons throughout the series. Additional student activities connect the lessons to the other arts, as well as provide a consistent historical and cultural context.

Experiencing Choral Music connects to . . . Skill Development

Through the Links to Learning exercises, students build vocal, theory and artistic expression skills necessary to perform each piece. Rhythmic, melodic and articulation skills are developed as needed for expressive interpretation. Students are encouraged to develop listening skills and use their perceptions to improve individual and group performance.

Experiencing Choral Music connects to . . . Creative Expression/Performance

Student performance provides opportunities for young musicians to demonstrate musical growth, to gain personal satisfaction from achievement, and to experience the joy of music making. To help develop skills, *Experiencing Choral Music* provides vocal, theory and artistic expression exercises which help prepare students to successfully sing each piece. Conceptual understanding is built throughout the teaching/learning sequence, as the performance is prepared.

Experiencing Choral Music connects to . . . Historical and Cultural Heritage

Experiencing Choral Music provides a vehicle to help students gain knowledge and understanding of historical and cultural contexts across the curriculum. These concepts are presented in the Getting Started section of each lesson. Also, historical connections through art, history, timelines, performance practices and listening examples are made in Music & History.

Experiencing Choral Music connects to . . . the Arts and Other Curriculum Areas

Choral music provides a rich opportunity to connect the musical experience to other art disciplines (dance, visual arts, theater), and to enhance the learning in other subject areas.

PROGRAM PHILOSOPHY

Responding to New Trends in Choral Music Education

Experiencing Choral Music is consistent with current educational philosophy that suggests:

- Performance is a product that should be the end result of a sound educational process, building conceptual understanding and skills as the performance is prepared.
- Students are motivated through materials and concepts that are connected to their own lives and interests, and should be exposed to high-quality, challenging musical literature.
- Students learn best when they are active participants in their learning, and when they clearly understand and help set the goals and objectives of the learning outcome.
- Students understand concepts better when they have background information and skills that allow them to place their learning into a larger context.
- Students need to actively manipulate musical concepts and skills through improvisation and/or composition in order to fully assimilate and understand them.

- Students improve when they receive fair, honest and meaningful feedback on their success and failures.
- Students should be encouraged to assess themselves individually and as a group, learning to receive and process constructive criticism, leading to independent self-correction and decision making.

Scope and Depth of Music Literature

Most students are capable of performing more difficult material than they can sight-read. Therefore, the literature in *Experiencing Choral Music* is drawn from many periods and styles of music. The wide range of composers and publishers ensures variety, and allows for various skills and concepts to be developed as each new piece is encountered. The high standards set in *Experiencing Choral Music* provide selections that are inherently powerful and exciting for students. The *Sight-Singing* textbooks provide additional literature for sight-singing purposes. Written in a sequential manner, this component will present students with a developmental process for learning to read music.

Addressing the National Standards

The National Standards for Arts Education, published in 1994, launched a national effort to bring a new vision to arts education for all students. The National Standards provide a framework for achievement in music, with outcomes suggested for grades 4, 8, and 12. *Experiencing Choral Music* addresses the National Standards in several ways.

The most obvious and predominant National Standards addressed in choral ensemble are: (1) singing and (5) reading and notation. However, good performance requires musical understanding that only occurs when all aspects of musical experience are incorporated. The preparation of vocal performance is enriched and deepened by involvement in all nine of the National Standards.

As you teach with *Experiencing Choral Music*, there will be frequent opportunities to deepen or extend student learning through: (2) playing through creating accompaniments, (3) improvisation, (4) composition and arranging, (6) analyzing, (7) assessing, (8) linking with other arts and other academic disciplines, and (9) understanding historical and cultural contexts. The National Standards identified for each lesson and the Extension activities provided in the Teacher Wraparound Edition help you become aware of the National Standards, and the depth of learning that will occur as you implement this choral music program.

Promoting Music Literacy

Experiencing Choral Music promotes music literacy throughout the lessons. Literacy includes oral and aural aspects of music communication—reading, writing, singing and listening. Each lesson begins with Getting Started that (1) connects the song to the student, and (2) frames the historical and cultural aspect of the music to be performed. From there the students are directed to the Links to Learning that is divided into three categories: Vocal, Theory and Artistic Expression. These exercises emphasize reading development and artistic expression. These may be rhythmic, melodic, harmonic or a combination thereof; and are directly related to the objectives of the lesson. The exercises lead directly into the musical selection. Students are encouraged to sight-sing in every lesson. Sight-singing is approached as a challenge and a means to musical independence for the student.

Literacy goes beyond simply reading pitch and rhythm, extending to the expressive elements of music and appropriate interpretation. Through Artistic Expression, students will be asked to explore interpretive aspects of music making, and are encouraged to suggest their own ideas for phrasing, dynamics, and so on. Through careful listening and constructive critique of their own work, they will gradually become more discriminating about the quality of performance and the impact of that performance on the audience.

Including Authentic Student Assessment

The assessment in *Experiencing Choral Music* is systematic, objective and authentic. There is ongoing informal assessment by teacher observation throughout the lessons. The text is written as a series of action steps for the student, so there are many opportunities for the director to hear and see the level of accomplishment.

Students will find objectives at the beginning of each lesson, and evaluation activities at the end. The Evaluation questions and activities are always related directly to the lesson objectives, and allow students to demonstrate their understanding. By answering the questions, and demonstrating as suggested, students are involved in *self-assessment*. Many times students are involved in their own assessment, constructing rubrics or critiquing their performance to determine what level of success has been achieved, and identifying the next challenge.

The *Teacher Wraparound Edition* includes lesson objectives, and each lesson is taught so the concepts and skills are experienced, labeled, practiced and reinforced, then measured through *formal assessment*. These assessment tasks match the lesson objectives, allowing students to demonstrate understanding of concepts and skills through performance, composition, or writing. Students are frequently required to produce audio- or videotapes. This authentic assessment keeps testing of rote learning to a minimum, and allows measurement of higher-level application of knowledge and skills. A portfolio can be constructed for individual students, groups, or the whole ensemble, demonstrating growth over time.

Connecting the Arts and Other Curriculum Areas

Lessons in *Experiencing Choral Music* integrate many appropriate aspects of musical endeavor into the preparation of a piece. Students compose, improvise, conduct, read, write, sing, play, listen/analyze and assess on an ongoing basis that builds understanding, as well as high standards. In this way, the many aspects of music are integrated for deeper learning.

As one of the arts, music can be linked to other arts through similarities and differences. Throughout the text, and particularly in the historical section, music is compared and contrasted with other arts to determine aspects of confluence and the unique features of each art.

As one way of knowing about the world, music can be compared with concepts and skills from other disciplines as seemingly different as science or mathematics. The integrations between music and other disciplines are kept at the conceptual level, to maintain the integrity of both music and the other subjects. For example, mathematical sets of 2, 3, 4, 5 and 6 might be explored as a link to pieces with changing meter; or the text of a piece might become a starting point for exploration of tone painting. In Music & History, a time line connects music to social studies, and a list of authors for each period provides a link to language and literature.

Providing a Variety of Student Activities

Experiencing Choral Music begins with the choral experience, and builds understanding through active participation in a range of activities including singing, playing, improvising, composing, arranging, moving, writing, listening, analyzing, assessing and connecting to cultures, periods or disciplines. Lessons are written with the heading "Direct students to . . ." so there is always an emphasis on learning by doing. In this way the teacher becomes a guide and places the responsibility for learning on the student. When students are engaged in meaningful and challenging activity, they are more likely to learn.

Fitting Your Classroom Needs

With *Experiencing Choral Music*, your students will be clear about purpose and direction, have multiple routes to success, and be involved in their own learning. The lessons will guide you and your students to share in the excitement of music making, and help you to grow together. The lessons are written the way you teach, and allow you to maintain and strengthen your routines, while adding flexibility, variety and depth.

ORGANIZATION AND FLEXIBILITY

Each *Experiencing Choral Music* text is divided into the following sections:

- Lessons
- Music & History
- Choral Library

Lessons

The Lessons are designed to be taught over a period of time. They are divided into three categories: Beginning of the Year, Mid-Winter, and Concert/Festival. Each lesson is developed around a piece of authentic and quality music literature. The lesson includes background information, vocal examples, sight-reading and rhythmic or melodic drills, all of which are directly related to preparation of the piece. Objectives are clearly stated, and a motivational opening activity or discussion is provided. The Teacher Wraparound Edition outlines a carefully sequenced approach to the piece and clear assessment opportunities to document achievement and growth.

Music & History

Music & History provides narrative and listening experiences for each of the five main historical periods. A *narrative lesson* provides a brief and interesting exposition of the main characteristics of the period outlining the achievements and new styles that emerged. A time line guides the student to place the musical characteristics into a larger historical and cultural context. The listening lesson includes both vocal and instrumental *listening selections* from the period, with a guide to student listening. A listing of the historical pieces to be sung from the period are cross-referenced from the Music & History divider page. Combined, these components give historical context of the period across the arts, then apply the context to musical literature.

Choral Library

The Choral Library provides the same comprehensive student lesson featured in the Lessons. The additional literature features multicultural selections, patriotic and seasonal selections, American folk music, African American spirituals, Broadway show tunes, and light concert pieces that can be used to enhance the repertoire of your choral music performance.

Overview of Lesson Objectives

Each lesson has objectives that emphasize and build conceptual understanding and skills across the lessons. The objectives in this book are:

LESSON OBJECTIVES	
Title	**Objective**
Rise Up This Day To Celebrate	• Describe and perform music from the Classical period. • Sing phrases using repetition and contrast. • Identify and perform cadences.
Down In The Valley	• Read and perform music in 3/4 meter. • Define and demonstrate accurate intonation. • Read, write and perform music in the key of E♭ major.
Elijah Rock!	• Read and perform syncopated rhythms. • Perform music that represents the African American spiritual.
America The Beautiful	• Demonstrate musical artistry and appropriate performance practice. • Describe suspension using music terminology. • Identify the relationships between the other fine arts and those of music.
Cantemos Alleluia	• Identify and perform music in ABA form. • Describe and perform parallel sixths. • Interpret the text in an expressive manner.
Winter Storm	• Relate music to other subjects. • Use standard terminology to describe a chord. • Read and perform syncopated rhythmic patterns.
Shalom Aleichem	• Sing music using various articulation styles. • Write and perform music in the key of A minor. • Perform music that represents the Jewish culture.
Calypso Gloria	• Sing in Latin using tall, pure vowel sounds. • Perform music that contains calypso rhythms. • Create and perform rhythmic phrases.
Innsbruck, ich muss dich lassen	• Describe and perform music from the Renaissance period. • Read and write music in 3/2 meter and 2/2 meter.
Come Joyfully Sing	• Describe and perform music from the Baroque period. • Perform music with accurate dynamics. • Read and conduct rhythmic patterns in 3/4 meter.
Bless The Lord, O My Soul	• Read, write and perform rhythmic patterns with syncopation. • Read and perform music in the key of E♭ major. • Describe and perform music from the Romantic period.
Sing To The Lord	• Perform music in mixed meter. • Identify musical symbols. • Perform music that represents the Contemporary period.
¡Aleluya, Amén!	• Perform music in mixed meter. • Perform music representing the Dominican Republic culture.

LESSON OBJECTIVES	
Title	**Objective**
Bound For The Rio Grande	• Identify the melody line in music. • Read and perform music in 6/8 meter. • Perform music in the character in which it was written.
City Called Heaven	• Read and perform music in 9/8 meter. • Identify and perform tenuto markings. • Perform music that represents the gospel style.
Duond Akuru	• Read and perform rhythmic patterns that contain syncopation. • Sing in a foreign language using proper diction (Duoluo). • Perform music written in the style of African music.
I Know Where I'm Goin'	• Perform two-part music. • Sing phrases expressively. • Perform music representing the Irish culture.
Kyrie	• Perform music with accurate pitch matching. • Identify ABA form and coda. • Perform music that represents the Contemporary period.
Lakota Wiyanki	• Sing with proper vowel sounds. • Perform music that represents the Native American culture.
Miserere Nobis	• Sing with pure Latin vowels. • Perform music with understanding of the Latin text.
The River Sleeps Beneath The Sky	• Demonstrate musical artistry. • Read and perform dotted rhythms. • Relate music to poetry.
Set Me As A Seal	• Identify compositional techniques found in the music. • Read and write music in 4/4 meter. • Demonstrate musical artistry through the use of proper breath management.
Sing Out This Maytime	• Identify music forms found in music (ABA). • Perform independently with accurate rhythm. • Perform music with varying dynamics.
The Wells Fargo Wagon	• Demonstrate musical artistry through the use of proper diction. • Read and perform syncopated rhythmic patterns. • Perform music that represents the musical theater genre.

STUDENT TEXT

The comprehensive student lessons are structured as follows:

- **FOCUS . . .** tells the student the main concepts and skills addressed in the lesson. By having only a few main goals, students and teacher will keep focused on these objectives as work progresses.

- **VOCABULARY . . .** gives the student an opportunity to build a musical vocabulary essential for clarity of thought in communicating about music to others.

- **LINKS TO LEARNING**

  Vocal . . . allows the student to explore the melodic and vocal skills that are directly related to some aspect of the upcoming musical selection. Also includes melodic sight-singing examples.

  Theory . . . builds rhythmic, theory and basic reading skills through exercises that are directly related to the musical selection about to be learned. Through sight-reading practice every day, students gain confidence and skills to become independent readers.

  Artistic Expression . . . provides interpretive aspects of music making, such as phrasing, dynamics, stylistic performance practices, movement, and artistic expression through drama, writing and the visual arts. Through interest and active participation, the student is then led logically into the piece.

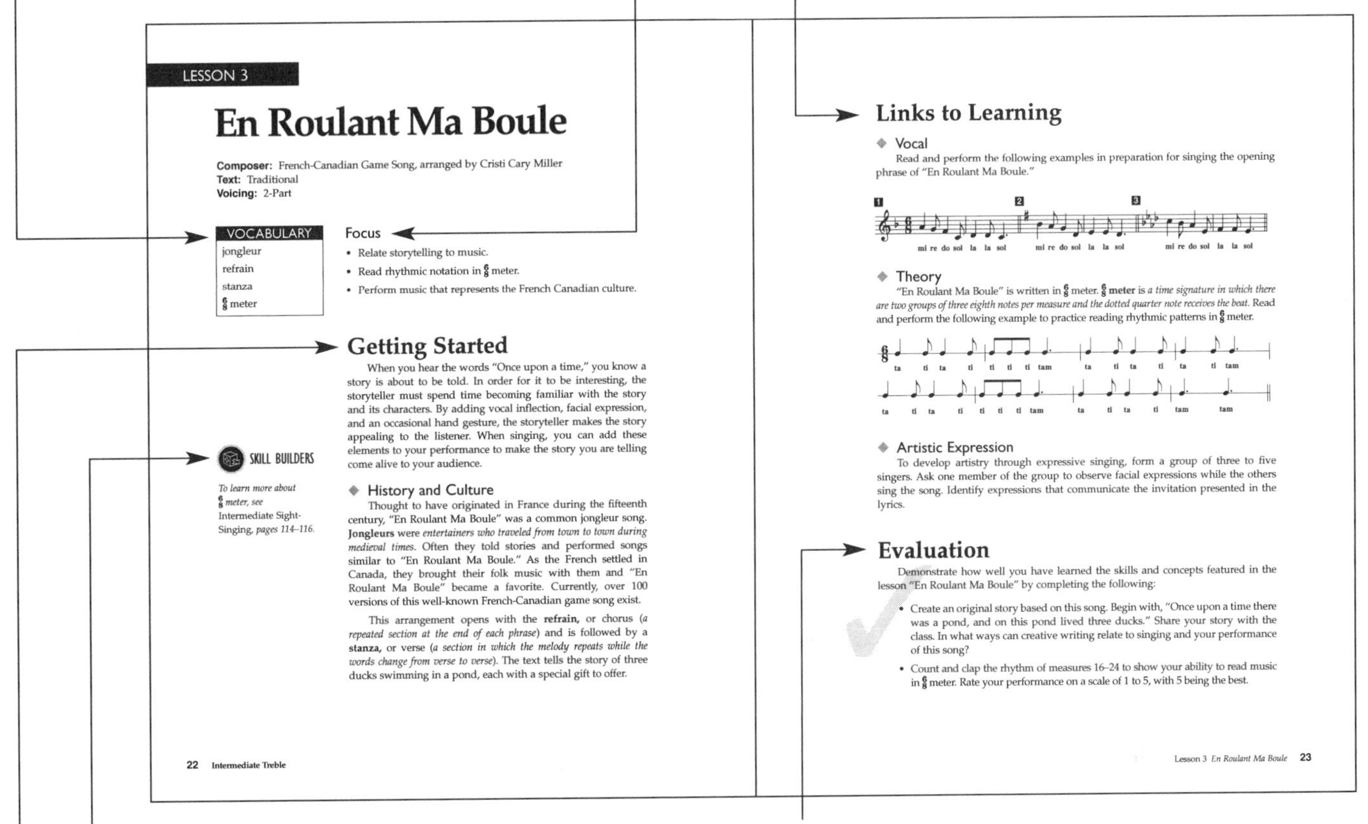

LESSON 3

En Roulant Ma Boule

Composer: French-Canadian Game Song, arranged by Cristi Cary Miller
Text: Traditional
Voicing: 2-Part

VOCABULARY
jongleur
refrain
stanza
$\frac{6}{8}$ meter

Focus

- Relate storytelling to music.
- Read rhythmic notation in $\frac{6}{8}$ meter.
- Perform music that represents the French Canadian culture.

Getting Started

When you hear the words "Once upon a time," you know a story is about to be told. In order for it to be interesting, the storyteller must spend time becoming familiar with the story and its characters. By adding vocal inflection, facial expression, and an occasional hand gesture, the storyteller makes the story appealing to the listener. When singing, you can add these elements to your performance to make the story you are telling come alive to your audience.

SKILL BUILDERS

To learn more about $\frac{6}{8}$ meter, see Intermediate Sight-Singing, *pages 114–116.*

History and Culture

Thought to have originated in France during the fifteenth century, "En Roulant Ma Boule" was a common jongleur song. **Jongleurs** were *entertainers who traveled from town to town during medieval times*. Often they told stories and performed songs similar to "En Roulant Ma Boule." As the French settled in Canada, they brought their folk music with them and "En Roulant Ma Boule" became a favorite. Currently, over 100 versions of this well-known French-Canadian game song exist.

This arrangement opens with the **refrain,** or chorus (*a repeated section at the end of each phrase*) and is followed by a **stanza,** or verse (*a section in which the melody repeats while the words change from verse to verse*). The text tells the story of three ducks swimming in a pond, each with a special gift to offer.

22 Intermediate Treble

Links to Learning

Vocal

Read and perform the following examples in preparation for singing the opening phrase of "En Roulant Ma Boule."

Theory

"En Roulant Ma Boule" is written in $\frac{6}{8}$ meter. $\frac{6}{8}$ **meter** is *a time signature in which there are two groups of three eighth notes per measure and the dotted quarter note receives the beat.* Read and perform the following example to practice reading rhythmic patterns in $\frac{6}{8}$ meter.

Artistic Expression

To develop artistry through expressive singing, form a group of three to five singers. Ask one member of the group to observe facial expressions while the others sing the song. Identify expressions that communicate the invitation presented in the lyrics.

Evaluation

Demonstrate how well you have learned the skills and concepts featured in the lesson "En Roulant Ma Boule" by completing the following:

- Create an original story based on this song. Begin with, "Once upon a time there was a pond, and on this pond lived three ducks." Share your story with the class. In what ways can creative writing relate to singing and your performance of this song?
- Count and clap the rhythm of measures 16–24 to show your ability to read music in $\frac{6}{8}$ meter. Rate your performance on a scale of 1 to 5, with 5 being the best.

Lesson 3 *En Roulant Ma Boule* 23

- **SIDEBAR REFERENCES . . .** provide additional information about the lesson through:
  Skill Builders . . . reference to *Sight-Singing* textbook
  Music & History . . . reference to the History section
  Spotlights . . . reference to a featured Spotlight page

- **GETTING STARTED. . .** provides a motivating introduction to the piece of music, related to the student's perspective. The History and Culture provides background information on the selection, the composer and/or the cultural context.

- **EVALUATION . . .** gives the student ways to assess accomplishment, growth and needs, for both self and group. Through careful listening and constructive critique of their own work, they will gradually become more discriminating about the quality of performance and the impact of that performance on the audience.

Lessons

The student lessons, through which students systematically build musical skills and conceptual understanding, comprise the first twelve selections of the text. They are presented in three general categories: Beginning of the Year, Mid-Winter, and Concert/Festival.

Music & History

The Historical section of the text provides a survey of Western music history through exploration of the culture and music of the five overarching periods: Renaissance, Baroque, Classical, Romantic and Contemporary. Each period is addressed in the following ways:

- **Historical Narrative Lesson . . .** provides a brief, student-oriented historical context of the period through visual art, architecture, historical events, musical developments, artistic characteristics, musical personalities and listening selections.
- **Historical Listening Lesson . . .** provides one choral and one instrumental listening selection to give students an aural experience with the styles, sounds and forms of the period. Recordings are provided to aid student learning.

Choral Library

The Choral Library maintains the same comprehensive lesson format of the Lessons and comprises the final twelve selections of the text. The additional literature features multicultural selections, patriotic and seasonal selections, American folk music, African American spirituals, Broadway show tunes and light concert pieces.

Glossary

The glossary provides brief, accurate definitions of musical terms used in the text.

TEACHER WRAPAROUND EDITION

National Standards Connections

Experiencing Choral Music affords multiple opportunities to address the National Standards. Correlations among lesson content, extension activities and bottom-page activities are listed to make obvious the relationship between lesson activities and the standards.

Suggested Teaching Sequence

Each lesson is organized to follow a logical progression from Getting Started through Evaluation, while providing maximum flexibility of use for your individual situation. Each lesson is linked to one musical selection, and provides learning opportunities based on the inherent concepts and skills required to understand and perform the piece. The lessons of the Teacher Wraparound Edition are structured as follows.

- **Overview . . .** Gives the teacher a brief analysis of the music being taught, including composer, text, voicing, key, meter, form, style, accompaniment, programming ideas and vocal ranges for each voice part.
- **Objectives . . .** Two or three concrete, measurable objectives form the skeletal structure for the lesson, allowing an interconnected approach to lesson segments.
- **Vocabulary . . .** Vocabulary terms are those used during the lesson and music terms used in the music to build understanding and skills.
- **Links to Learning . . .** The Links to Learning of the lesson includes exercises that focus on vocal, theory and artistic expression elements of the upcoming song. It provides rhythm and vocal, as well as sight-singing exercises. They are designed to sequentially develop vocal and sight-singing skills, and lead directly into the upcoming piece. These exercises may all be done before the piece is introduced, or they may be presented cumulatively, one each day, and concurrent with developing understanding of the piece.
- **The Lesson Plan: Suggested Teaching Sequence . . .** The Suggested Teaching Sequence is divided into three section: Introduce, Rehearse, and Refine. At the end of each section, Progress Checkpoints are provided for quick informal assessment of the materials covered to that point. Introduce often refers to the Links to Learning exercises on the student page and provides meaningful ways to introduce a new song to students. Rehearse includes a list of recommended steps to teach the piece through a variety of teaching techniques. Refine puts it all together and prepares the students for performance of the piece. The Performance Tips provide teachers with the polishing nuances that transform the notes on the page into an expressive performance experience.

Informal Assessment, Student Self-Assessment, and Individual and Group Performance Evaluation

Informal Assessment is done by teacher observation during the lesson. Each objective is observable, and the text indicates the checkpoint for teacher assessment.

Student Self-Assessment is accomplished through student evaluation of their individual performance based on an established set of criteria.

Individual and Group Performance Evaluation requires the student to demonstrate a skill or understanding through individual or group evaluation. This is directly related to the Evaluation found in the student lesson. Individual and Group Performance Evaluation can be done by the teacher, student, peers or a combination thereof. Frequent audio- or videotaping is suggested as an effective means of evaluation. The tapes may be compiled into a portfolio that shows growth and developing understanding over time.

Bottom-Page Activities

Bottom-page activities in each lesson afford a plethora of background information, teaching strategies and enrichment opportunities.

- *Teacher 2 Teacher* provides a brief description of the main features of the lesson.
- *Enrichment activities* provide musical activities that go beyond the basic lesson including composition, improvisation, and so forth.
- *Extension activities* expand the lesson to the other arts or other disciplines.
- *Teaching strategies* reinforce concepts or skills presented in the lesson, or elaborate on classroom management techniques.
- *More about* boxes provide background historical, cultural, and/or biographical information.
- *Curriculum connections* provide strategies to help students build bridges between music and other disciplines.
- *Vocal development strategies* give detailed information about specific techniques that facilitate vocal production and style.
- *Music literacy strategies* help students expand their ability to read and analyze music.
- *Cultural connections* provide cultural information related to the lesson.
- *Connecting to the arts* boxes provide strategies to help students connect music to the other arts.
- *Community connections* provide activities that extend into the community.
- *Careers in music* boxes provide information about career opportunities in music.
- *Online* directs students and teachers to **music.glencoe.com**, the website for *Experiencing Choral Music.*

TEACHER RESOURCE BINDER

The *Teacher Resource Binder* contains teaching materials designed to reduce teacher preparation time and maximize students' learning. The following categories are provided to assist with meeting the individual needs and interests of your students.

- **Teaching Masters.** The *Teaching Masters* support, extend and enhance the musical concepts and skills presented in the text lessons. Included are strategied focusing on composing, arranging, evaluating, analyzing, writing, multi-arts, culture and language pronunciation guides.
- **Evaluation Masters.** The *Evaluation Masters* provide performance assessment criteria, rubrics and other pages to help teachers and students with individual group, and ensemble assessment.
- **Music & History.** The *Music & History Masters* include full-color overhead transparencies of the visual art pieces introduced in each of the historical sections. They also include characteristics of the period, biographies of composers and other teaching strategies.
- **Vocal Development Masters.** The *Vocal Development Masters* provide important information about the voice. Included are numerous warm-up exercises that may be used throughout the year. Each exercise is recorded and included on the *Sight-Singing CD.*
- **Skill Builders Masters.** The *Skill Builders Masters* reinforce the development of fundamental skills, knowledge and understanding in areas such as rhythm, notation, music symbols, conducting patterns, improvisation, Kodály hand signs, time signatures and meter.
- **Sight-Singing Masters.** The *Sight-Singing Masters* are directly correlated to the *Sight-Singing* textbooks. They provide reproducible evaluation activity sheets for assessment and review.
- **Kodály, Dalcroze, Interdisciplinary.** Teaching strategies with a focus on Kodály, Dalcroze and Interdisciplinary are presented in this section.
- **Reference Resources.** The *Reference Resource Masters* serve as a resource bank for the teacher and provides a library of resource materials useful in supporting instruction.
- **Listening Selections CD.** *Listening Selections CD* provides full recordings of the vocal and instrumental historical listening lessons from the student text.
- **Sight-Singing CD.** The *Sight-Singing CD* provides a piano accompaniment track for practice songs and sight-singing exercises found in the student text of *Experiencing Choral Music: Sight-Singing*. The CD also includes the accompaniment track to the vocal warm-up exercises in the Vocal Development section.

EFFECTIVE TEACHING CHECKLIST

Teaching can be a rewarding as well as a challenging experience. The following is a compilation of suggestions and tips from experienced teachers. Review this list often.

Preparation

- Good planning leads to a successful rehearsal.
- Establish high expectations from the start – students want to succeed.
- Establish a routine and basic standards of behavior – and stick to it!
- Follow your planned routine every rehearsal (e.g. opening cue that rehearsal has begun, warm-up, sight-reading, repertoire, evaluation). Younger choirs in particular respond well to structure in a rehearsal.
- Plan, plan, plan.
- Develop long-range planning (the entire year's goals and activities, the semester, the month) and short-range planning (weekly plans and the daily lesson as they fit within the entire year's goals).
- Vary teaching strategies: modeling, peer coaching, large group, small group, cooperative learning, individual instruction, student conductors, independent practice.
- Study the score well. Anticipate problem areas.
- Be able to sing any one part while playing another.
- Know the vocal ranges of each member of the chorus.
- Select appropriate music to fit those vocal ranges.
- Remember: out-of-range results in out-of-tune singing.
- Select music of appropriate difficulty for the group.
- Plan evaluation techniques in advance.
- Have all necessary supplies and equipment ready (music in folders or ready to pass out, tapes cued, director's folder handy, recording equipment set, etc.) before the lesson begins.
- Plan to make beautiful music at least once during every rehearsal.

Presentation

- Begin each lesson with singing rather than talking.
- Make all parts of the lesson musical—including warm-ups and sight-reading.
- Rehearse a cappella. Use the piano as little as possible.
- Remember: Delivering information is not necessarily teaching.
- Display a positive attitude.
- Communicate effectively and concisely.
- Enthusiasm is essential.
- Make learning an enjoyable experience.
- Respect legitimate effort on the part of every student.
- Be the best musician you can be.
- Laugh often.

Pacing

- Be 30 seconds mentally ahead of the class at all times.
- Know where the lesson is going before it happens.
- Vary activities and standing/sitting positions.
- Plan a smooth transition from one activity to the next.
- Avoid "lag" time.
- If a "teachable" moment occurs, make the most of it.
- Avoid belaboring any one exercise, phrase, or activity—come back to it at another time.
- Always give students a reason for repeating a section.
- Provide at least one successful musical experience in every rehearsal.

Evaluation

- Assess student learning in every lesson (formally or informally).
- Vary the assessment activities.
- Consider evaluating individual as well as group effort.
- Tape the rehearsals often (audio and/or video).
- Study the rehearsal tapes: (1) to discover where overlooked errors occur, (2) to assist in planning the next rehearsal, or (3) to share findings with the students.
- Provide students with opportunities to evaluate themselves.
- Teach critical listening to the students by asking specific students or a group of students to listen for a specific thing (balance of parts in the polyphonic section, a correct uniform vowel sound on a particular word or words, rise and fall of phrase, and so forth).
- Constantly evaluate what's really happening. (We often hear what we want to hear!)
- Listen, listen, listen.

TEACHER WRAPAROUND EDITION
INTERMEDIATE

Experiencing Choral Music

MIXED

Developed by

New York, New York Columbus, Ohio Chicago, Illinois Peoria, Illinois Woodland Hills, California

A portion of the sales of this material goes to support music education programs through programs of MENC–The National Association for Music Education.

The McGraw·Hill Companies

Printed in the United States of America.

Send all inquiries to:
Glencoe/McGraw-Hill
21600 Oxnard Street, Suite 500
Woodland Hills, CA 91367

ISBN 0-07-861108-3 (Student Edition)
ISBN 0-07-861109-1 (Teacher Wraparound Edition)

1 2 3 4 5 6 7 8 9 045 09 08 07 06 05 04

Credits

LEAD AUTHORS

Emily Crocker
Vice President of Choral Publications
Hal Leonard Corporation, Milwaukee, Wisconsin
Founder and Artistic Director, Milwaukee Children's Choir

Michael Jothen
Professor of Music, Program Director of Graduate Music Education
Chairperson of Music Education
Towson University, Towson, Maryland

Jan Juneau
Choral Director
Klein Collins High School
Spring, Texas

Henry H. Leck
Associate Professor and Director of Choral Activities
Butler University, Indianapolis, Indiana
Founder and Artistic Director, Indianapolis Children's Choir

Michael O'Hern
Choral Director
Lake Highlands High School
Richardson, Texas

Audrey Snyder
Composer
Eugene, Oregon

Mollie Tower
Coordinator of Choral and General Music, K-12, Retired
Austin, Texas

AUTHORS

Anne Denbow
Voice Instructor, Professional Singer/Actress
Director of Music, Holy Cross Episcopal Church
Simpsonville, South Carolina

Rollo A. Dilworth
Director of Choral Activities and Music Education
North Park University, Chicago, Illinois

Deidre Douglas
Choral Director
Labay Junior High, Katy, Texas

Ruth E. Dwyer
Associate Director and Director of Education
Indianapolis Children's Choir
Indianapolis, Indiana

Norma Freeman
Choral Director
Saline High School, Saline, Michigan

Cynthia I. Gonzales
Music Theorist
Greenville, South Carolina

Michael Mendoza
Professor of Choral Activities
New Jersey State University
Trenton, New Jersey

Thomas Parente
Associate Professor
Westminster Choir College of Rider University
Princeton, New Jersey

Barry Talley
Director of Fine Arts and Choral Director
Deer Park ISD, Deer Park, Texas

CONTRIBUTING AUTHORS

Debbie Daniel
Choral Director, Webb Middle School
Garland, Texas

Roger Emerson
Composer/Arranger
Mount Shasta, California

Kari Gilbertson
Choral Director, Forest Meadow Junior High
Richardson, Texas

Tim McDonald
Creative Director, Music Theatre International
New York, New York

Christopher W. Peterson
Assistant Professor of Music Education (Choral)
University of Wisconsin-Milwaukee
Milwaukee, Wisconsin

Kirby Shaw
Composer/Arranger
Ashland, Oregon

Stephen Zegree
Professor of Music
Western Michigan State University
Kalamazoo, Michigan

EDITORIAL

Linda Rann
Senior Editor
Hal Leonard Corporation
Milwaukee, Wisconsin

Stacey Nordmeyer
Choral Editor
Hal Leonard Corporation
Milwaukee, Wisconsin

Table of Contents

Lessons

Music & History

Choral Library

TO THE STUDENT

Welcome to choir!

By singing in the choir, you have chosen to be a part of an exciting and rewarding adventure. The benefits of being in choir are many. Basically, singing is fun. It provides an expressive way of sharing your feelings and emotions. Through choir, you will have friends that share a common interest with you. You will experience the joy of making beautiful music together. Choir provides the opportunity to develop your interpersonal skills. It takes teamwork and cooperation to sing together, and you must learn how to work with others. As you critique your individual and group performances, you can improve your ability to analyze and communicate your thoughts clearly.

Even if you do not pursue a music career, music can be an important part of your life. There are many avocational opportunities in music. **Avocational** means *not related to a job or career*. Singing as a hobby can provide you with personal enjoyment, enrich your life, and teach you life skills. Singing is something you can do for the rest of your life.

In this course, you will be presented with the basic skills of vocal production and music literacy. You will be exposed to songs from different cultures, songs in many different styles and languages, and songs from various historical periods. You will discover connections between music and the other arts. Guidelines for becoming a better singer and choir member include:

- Come to class prepared to learn.
- Respect the efforts of others.
- Work daily to improve your sight-singing skills.
- Sing expressively at all times.
- Have fun singing.

This book was written to provide you with a meaningful choral experience. Take advantage of the knowledge and opportunities offered here. Your exciting adventure of experiencing choral music is about to begin!

Lessons

Lessons for the Beginning of the Year

Lessons for Mid-Winter

Lessons for Concert/Festival

Rise Up This Day to Celebrate

OVERVIEW

Composer: Johann Michael Haydn (1737–1806), arranged by Patrick M. Liebergen
Text: English Text by Patrick M. Liebergen
Voicing: 3-Part Mixed
Key: B♭ major
Meter: Cut Time
Form: ABA
Style: German Classical Anthem
Accompaniment: Piano, Trumpet
Programming: Concert Opener

Vocal Ranges:

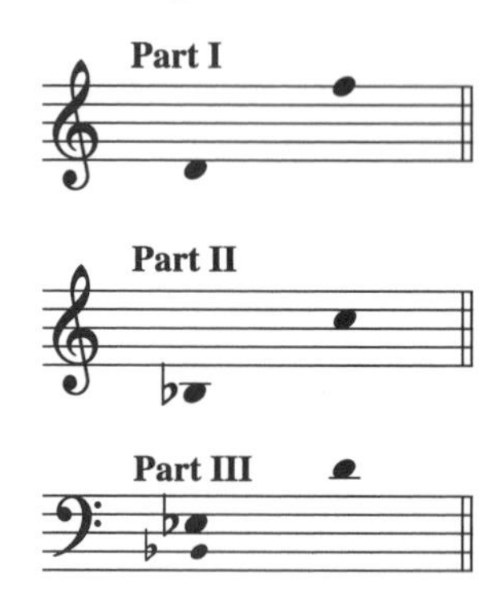

OBJECTIVES

After completing this lesson, students will be able to:

- Describe and perform music from the Classical period.
- Interpret music symbols referring to dynamics when performing.
- Analyze harmonic endings (cadences).

VOCABULARY

Have students review vocabulary in student lesson. Introduce terms found in the music. A complete glossary of terms is found on page 240 of the student book.

LESSON 1

Rise Up This Day To Celebrate

Composer: Johann Michael Haydn (1737–1806), arranged by Patrick M. Liebergen
Text: English Text by Patrick M. Liebergen
Voicing: 3-Part Mixed

VOCABULARY

- Classical period
- mass
- phrase
- cadence
- trio

Focus

- Describe and perform music from the Classical period.
- Sing phrases using repetition and contrast.
- Identify and perform cadences.

Getting Started

Have you ever noticed that great talent sometimes runs in families?

Venus & Serena Williams	*Professional tennis players*
Donny & Marie Osmond	*Professional singers*
Charlotte & Emily Bronte	*English novelists*
Wilhelm & C.P.E. Bach	*Composers (sons of J.S. Bach)*

The talent and skills of the famous siblings mentioned above are extraordinary. The same could also be said of the Haydn brothers. Although we remember Franz Joseph (1732–1809) for his "Surprise Symphony," his younger brother Johann Michael was a prolific composer, as well.

MUSIC & HISTORY

To learn more about the Classical period, see page 116.

◆ History and Culture

Johann Michael Haydn (1737–1806) was a well-known Austrian composer during the **Classical period** *(1750–1820).* Like the best male singers of his time, he left home at the age of eight or nine to attend St. Stephen's Cathedral school in Vienna. As an adult, he held the important position of court musician and composer for the Archbishop of Salzburg.

Among his compositions, Haydn wrote 38 masses for choir and orchestra. A **mass** is *a religious service of prayers and ceremonies consisting of spoken and sung sections.* This arrangement of "Rise Up This Day To Celebrate" is from his *Deutsche Messe* of 1777.

RESOURCES

Intermediate Sight-Singing

- Sight-Singing in B♭ major, pages 121–129
- Rhythm Reading Eighth Notes/Rests, pages 26–27
- Rhythm Reading Dotted Notes, pages 45, 48, 49
- Rhythm Reading in 2/2 Meter and Cut Time, page 140

Teacher Resource Binder

- Teacher Master 1, *Analyzing Cadences*
- Evaluation Master 4, *Checking Out Phrasing*
- Evaluation Master 7, *Evaluating Musical Expression*
- Skill Builder 29, *Singing in Three Parts*
- For additional resources, see TRB Table of Contents.

Links to Learning

◆ Vocal

Music of the Classical period sometimes features repetition with contrasts. One such contrast is to repeat a **phrase,** or *a musical idea with a beginning and an end,* using a change in dynamics. In "Rise Up This Day To Celebrate," each phrase is repeated at a softer dynamic level. Perform the following phrase twice, first time *forte* (loud) and second time *piano* (soft), to practice these contrasts.

◆ Theory

Just as a period indicates the end of a sentence, a **cadence** is *a melodic or harmonic structure that marks the end of a phrase or the completion of a song.* The first cadence in "Rise Up This Day To Celebrate" appears in measures 7–8. Perform the following example on "loo" to practice singing this cadence.

Evaluation

Demonstrate how well you have learned the skills and concepts featured in the lesson "Rise Up This Day To Celebrate" by completing the following:

- Discuss the musical characteristics of the Classical period.
- As a **trio** *(three singers)* with one singer on a part, perform measures 17–28 with accuracy, showing your understanding of dynamic contrast in each phrase. How well did you show dynamic contrast?
- With two or three classmates, analyze the music and locate the cadences similar to the example found in the Theory section above. Share your findings. In what ways do the cadences provide organization and structure to this piece?

LINKS TO LEARNING

Vocal

The Vocal section is designed to prepare students to:

- Sing a phrase *forte.*
- Sing the same phrase *piano.*

Have students:

- Learn their part of the Vocal exercise.
- Sing the phrase in three-part harmony.
- Vary the dynamic by first singing *forte,* then *piano.*

Theory

The Theory section is designed to prepare students to:

- Understand a cadence.
- Sing a cadence in three-part harmony.

Have students:

- Learn their part of the Theory exercise.
- Sing the phrase in three-part harmony.
- Listen carefully to tune the cadence.

RESOURCES

Intermediate Mixed Rehearsal/Performance CD

CD 1:1 Voices
CD 1:2 Accompaniment Only
CD 3:1 Vocal Practice Track—Part I
CD 4:1 Vocal Practice Track—Part II
CD 6:1 Vocal Practice Track—Part III

National Standards

1. Singing, alone and with others, a varied repertoire of music. **(a, b, c, d)**
5. Reading and notating music. **(c)**
6. Listening to, analyzing, and describing music. **(a, b)**

LESSON PLAN

Suggested Teaching Sequence and Performance Tips

1. Introduce

Direct students to:

- Read and discuss the information found in the Getting Started section on page 2.
- Practice singing the phrase in the Vocal section on page 3 *forte* and *piano*. Relate to measures 21–28. What are the dynamic levels marked in the score? Sing measures 21–28 following the dynamics marked in the score.
- Practice singing the cadence in the Theory section on page 3. Relate to measures 7–8, 11–12, 33–34, 37–38 in the score.

Progress Checkpoints

Observe students' progress in:

✓ Repeating a phrase using contrasting dynamic levels.

✓ Singing a cadence.

Rise Up This Day To Celebrate

For 3-Part Mixed and Piano with Optional B♭ Trumpet*

Arranged with English Text by
PATRICK M. LIEBERGEN

JOHANN MICHAEL HAYDN
(1737–1806)

*Part for B♭ Trumpet may be found on page 9.

TEACHER 2 TEACHER

Celebrate! The lyrics of "Rise Up This Day To Celebrate" are joyous! With the trumpet part, this song is a wonderful concert opener, particularly because the lyrics invite all to "unite and gladly sing." Keep the rhythms energetic and the diction crisp. The harmonic progressions are basic, and, thereby, are useful for teaching young choirs to sing in three-part harmony.

ENRICHMENT

Patronage in the Arts

Today, most orchestras and professional choirs are organized as nonprofit entities. To raise funds, they rely on ticket sales as well as donations from individuals, foundations and businesses. During Johann Michael Haydn's lifetime, however, wealthy individuals hired musicians as employees, who could then be available as needed to provide musical entertainment. This was known as the patronage system. Patrons not only provided musicians with a salary, but also housing and food, as well as the opportunity to compose and to perform regularly.

2. Rehearse

Direct students to:

- Count aloud the rhythms in measures 5–12. When correct, add pitches part by part. Identify the cadences at measures 7–8 and 11–12 as the one shown in the Theory section. Notice that measures 5–8 repeat in measures 9–12. Combine all three parts together.
- Count the rhythms in measures 13–16. When correct, add pitches part by part. Notice that measures 13–14 repeat in measures 15–16. Combine all three parts together.
- Count the rhythms in measures 17–20. When correct, add pitches part by part. Notice that measures 17–18 repeat in measures 19–20. Combine all three parts.
- Identify measures 21–28 as those shown in the Vocal section. Rehearse as needed.
- Identify measures 31–38 as a repetition of measures 5–12. Rehearse as needed.
- Count the rhythms in measures 39–42. When correct, add pitches part by part. Combine all three parts.

Progress Checkpoints

Observe students' progress in:

✓ Singing the correct rhythms and pitches.

✓ Recognizing repeated phrases.

✓ Singing three-part harmony.

3. Refine

Direct students to:

- Apply the dynamic markings provided in the score.
- Sing tall, round vowel sounds, particularly through sustained notes.
- Listen for vowel sounds being shared by the whole choir.
- Articulate final consonants of words and phrases together.

Progress Checkpoints

Observe students' progress in:

✓ Varying the dynamic levels.
✓ Singing tall, round vowel sounds.
✓ Ending final consonants together.

6 Intermediate Mixed

MORE ABOUT...

Form

Form is the design of a musical composition as defined by all of its pitches, rhythms and dynamics. "Rise Up This Day To Celebrate" is in ABA form, a design in which the opening phrases (Section A) are followed by contrasting phrases (Section B) and a repetition of the opening phrases (Section A). Measures 1–12 are Section A and measures 13–30 are Section B, while measures 31 to the end are the repetition of Section A. Knowledge of form can aid in both learning and memorizing a new piece of music.

ASSESSMENT

Informal Assessment

In this lesson, the students showed the ability to:

- Sing a repeated phrase *forte* and *piano.*
- Sing and identify cadences in the key of B♭ major.

Student Self-Assessment

Have students evaluate their individual performances based on the following:

- Posture
- Phrasing
- Dynamics
- Accurate Pitches
- Accurate Rhythms

Have each student rate his/her performance of this song in the areas above on a scale of 1–5, 5 being the best.

MORE ABOUT...

Sol–Do

Do and *sol* are the most important structural tones in the major and minor scales. Thereby, it is not atypical to find these two tones present at the beginning and end of a phrase. In "Rise Up This Day To Celebrate," the perfect fourth *sol* up to *do* occurs at the beginning of many phrases. Parts I and III approach measures 5, 9, 17, 19, 21, 25, 31 and 35 by ascending this perfect fourth. And the perfect fifth *sol* down to *do* occurs at the end of several phrases in Part III in measures 8, 12, 24, 28, 34, 38 and 41.

Individual and Group Performance Evaluation

To further measure growth of musical skills presented in this lesson, direct students to complete the Evaluation section on page 3.

- After discussing the musical characteristics of the Classical period, create a poster or bulletin board listing these characteristics to serve as a reminder for future Classical pieces.
- After singing measures 17–28 with a trio, review each performance by asking, "Did this trio perform a dynamic contrast between repeated phrases?"
- After singing the cadences in the Theory section, locate similar cadences in the choral score by marking them with a symbol. Have students exchange books and evaluate each other's ability to locate these cadences.

MORE ABOUT...

Composer Johann Michael Haydn

Johann Michael Haydn (1737–1806) was a prolific Austrian composer of both sacred and secular works. The younger brother of Franz Joseph Haydn (1732–1809) and a friend of Wolfgang Amadeus Mozart (1756–1791), he was best known for his numerous sacred compositions.

Rise Up This Day To Celebrate

B♭ TRUMPET

JOHANN MICHAEL HAYDN (1737–1806)
Edited and Arranged by PATRICK M. LIEBERGEN

EXTENSION

Repetition

"Rise Up This Day To Celebrate" is a joyful song whose design employs repetition. For example, the first phrase in measures 5–8 repeats in measures 9–12, 31–34, and 35–38. These repetitions are exact, in that the words and pitches are identical. As you look through the song, notice that every phrase is repeated. The notes in measures 13–14 appear with new words in measures 15–16. Both the words and pitches in measures 17–18 recur in measures 19–20; and measures 21–24 are restated in measures 25–28. Encourage students to use knowledge of these repetitions to memorize "Rise Up This Day To Celebrate."

Additional National Standards

The following National Standards are addressed through the Assessment, Extension, Enrichment and bottom-page activities:

2. Performing, alone and with others, a varied repertoire of music. **(a)**

5. Reading and notating music. **(e)**

7. Evaluating music and music performances. **(a, b)**

9. Understanding music in relation to history and culture. **(b)**

LESSON 2

Down In The Valley

OVERVIEW

Composer: American Folk Song, arranged by Linda Spevacek
Text: Traditional
Voicing: 3-Part Mixed
Key: E♭ major
Meter: 3/4
Form: ABB′
Style: American Folk Song
Accompaniment: A cappella
Programming: Festival/Competition

Vocal Ranges:

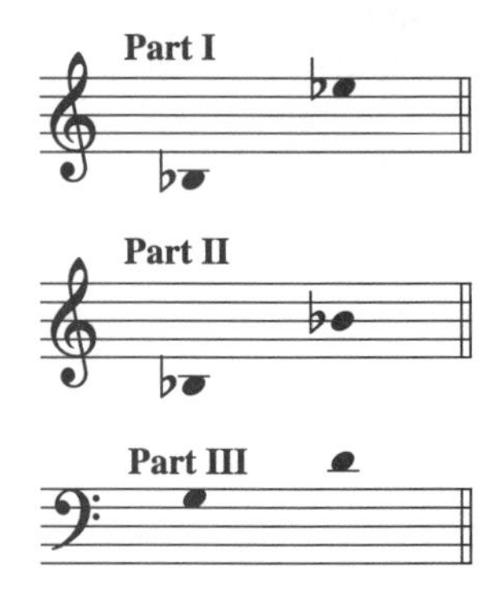

Objectives

After completing this lesson, students will be able to:

- Sight-read and perform music in various meters, including 3/4 meter.
- Perform individually or in groups using basic performance techniques to achieve accurate intonation.
- Sight-read and perform music in various keys, including E♭ major.

VOCABULARY

Have students review vocabulary in student lesson. Introduce terms found in the music. A complete glossary of terms is found on page 240 of the student book.

LESSON 2

Down In The Valley

Composer: American Folk Song, arranged by Linda Spevacek
Text: Traditional
Voicing: 3-Part Mixed

VOCABULARY

lyrics
folk song
intonation
breath support
$\frac{3}{4}$ meter

Focus

- Read and perform music in $\frac{3}{4}$ meter.
- Define and demonstrate accurate intonation.
- Read, write and perform music in the key of E♭ major.

Getting Started

Roses love sunshine, violets love dew
Angels in heaven know I love you.

What is the theme or subject matter of this short poem? If you guessed "love," then you are correct. More songs have been written about love than any other subject. Some people find it easier to express their feelings and emotions through music then through the spoken word. "Down In The Valley" is a beautiful song that expresses love through the words and music. Look at the **lyrics** *(the words to a song)*, and find other passages that express one's love in a unique way.

SKILL BUILDERS

To learn more about $\frac{3}{4}$ *meter, see* Intermediate Sight-Singing, *page 17.*

◆ History and Culture

"Down In The Valley" is an American folk song. **Folk songs** are *songs that have been passed down by word of mouth from generation to generation.* They sometimes reflect a local place or event, and they were often the popular songs of the day. Although the exact origin of "Down In The Valley" is unknown, it is believed to be from the Kentucky area. Many versions of this song exist.

The lyrics of "Down In The Valley" read like a poem. Many song texts are taken from poetry. Create your own lyrics by writing an original poem in the style and format of the verses of this song. The last word of each line should rhyme. Share your new lyrics with the class.

RESOURCES

Intermediate Sight-Singing

Sight-Singing in E♭ major, pages 141–143

Reading Rhythms in 3/4 Meter, pages 17–22

Teacher Resource Binder

Teaching Master 2, *Creating Lyrics for "Down in the Valley"*

Teaching Master 3, *Creating a Melody in 3/4 Meter*

Skill Builder 21, *Pitch and Kodály*

Skill Builder 23, *Rhythm and Kodály*

Skill Builder 26, *Rhythm Challenge in 3/4 Meter*

For additional resources, see TRB Table of Contents.

Links to Learning

◆ Vocal

Good **intonation,** or *in-tune singing,* is the product of proper breath support and vowel shape. **Breath support** refers to *the constant airflow necessary to produce sound for singing.* You can help develop this skill by doing the following:

> Breathe in air through an imaginary straw. Exhale on a hissing sound. First inhale on 4 counts, and then exhale over 6 counts, then 10 counts, then 12.

"Down in the Valley" is in the key of E♭ major and is based on the E♭ major scale. This scale uses the notes E♭, F, G, A♭, B♭, C, D, E♭. Sing the following E♭ major scale.

◆ Theory

3/4 meter is *a meter in which there are three beats per measure and the quarter note receives the beat.* Read and perform the following example to practice reading rhythmic patterns in 3/4 meter.

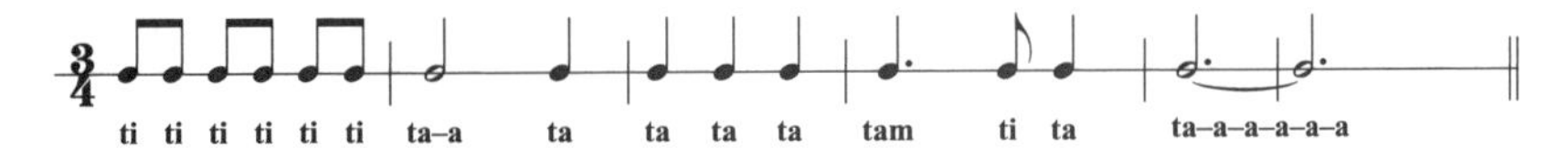

Evaluation

Demonstrate how well you have learned the skills and concepts featured in the lesson "Down In The Valley" by completing the following:

- Sing your part in measures 9-20 to show your understanding of 3/4 meter and accurate intonation. How did you do?
- Using the pitches *do, re, mi, sol* and *la,* of the E♭ major scale, compose a melody in 3/4 meter that begins and ends on *do.* Use rhythms found in "Down In The Valley." Notate your melody on staff paper or computer. With a classmate, check your work for correct rhythm and pitch notation.

LINKS TO LEARNING

Vocal

The Vocal section is designed to prepare students to:

- Sing melodic lines with pure vowel sounds, using adequate breath control and breath support to aid intonation.
- Sing a scale in the key of E♭ major using solfège.
- Have students sing their parts on a neutral vowel.
- Have students sing the scale using solfège.
- Have students sing the introduction in solfège.

Theory

The Theory section is designed to prepare students to:

- Understand 3/4 meter.
- Read and perform with rhythmic accuracy in 3/4 meter.

Have students:

- Speak the rhythmic example.
- Perform the rhythmic example by clapping and speaking the rhythm-note names.
- Perform the rhythmic example by clapping only, internalizing the note names.

RESOURCES

Intermediate Mixed Rehearsal/Performance CD

CD 1:3 Voices
CD 1:4 Accompaniment Only
CD 3:2 Vocal Practice Track—Part I
CD 4:2 Vocal Practice Track—Part II
CD 6:2 Vocal Practice Track—Part III

National Standards

1. Singing, alone and with others, a varied repertoire of music. **(a, b, c, d, e)**
5. Reading and notating music. **(a, b, c, d, e)**
6. Listening to, analyzing, and describing music. **(a, b, c)**

LESSON PLAN

Suggested Teaching Sequence and Performance Tips

1. Introduce

Direct students to:

- Read and discuss the information found in the Getting Started section found on page 10.
- Review 3/4 time signature. Practice reading the examples in 3/4 meter on student page 11.
- Review solfège scale tones and sing in the key of E♭ from the Vocal section on student page 11.
- Review the repeat sign and first and second ending. Have students identify the introduction, first and second verse, and coda.
- Label the form of the piece with appropriate letters. (Intro. AA Coda)
- Mark the breaths for each section.
- Circle all dynamic markings. Review the English meaning of the circled dynamics. *(piano, mezzo forte, crescendo)*
- Define and discuss *molto ritard.*

Progress Checkpoints

Observe students' progress in:

✓ Their ability to mark breath marks, the letters showing the form, and the circling of the dynamics.

✓ Their accuracy when reading the theory example.

✓ Their ability to sing with breath control, staggered breathing, and breath support when performing the vocal example.

Down In The Valley

For 3-Part Mixed, a cappella

Arranged by
LINDA SPEVACEK

American Folk Song

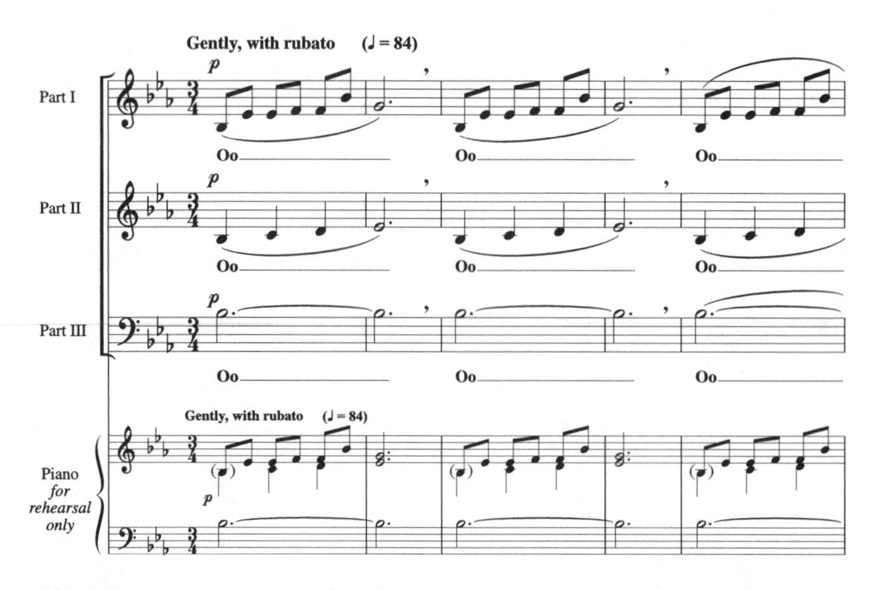

12 Intermediate Mixed

TEACHER 2 TEACHER

"Down In The Valley" is an American folk song that many students may already know. Because of the slight melodic changes, those who already know the traditional melody will be challenged. The harmony is written to enhance the ease of learning for young three-part choirs.

Lesson 2 *Down In The Valley* **13**

2. Rehearse

Direct students to:

- Chant the rhythm of each section. Reinforce the students breathing in the correct place while chanting rhythm.
- Begin learning the piece on solfège. In sections with complex rhythmic patterns, have students write solfège in their music. In the easier rhythmic places allow students to read without the aid of written syllables. This can strengthen their reading ability. Remember to continue to reinforce breathing in designated places to enhance intonation.

Progress Checkpoints

Observe students' progress in:

✓ Their rhythmic accuracy—especially in the sections with complex rhythmic patterns.

✓ Singing with pure vowel sounds when reading the piece on solfège.

MORE ABOUT...

Developing Vocal Resonance

Resonance is the unique sound of a voice that gives it rich beauty. Ask students to think of their mouths, throats, nasal passages, and sinuses as a resonator chamber, similar to a large dome-shaped building such as a cathedral or church. The sound is amplified without mechanical means when it can resonate in a large space with firm walls. Your head is your resonating chamber for sound and needs large spaces with firm walls (your facial bone structure) to ring and sound out.

3. Refine

Direct students to:

- Underline words in the music that require them to sing on one vowel sound for several pitches. Have them write the vowel sound underneath that series of pitches to aid in remembering to keep the vowel sound pure throughout each pitch.
- Speak through the text using desired pronunciation of each word. Beware of diphthongs. (...shine) Have the students model. Speak the text in rhythm.
- Echo as you model musical phrasing of each melodic line. Ask students to sing each line as modeled using solfège.
- Begin substituting solfège with text, once the students are consistently singing phrases musically.
- Begin adding dynamics to the phrases to increase expressiveness of the text.

Progress Checkpoints

Observe students' progress in:

- Continuing to adjust vowel sounds to aid good intonation and tone quality.
- Listening for adequate breath control with the use of staggered breathing.
- Checking for accuracy of dynamic changes in the musical phrases as indicated in the music.

MUSIC, SOCIETY AND CULTURE

Have students perform additional songs representing diverse cultures, including American and Texas heritage. Go to **music.glencoe.com**, the Web site for Glencoe's choral music programs, for additional music selections students can perform.

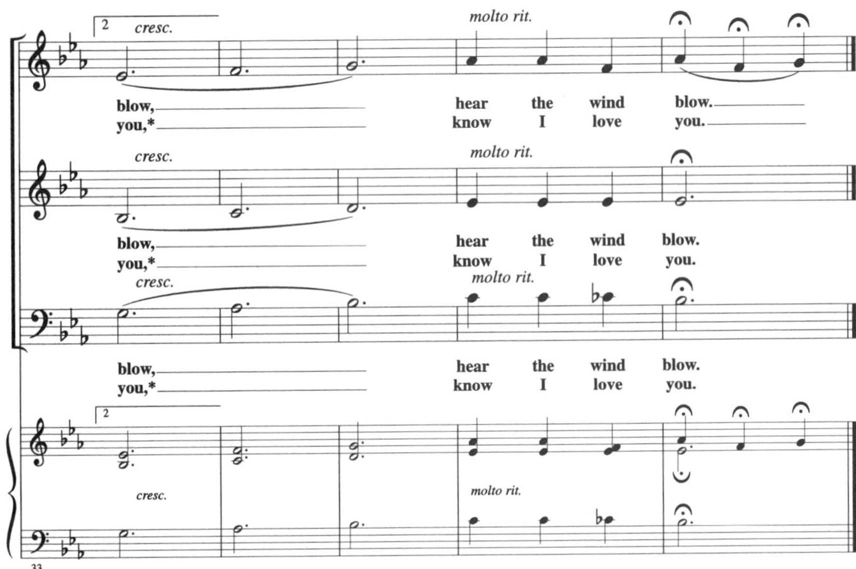

*Adjust text to fit choice of verses.

3. Build me a castle forty feet high.
So I can see him (her) as he (she) rides by.
As he (she) rides by, love, as he (she) rides by,
So I can see him (her) as he (she) rides by.

4. If you don't love me, love whom you please
Put your arms 'round me, give my heart ease.
Give my heart ease, love, give my heart ease.
Throw your arms 'round me, give my heart ease.

5. Write me a letter, send it by mail.
Send it in care of Birmingham jail.
Birmingham jail, love, Birmingham jail.
Send it in care of Birmingham jail.

Repeat first verse

Additional National Standards

The following National Standards are addressed through the Assessment, Extension, Enrichment and bottom-page activities:

3. Improvising melodies, variations, and accompaniments **(a)**

4. Composing and arranging music within specific guidelines. **(b)**

7. Evaluating music and music performances **(a, b, c)**

ASSESSMENT

Informal Assessment

In this lesson, students showed the ability to:

- Read and perform with accuracy in 3/4 meter.
- Sing a musical phrase with pure vowel sounds and good breath control and support.

Student Self-Assessment

Have students evaluate their individual performances based on the following:

- Phrasing
- Diction
- Accurate Pitches
- Accurate Rhythms
- Expressive Singing

Have each student rate his/her performance of this song in the areas above on a scale of 1–5, 5 being the best.

Individual and Group Performance Evaluation

To further measure growth of musical skills presented in this lesson, direct students to complete the Evaluation section on page 11.

Have students:

- Sing individually measures 9–20 using proper vowel sounds, trying only to breathe in designated places.
- After students have written a pentatonic melody in 3/4 meter, have them exchange it with a classmate and check their work.

Elijah Rock!

OVERVIEW

Composer: Traditional Spiritual, arranged by Roger Emerson
Text: Traditional
Voicing: 3-Part Mixed
Key: G minor
Meter: 4/4
Form: Intro. ABCABC'A Coda
Style: Traditional Spiritual
Accompaniment: Piano
Programming: Contest/Festival

Vocal Ranges:

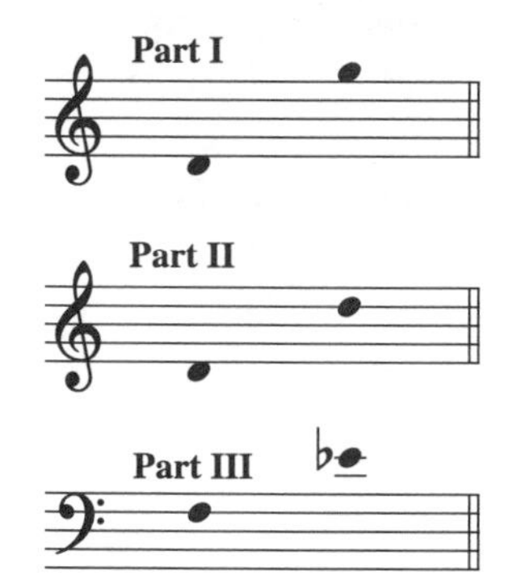

Objectives

After completing this lesson, students will be able to:

- Perform music representing styles from diverse cultures.
- Read and perform music notation that includes complex syncopated rhythms.
- Demonstrate musical artistry in the style of an African American spiritual.

VOCABULARY

Have students review vocabulary in student lesson. Introduce terms found in the music. A complete glossary of terms is found on page 240 of the student book.

LESSON 3

Elijah Rock!

Composer: Traditional Spiritual, arranged by Roger Emerson
Text: Traditional
Voicing: 3-Part Mixed

VOCABULARY

syncopation
spiritual
minor scale
rest

Focus

- Read and perform syncopated rhythms.
- Perform music that represents the African American spiritual.

Getting Started

When you hear music that has catchy rhythms and a strong beat, you might find yourself tapping your foot, nodding your head or snapping your fingers. This excitement in music is often caused by syncopation. **Syncopation** occurs when *the accent is moved from the strong beat to a weak beat or the weak portion of the beat.* As you sing "Elijah Rock!" listen for the syncopated rhythms.

SKILL BUILDERS

To learn more about syncopation, see Intermediate Sight-Singing, *page 126.*

History and Culture

"Elijah Rock!" is an example of a spiritual. Part of the African American traditions are **spirituals,** *songs that are often based on biblical themes or stories and were first sung by African American slaves.* These spirituals were probably sung while the slaves were working in the fields, engaging in social activities, or participating in worship. Syncopation and complex rhythms are common features found in spirituals.

Arranger Roger Emerson has added unique features to this arrangement. The slow, pensive introduction is followed by the driving syncopated chorus. Repeated sections are used to build momentum to the rousing final note.

RESOURCES

Intermediate Sight-Singing

Sight-Singing in G Minor, pages 133–136

Reading syncopation, pages 126–129

Teacher Resource Binder

Evaluation Master 3, *Assessing Performing Syncopated Rhythms*

Skill Builder 18, *Major and Minor Scales*

Dalcroze 12, *Moving to the Beat and Beat Subdivisions*

For additional resources, see the TRB Table of Contents.

Links to Learning

◆ Theory

This arrangement of "Elijah Rock!" is in the key of G minor and is based on the G minor scale. A **minor scale** is *a scale that has* la *as its keynote or home tone.* To locate "G" on the piano, find any set of three black keys. "G" is the white key just below the middle black key. This scale uses the notes G, A, B♭, C, D, E♭, F, G. Using the keyboard below as a guide, play the G minor scale.

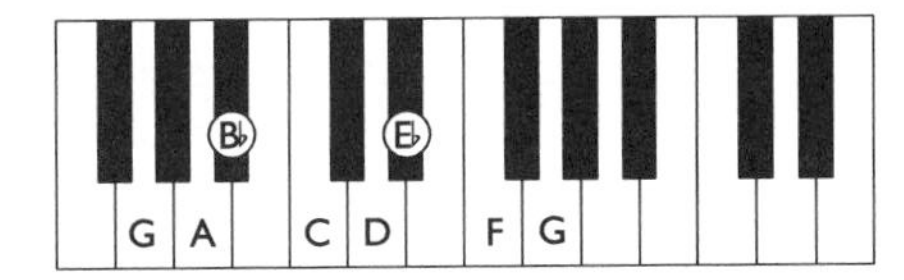

Syncopated rhythmic patterns sometimes contain rests. A **rest** is *a symbol used in music notation to indicate silence.* Read and perform the following example to practice shifting the accent from the strong beat to the weak portion of the beat. Find these patterns in the music.

◆ Artistic Expression

Movement can enhance the interpretation or character of a song. Form two or more circles in the room. Walk to the beat of a drum. Once you are secure in walking the beat, begin singing "Elijah Rock!" Notice the words that fall on the beat and those that fall off the beat. This will help you discover where syncopation occurs in this song.

Evaluation

Demonstrate how well you have learned the skills and concepts featured in the lesson "Elijah Rock!" by completing the following:

- Alone or in a small group, sing measures 17–24 to show your ability to perform syncopated rhythms correctly. How well did you do?
- In what measures do the rests move the accent from the strong beat to the weak portion of the beat?

LINKS TO LEARNING

Theory

The Theory section is designed to prepare students to:

- Read and perform music in the key of G minor.
- Read and perform syncopated rhythms.
- Read and perform rhythmic patterns that contain rests.

Have students:

- Sing the G minor scale on solfège, starting on *la. (la, ti, do, re, mi, fa, sol, la)*
- Play the G minor scale at the keyboard.
- Read and perform the rhythmic excerpt.

Artistic Expression

The Artistic Expression section is designed to prepare students to discover which words are syncopated.

Have students:

- Walk in a circle, so that each step is a beat. Sing a phrase that contains syncopation.
- Identify which words are syncopated.

RESOURCES

Intermediate Mixed Rehearsal/Performance CD

CD 1:5 Voices
CD 1:6 Accompaniment Only
CD 3:3 Vocal Practice Track—Part I
CD 4:3 Vocal Practice Track—Part II
CD 6:3 Vocal Practice Track—Part III

National Standards

1. Singing, alone and with others, a varied repertoire of music. **(b, c, d)**
5. Reading and notating music. **(a)**
6. Listening to, analyzing, and describing music. **(b)**

LESSON PLAN

Suggested Teaching Sequence and Performance Tips

1. Introduce

Direct students to:

- Read and discuss the information found in the Getting Started section on page 16.
- Sing the G minor scale in the Theory section on page 17.
- Sing the following melodic patterns extracted from the music: *la–do–la, la–mi–do, do–re–do–la, do–mi–sol–la, mi–fa–mi–do.*
- Read and perform the rhythmic excerpt in the Theory section on page 17.
- Locate the rhythmic excerpt in the music at measures 17–18, 21–22, 43–44, 47–48.
- Read the lyrics and locate repetitions of textual phrases that form the A, B, and C sections.
- Identify and label Section A and its varied repetitions as measures 17–24, 43–50.

Elijah Rock!

For 3-Part Mixed and Piano

Adapted and Arranged by
ROGER EMERSON

Traditional Spiritual

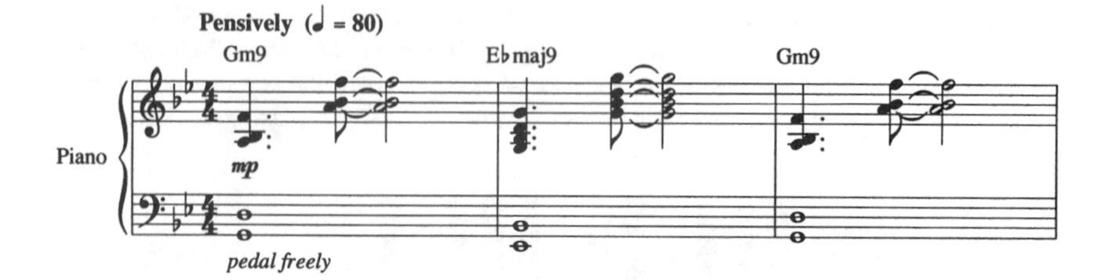

TEACHER 2 TEACHER

Keeping a Resonant Sound

Singers often feel that to sing folk, pop or spiritual music they need to compromise the bel canto style of singing. While this is not always the case, the driving force of the music sometimes causes singers to "belt" or "let loose." The vocal range should dictate whether a heavier voice should be used. "Elijah Rock!" is not written for a heavy voice. Often a hushed and articulated sound gives the most drama.

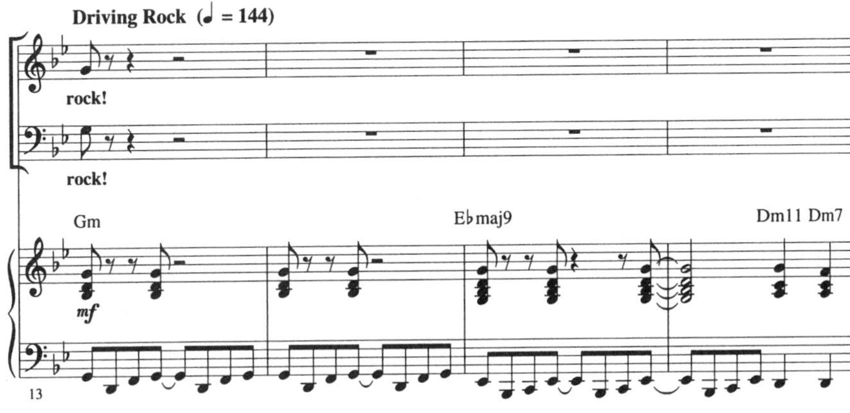

- Identify and label Section B as measures 33–42 and 51–58.
- Identify and label Section C and its varied repetitions as measures 33–42 and 59–68.
- Locate and identify the Introduction (measures 1-13) and the Coda (measures 69-72)
- Locate and identify the D. S. al Coda indication at measure 68, the sign at measure 43, and the Coda sign at measure 59. Instruct the students as to the sequence of the printed song.

Progress Checkpoints

Observe students' progress in:

✓ Singing the G minor scale in tune.

✓ Singing the melodic patterns extracted from the music in tune: *la–do–la, la–mi–do, do–re–do–la, do–mi–so–la, mi–fa–mi–do.*

✓ Performing the rhythmic excerpt.

✓ Locating the rhythmic excerpt in the score.

✓ Identifying textural repetitions.

✓ Labeling the A, B, and C sections.

ENRICHMENT

Performance evaluation

Record the class singing "Elijah Rock!" with learned and added qualities from the Extension on page 24. Provide a checklist worksheet for them to complete as they are listening. Have them check off the criteria that were met during the performance and rate the choir. Share the data with the class, including the ratings.

2. Rehearse

Direct students to:

- Speak the text of measures 17–18 of Part I, relating it to the first measure in the Theory section's rhythmic excerpt.
- Speak the text of measures 7–8 of Part I. Contrast the on-the-beat rhythmic pattern in these measures with the syncopated rhythmic pattern of measures 5-6.
- Sing measures 5–8 of Part I on solfège. Notice that Part III imitates Part I in measures 7–9. Sing as written in parts on solfège. When accurate, progress to singing the lyrics.
- Learn Section A in measures 17–24 by reading the rhythm. When accurate, speak the text in rhythm. Sing the pitches on solfège. When rhythms and pitches are accurate, progress to singing the lyrics.

MORE ABOUT...

The Pentatonic Scale and Folk Music

Many people think that the sound of the pentatonic scale is unique to Asian culture. Not so! Using the five black keys on the piano, play the melody of "Elijah Rock!" by ear. The five black keys are the pentatonic scale. *(do, re, mi, sol, la)* Encourage students to discover other folk songs that are limited to the pentatonic scale. Have them arrange one in a style of their choice within your guidelines.

- Learn the varied repetition of Section B in measures 25–32, noticing that imitation has been replaced by three-part harmony. Part by part, sing the pitches on solfège. Combine parts and sing on solfège. When rhythms and pitches are accurate, progress to singing the lyrics.
- Learn Section C in measures 33-42, its repetition in measures 59–68, and the Coda in measures 69–72, engaging a procedure similar to that used to learn Sections A and B: rhythm, chant text in rhythm, solfège, and lyrics.

Progress Checkpoints

Observe students' progress in:

✓ Labeling the sections in the piece.

✓ Performing correct rhythms throughout, giving particular emphasis to syncopations.

✓ Performing correct pitches throughout.

✓ Singing three-part harmonies in tune.

✓ Singing unisons as one voice, with a shared, centered pitch and a unified vowel sound.

✓ Pronouncing lyrics energetically.

MORE ABOUT...

Spirituals

The enslaved Africans brought music with the following elements to the New World: syncopation, polyrhythm, pentatonic and gap scales, and the idea of music combined with body movements. From the suffering of the ocean crossing and a life of subjugation, they create a new genre, the spiritual, or religious folk song of the slave. It revealed their unhappiness and suffering, taught facts, sent messages, provided a common language, and shared religious rituals and beliefs. In the spiritual, the singer must express a personal connection with a deity of God. The spiritual reflects a true historical picture of the lives of slaves as told by slaves themselves.

3. Refine

Direct students to:

- Count-sing the entire piece, returning to lyrics after verifying accurate pitches and rhythms.
- Circle the dynamic markings in the score. Sing, giving particular attention to the dynamic levels.
- Rehearse the tempo change at measure 13 until smooth.
- Practice in measures 25 and 51 ending Section A and beginning Section B smoothly, transitioning from singing unison to three-part harmony.
- Isolate Part III in measures 59–68 to verify rhythmic accuracy. When correct, sing all parts together, listening for rhythmic independence between the melody in Parts I and II and the vocal accompaniment in Part III.

Progress Checkpoints

Observe students' progress in:

- Singing correct pitches and rhythms in solfège, counting rhythms and lyrics.
- Making an audible difference when dynamic levels change.
- Transitioning smoothly from the initial tempo to the faster tempo, and from sections sung in unison to those in three-part harmony

MUSIC, SOCIETY AND CULTURE

Have students perform additional songs representing diverse cultures, including American and Texas heritage. Go to **music.glencoe.com**, the Web site for Glencoe's choral music programs, for additional music selections students can perform.

ASSESSMENT

Informal Assessment

In this lesson, the students showed the ability to:

- Sing and read music with accurate intonation in the key of G minor.
- Count syncopated rhythms accurately.
- Sing lyrics with syncopated rhythms.
- Sing three-part harmony in the key of G minor.

Student Self-Assessment

Have students evaluate their individual performances based on the following:

- Accurate Rhythms
- Accurate Pitches
- In-tune Singing
- Dynamics
- Facial Expressions

Have each student rate his/her performance of this song in the areas above on a scale of 1–5, 5 being the best.

MORE ABOUT...

The Cambiata Voice

As a male's voice changes, it reaches a stage called the *cambiata voice,* which begins to stretch lower but is still able to sing into the higher pitches of the male's voice. It is important not to stretch this voice too low, as it can become strained. It is fascinating for young men to track their development through the year, as they are able to sing lower and lower. This song, with its limited range and high interest, is very accessible to the cambiata voice.

Individual and Group Performance Evaluation

To further measure growth of musical skills presented in this lesson, direct students to complete the Evaluation section on page 17.

- Evaluate student performance of measures 17–24 by asking questions. Are the rhythms accurate? Are the pitches in tune? Is the dynamic level appropriate? Is the diction clear?
- Evaluate student ability to analyze the rhythms and to discern where syncopated rhythms displaced on-the-beat syllables to be off the beat.

EXTENSION

Professional Recording

Play a recording of a group singing a spiritual. As the students listen, have them write down qualities that they like about the piece. Encourage them to be specific. Compile a list on the board of the most repeated qualities. Ask the students which ones could be added to their performance of "Elijah Rock!". Ask for volunteers to perform passages from "Elijah Rock!". using one of the qualities listed on the board. Based upon the performances, ask students which qualities should be added to the choir's performance.

24 Intermediate Mixed

Additional National Standards

The following National Standards are addressed throughout the Assessment, Extension Enrichment and bottom-page activities:

4. Composing and arranging music within specified guidelines. **(b)**

5. Reading and notating music. **(c)**

6. Listening to, analyzing, and describing music. **(a)**

7. Evaluating music and music performances. **(a, b)**

9. Understanding music in relation to history and culture. **(a, c,)**

Diction

Singing is a form of communication. To communicate well while singing, you must not only form your vowels correctly, but also say your consonants as clearly and cleanly as possible.

There are two kinds of consonants: voiced and unvoiced. Consonants that require the use of the voice along with the **articulators** *(lips, teeth, tongue, and other parts of the mouth and throat)* are called voiced consonants. If you place your hand on your throat, you can actually feel your voice box vibrate while producing them. Unvoiced consonant sounds are made with the articulators only.

In each pair below, the first word contains a voiced consonant while the second word contains an unvoiced consonant. Speak the following word pairs, then sing them on any pitch. When singing, make sure the voiced consonant is on the same pitch as the vowel.

Voiced:	Unvoiced Consonants:	More Voiced Consonants:
[b] bay	[p] pay	[l] lip
[d] den	[t] ten	[m] mice
[g] goat	[k] coat	[n] nice
[ʤ] jeer	[ʧ] cheer	[j] yell
[z] zero	[s] scenic	[r] red
[ʒ] fusion	[ʃ] shun	
[ð] there	[θ] therapy	More Unvoiced Consonants:
[v] vine	[f] fine	[h] have
[w] wince	[hw] whim	

The American "r" requires special treatment in classical choral singing. To sing an American "r" at the end of a syllable following a vowel, sing the vowel with your teeth apart and jaw open. In some formal sacred music and English texts, you may need to flip or roll the "r." For most other instances, sing the "r" on pitch, then open to the following vowel quickly.

RESOURCES

Teacher Resource Binder

Evaluation Master 6, *Diction Checkup*
Vocal Development 9, *Diction*
Vocal Development 13, *Posture & Breathing*
Reference 12, *Diction Guide*
Reference 16, *My Music Dictionary*

National Standards

1. Singing, alone and with others, a varied repertoire of music. **(b)**
8. Understanding relationships between music, the other arts, and disciplines outside the arts. **(b)**

DICTION

Objectives

- Demonstrate basic performance techniques using proper diction.

Suggested Teaching Sequence

Direct students to:

- Read the Spotlight on Diction on student page 25 and identify the importance of diction in singing.
- Define *articulators*.
- Describe the difference between voiced and unvoiced consonants.
- Speak the voiced and unvoiced consonants out loud and find examples in music.
- Compare the concept of proper diction to effective performance practices.
- Discuss the proper use of the "r" consonant when singing.

Progress Checkpoints

Observe students' progress in:

✓ Their ability to speak voiced and unvoiced consonants properly.
✓ Their ability to name the parts of the body that are the articulators.
✓ Their ability to recognize voiced and unvoiced consonants in other music they are studying.
✓ Their ability to relate the importance of proper diction in other areas such as drama, speech and public speaking.

America The Beautiful

OVERVIEW

Composer: Samuel A. Ward, arranged by Joyce Eilers
Text: Katharine Lee Bates
Voicing: 3-Part Mixed
Key: B♭ Major
Meter: 4/4
Form: Strophic
Style: Patriotic
Accompaniment: Piano
Programming: Patriotic

Vocal Ranges:

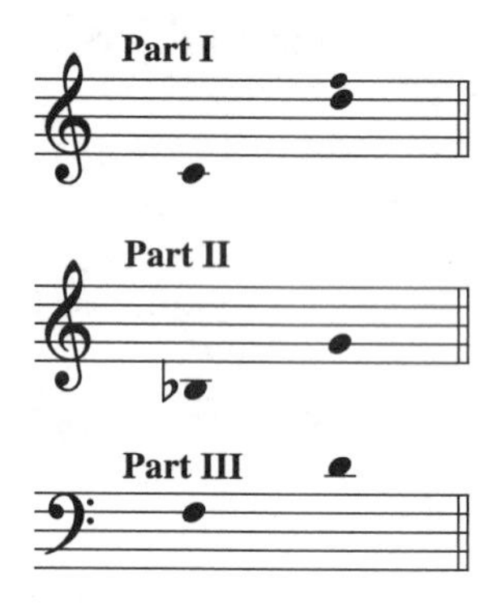

OBJECTIVES

After completing this lesson, students will be able to:

- Demonstrate musical artistry (singing legato).
- Demonstrate knowledge of harmonic expressions (suspensions).
- Identify the relationships between the content of the other fine arts and those of music.

VOCABULARY

Have students review vocabulary in student lesson. Introduce terms found in the music. A complete glossary of terms is found on page 240 of the student book.

LESSON 4

America The Beautiful

Composer: Samuel A. Ward, arranged by Joyce Eilers
Text: Katharine Lee Bates
Voicing: 3-Part Mixed

VOCABULARY

stage presence
legato
suspension

Focus

- Demonstrate musical artistry and appropriate performance practice.
- Describe suspension using music terminology.
- Identify the relationships between the other fine arts and those of music.

Getting Started

Choose the correct definition for the words listed below.

1. alabaster	**a.** magical saying	**b.** white granite
2. spacious	**a.** with lots of space	**b.** gracious
3. amber	**a.** a hot fire	**b.** golden in color
4. fruited plain	**a.** a nutty place	**b.** a field filled with fruit

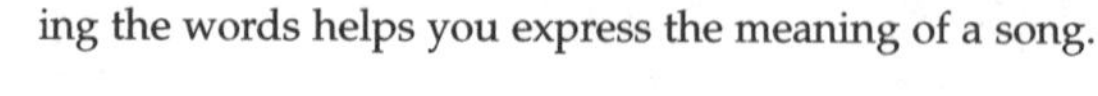

Find these words in "America the Beautiful." Understanding the words helps you express the meaning of a song.

SPOTLIGHT

To learn more about singing posture, see page 35.

◆ History and Culture

In 1893, Katharine Lee Bates, a professor at Wellesley College in Massachusetts, traveled to Colorado to present a series of lectures. Upon viewing the Rocky Mountains for the very first time, Ms. Bates was overwhelmed. She had never seen such tall and majestic mountains. She hiked to the top of Pike's Peak, and as she looked over the wide, fertile land below, the opening lines of "America The Beautiful" came to her. The poem was first published on July 4, 1895, and was later put to music.

When you sing, your **stage presence** *(a performer's overall appearance on stage, including enthusiasm, facial expression and posture)* affects the outcome of the performance. An enthusiastic stage presence will show your audience how important singing about America is to you.

RESOURCES

Intermediate Sight-Singing

Sight-Singing in B♭ major, pages 121–129

Reading Dotted Notes, pages 45, 48–49

Teacher Resource Binder

Teaching Master 4, *Developing Stage Presence*

Evaluation Master 7, *Evaluating Musical Expression*

Evaluation master 13, *Judging Stage Presence*

For additional resources, see TRB Table of Contents.

Links to Learning

◆ Vocal

Perform the following example to practice singing **legato** *(a connected and sustained style of singing)*. A successful legato sound requires a constant and steady flow of air.

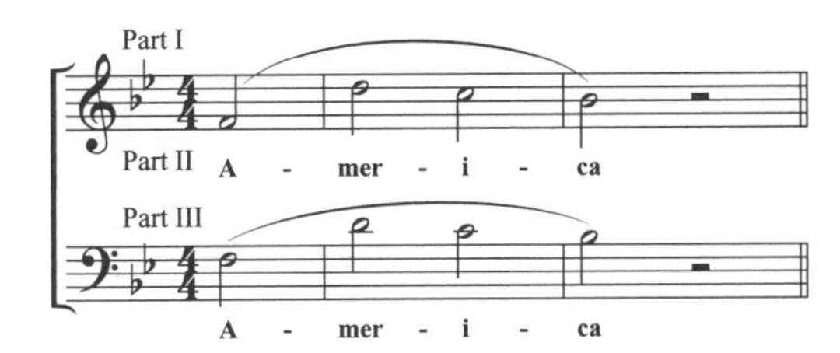

◆ Theory

Perform the three examples below to practice singing a suspension. A **suspension** is *the holding over of one or more musical tones of a chord into the following chord, producing a momentary discord.* In each example, Part III provides the suspended tone, which resolves downward (C to B♭, or *re* to *do*).

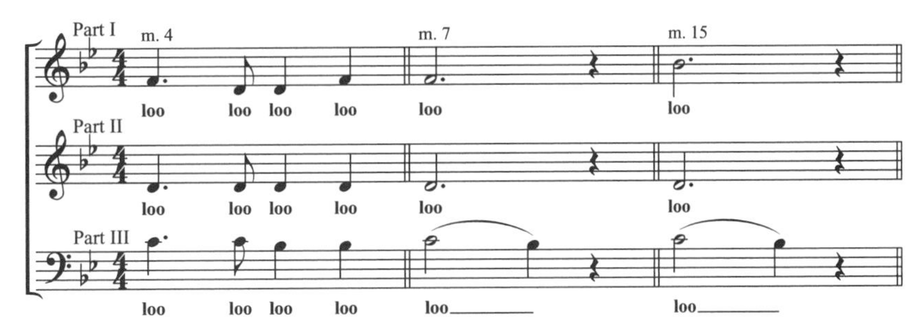

◆ Artistic Expression

Using colored pencils, crayons, or markers, create artwork that portrays an image or scene described in Katharine Lee Bates' poem.

Evaluation

Demonstrate how well you have learned the skills and concepts featured in the lesson "America The Beautiful" by completing the following:

- Sing measures 12–19 to show your ability to sing in a legato style.
- Listen to a recording of your choir singing measures 1–11 of "America The Beautiful." Raise your hand each time you hear Part III sing the suspension and its resolution.
- Share your artwork depicting a scene from "America The Beautiful" with the class. Explain what scene you chose to portray and why.

RESOURCES

Intermediate Mixed Rehearsal/Performance CD

CD 1:7 Voices
CD 1:8 Accompaniment Only
CD 3:4 Vocal Practice Track—Part I
CD 4:4 Vocal Practice Track—Part II
CD 6:4 Vocal Practice Track—Part III

National Standards

1. Singing, alone and with others, a varied repertoire of music. **(b, e)**
6. Listening to, analyzing, and describing music. **(a, b, c)**
8. Understanding music in relation to history and culture. **(b**

LINKS TO LEARNING

Vocal

The Vocal section is designed to prepare students to sing a legato line using steady air flow.

Have students:

- Sing the melody on "loo" making one initial articulation and maintaining the same vowel and dynamic throughout.
- Perform the example to practice singing legato.

Theory

The Theory section is designed to prepare students to participate in singing a suspension.

Have students:

- Practice the example given, noting the momentary dissonance and the subsequent resolution.
- Have the students find similar passages in the song, first by ear, then in print.

Artistic Expression

The Artistic Expression section is designed to expand the appreciation of the song.

Have students:

- Create visual representations of the images described in the lyrics.
- Have students illustrate a special "scene" from the text.

LESSON PLAN

Suggested Teaching Sequence and Performance Tips

1. Introduce

Direct students to:

- Read and discuss the information found in the Getting Started section on student page 26.
- Practice singing legato as instructed in the Vocal section on page 27.
- Learn to sing a suspension as shown in the Theory section on page 27.

America The Beautiful

For 3-Part Mixed and Piano

Arranged by JOYCE EILERS

Words by KATHARINE LEE BATES
Music by SAMUEL A. WARD

TEACHER 2 TEACHER

Joyce Eilers' lovely arrangement of "America The Beautiful" is appropriate to include in any concert! Although the opening block chords in the accompaniment are marked *forte,* they melt into a flowing rhythm of constant eighth notes which prepare the choral entrance. Strive to keep the melodic line lyrical throughout.

Progress Checkpoints

Observe students' progress in:

✓ Ability to sing legato.

✓ Ability to sing a suspension.

MORE ABOUT...

Katherine Lee Bates

Scholar, poet, and writer Katherine Lee Bates was born and bred in New England. Because of that, she was awestruck that day in 1893 as she traveled in a prairie wagon to the top of Pike's Peak in the Colorado Rockies. The spectacular views were unlike any she had ever seen. Bates was amazed by her poem's immediate and lasting success. She wrote, "That the hymn has gained, in these twenty odd years, such a hold as it has upon our people, is clearly due to the fact that Americans are at heart idealists, with a fundamental faith in human brotherhood."

2. Rehearse

Direct students to:

- Count the rhythm in measures 4–19, noting that the pattern repeats every four measures, beginning with two dotted-note rhythms and ending with even quarter notes.
- Sight-sing measures 4–19, repeating as necessary to gain correct pitches.
- Sight-sing the optional descant that begins in measure 38.
- Locate repetitions of measures 4–19 in the remainder of the piece before sight-singing the whole piece.

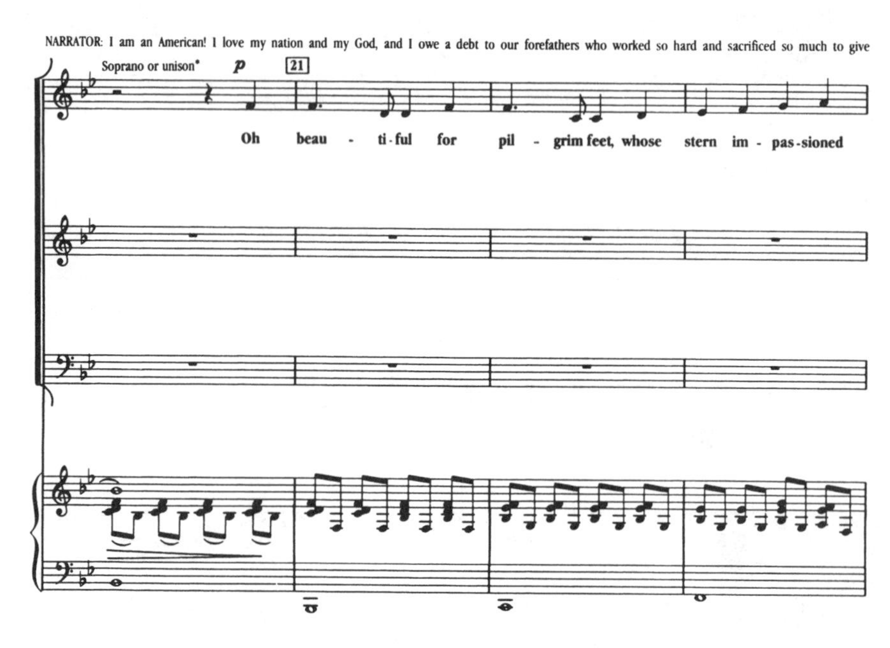

*Pace the narration to end before measure 29

30 Intermediate Mixed

TEACHING STRATEGY

Developing Repertoire

Children need to maintain a memorized repertoire of standard patriotic music. Be sure to review all of the beloved songs that our country has cherished. Warm-ups can include singing "America" in several keys, in parts and with improvised descants. "America The Beautiful" can be harmonized by ear in an improvisational-type singing.

Progress Checkpoints

Observe students' progress in:

✓ Singing accurate pitches throughout, particularly in measure 10 and its repetition in measure 44.

✓ Singing the descant in tune.

MORE ABOUT...

Visual Art/Video

If there are students who have interest, have them:

- Make a mural or banner, connecting the images that relate to the imagery in the song.
- Create transparencies or slides to be shown as the song is performed.
- Create a music video with students from the school as the performers and show it as the piece is performed.

3. Refine

Direct students to:

- Unify the phrase endings in measures 7, 11, 15, 32, 41, 45, 49 so that all parts sustain into beat 3 before breathing.
- Sustain energy and airflow through the dotted quarter-notes at the beginning of every phrase.
- Apply the dynamic marks as indicated throughout the piece to create an artistic shape to this arrangement.

Progress Checkpoints

Observe students' progress in:

✓ Singing legato throughout.

✓ Singing well-shaped phrases and unified phrase endings.

32 Intermediate Mixed

TEACHING STRATEGY

Posture

There are several approaches to achieving correct posture, which is a prerequisite and the most important aspect of breath support. Have students:

- Spread fingers of their right hand out over the abdomen, the little finger on the navel and the thumb on the breast bone.
- Stretch both hands over the head and reach slowly upward as if touching the ceiling. Gradually lower the hands and arms, leaving the chest high and the body tall.

Lesson 4 *America The Beautiful* 33

TEACHING STRATEGY

Staggered Breathing

The long phrases of "America The Beautiful" are good for teaching staggered breathing. Have students:

- Face one another and by gesture or eye contact make sure that staggered breathing is engaged. Sustain each phrase when singing on a neutral vowel, maintaining constant quality tone and dynamic level.
- Discuss the difference between the short, quick breath used in staggered breathing as opposed to the deeper, fuller breath taken as an ensemble. Notate each differently.

ASSESSMENT

Informal Assessment

In this lesson, students showed the ability to:

- Sing legato.
- Hear and sing suspensions.

Student Self-Assessment

Have students evaluate their individual performances based on the following:

- Posture
- Phrasing
- Dynamics
- Tall Vowels
- Expressive Singing

Have each student rate his/her performance of this song in the areas above on a scale of 1–5, 5 being the best.

Individual and Group Performance Evaluation

To further measure growth of musical skills presented in this lesson, direct students to complete the Evaluation section on page 27.

Have students sing their part as a solo with the accompaniment to verify individual ability to sing correct pitches and rhythms in a legato style.

- While listening to a recording of your choir singing the opeing measures of this piece, have students raise their hands each time they hear a suspension/resolution. Evaluate their ability.
- After creating the artwork assigned in the Artistic Expression section, have each student share his/her artwork and explain why he/she chose it.

EXTENSION

Invertible Counterpoint

Invertible counterpoint occurs when two lines can exchange position, that is, which is sung higher and which is sung lower, and yet still sound good together. Arranger Joyce Eilers has written a Bass line that is invertible with the melody. Give the Sopranos an opportunity to sing a harmony line and the Baritones to sing the melody; (the Altos must remain on their part). Consider performing measures 29-37 this way.

Music, Society and Culture

Have students perform additional songs representing diverse cultures, including American and Texas heritage. Go to **music.glencoe.com**, the Web site for Glencoe's choral music programs, for additional music selections students can perform.

Additional National Standards

The following National Standards are addressed through the Assessment, Extension, Enrichment and bottom-page activities:

1. Singing, alone and with others, a varied repertoire of music. **(d)**
3. Improvising melodies, variations and accompaniments. **(a)**
7. Evaluating music and music performances. **(b)**
8. Understanding relationships between music, the other arts, and disciplines in the arts.**(a)**

Posture

Posture is important for good singing. By having the body properly aligned, you are able to breathe correctly so that you have sufficient breath support needed to sing more expressively and for longer periods of time.

To experience, explore and establish proper posture for singing, try the following:

Standing

- Pretend someone is gently pulling up on a thread attached to the top of your head.
- Let out all of your air like a deflating balloon.
- Raise your arms up over your head.
- Take in a deep breath as if you were sipping through a straw.
- Slowly lower your arms down to your sides.
- Let all your air out on a breathy "pah," keeping your chest high.
- Both feet on floor, shoulder-width apart.
- Chest high, shoulders relaxed.
- Neck relaxed, head straight.

Sitting

- Sit on the edge of a chair with your feet flat on the floor while keeping your chest lifted.
- Hold your music with one hand and turn pages with the other.
- Always hold the music up so you can easily see the director and your music.

RESOURCES

Teacher Resource Binder

Vocal Development 13, *Posture and Breathing*

Evaluation Master 12, *Individual Performance Evaluation*

Reference 16, *My Music Dictionary*

National Standards

1. Singing, alone and with others. **(b)**

POSTURE

Objectives

- Demonstrate basic performance techniques including proper singing posture.

Suggested Teaching Sequence

Direct students to:

- Read the Spotlight On Posture on student page 35 and identify the importance of proper posture in singing.
- Perform the exercise for standing posture as presented on page 35.
- Perform the exercise for sitting posture as presented on page 35.
- Compare the concept of proper posture to basic performance techniques and the effect posture has on breath support, tone quality and overall stage presence.

Progress Checkpoints

Observe students' progress in:

✓ Their ability to stand in correct singing posture.

✓ Their ability to sit using correct singing posture.

✓ Their ability to explain the importance of proper posture in singing.

Cantemos Alleluia

OVERVIEW

Composer: Emily Crocker
Text: Based on Psalm 148
Voicing: SAB
Key: D major/E major
Meter: 4/4
Form: ABA
Style: Contemporary American Anthem
Accompaniment: Piano
Programming: Concert Opener, Festival

Vocal Ranges:

OBJECTIVES

After completing this lesson, students will be able to:

- Identify music form ABA aurally and through music notation.
- Describe and perform the interval of the parallel sixth.
- Interpret the text in an expressive manner.

VOCABULARY

Have students review vocabulary in student lesson. Introduce terms found in the music. A complete glossary of terms is found on page 240 of the student book.

LESSON 5

Cantemos Alleluia

Composer: Emily Crocker
Text: Based on Psalm 148
Voicing: SAB

VOCABULARY

concert etiquette
ABA form
descant
parallel sixths

Focus

- Identify and perform music in ABA form.
- Describe and perform parallel sixths.
- Interpret the text in an expressive manner.

Getting Started

If you were to listen to a live performance of "Cantemos Alleluia," you would most likely respond enthusiastically to the energy and excitement of this song. But as an audience member, it is also your responsibility to respond appropriately. **Concert etiquette** is *a term used to describe how we are expected to behave in formal musical performances.* Participation in choir will help you become not only a better singer, but also a more appreciative audience member.

SPOTLIGHT

To learn more about concert etiquette, see page 99.

◆ History and Culture

"Cantemos Alleluia" is written in ABA form. **ABA form** is *the design in which the opening phrases (section A) are followed by contrasting phrases (section B), which leads to a repetition of the opening phrases (section A).* Section A of "Cantemos Alleluia" (measures 1–29) consists of two melodies. First, the Baritones sing a melody in English. Then, the Sopranos and Altos introduce a new melody in Spanish. Section B (measures 30–55) has a contrasting melody. When section A returns, composer Emily Crocker combines the English melody and the Spanish melody. The song's rousing ending includes a **descant,** or *a special part that is usually sung higher than the melody.* Find these sections in the music.

RESOURCES

Intermediate Sight-Singing

Sight-Singing in D Major, pages 99–102
Sight-Singing in E Major, pages 188–189
Reading Rhythms in 4/4 Meter, pages 1–9

Teacher Resource Binder

Teaching Master 5, *Pronunciation Guide for "Cantemos Alleluia"*
Teaching Master 6, *Thoughts on "Cantemos Alleluia"*
Evaluation Master 5, *Concert Etiquette Quiz*
Vocal Development 15, *Vowels*
Dalcroze 16, *Musical Style*
For additional resources, see TRB Table of Contents.

Links to Learning

Vocal

Perform the following example to sing the word "Alleluia" with tall vowel sounds. Is this example most like the melody in section A or section B?

Theory

Perform the following example to experience singing parallel sixths. **Parallel sixths** are *a group of notes that are a sixth apart and move in parallel motion.* Find the parallel sixths in section B.

Artistic Expression

If you are not familiar with Spanish, memorize the English translation of the Spanish lyrics to this song. When singing in Spanish, think about the English translation so that you communicate the meaning of the text to your audience.

Evaluation

Demonstrate how well you have learned the skills and concepts featured in the lesson "Cantemos Alleluia" by completing the following:

- Make up simple motions to use while singing section A (swaying, tapping, clapping, etc.). Stand still during section B. To demonstrate your understanding of ABA form, perform the entire song moving or standing still during each section.
- Define *parallel sixths.* Find one example of parallel sixths in the music.
- Working with a partner, quiz each other's knowledge of the English translation for the Spanish lyrics.

RESOURCES

Intermediate Mixed Rehearsal/Performance CD

CD 1:9 Voices
CD 1:10 Accompaniment Only
CD 3:5 Vocal Practice Track—Soprano
CD 4:5 Vocal Practice Track—Alto
CD 6:5 Vocal Practice Track—Baritone

National Standards

1. Singing, alone and with others, a varied repertoire of music. **(a, b, c, d)**
5. Reading and notating music. **(a)**
6. Listening to, analyzing, and describing music. **(a, c)**

LINKS TO LEARNING

Vocal

The Vocal section is designed to prepare students to use proper diction when singing the word *alleluia.*

Have students:

- Read the rhythm of the Vocal exercise.
- Sing the Vocal exercise using solfège syllables.
- Sing the Vocal exercise using the word *alleluia* with tall vowels and avoiding diphthongs.

Theory

The Theory section is designed to prepare students to participate in singing parallel sixths.

Have students:

- Sing the Theory section, using solfège syllables.
- Sing the exercise as written.
- Find the parallel sixths in Section B of the song.

Artistic Expression

The Artistic Expression section is designed to prepare students to understand and memorize the English translation of the Spanish lyrics.

Have students:

- Read silently as you speak the words in Spanish.
- Listen to the recording for the lyrics to be sung in Spanish.
- Have students speak the lyrics in the correct rhythm.
- Memorize the Spanish lyrics for better performance.

LESSON PLAN

Suggested Teaching Sequence and Performance Tips

1. Introduce

Direct students to:

- Read and discuss the information found in the Getting Started section on student page 36.
- Practice singing the word *alleluia* with tall vowel sounds as instructed in the Vocal section on page 37.
- Practice singing parallel sixths as instructed in the Theory section on page 37.
- Read through the lyrics. Learn to pronounce the Spanish text. A pronunciation guide can be found in the Teacher Resource Binder, Teaching Master 5.

For the 1993 TMEA Region 19 Jr. High Choir, Houston, Texas

Cantemos Alleluia

For SAB and Piano

Text based on Psalm 148

Music by EMILY CROCKER

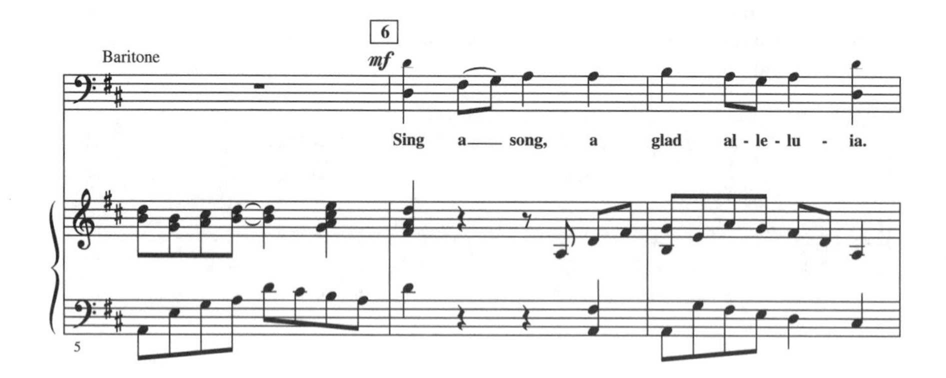

TEACHER 2 TEACHER

Emily Crocker is known nationally as a composer and hails from Texas. Her sensitivity to the developing voice, expanding the sequence of learning for the intermediate level student and the need for children to express the joy of music through singing can be found in many works written by her. She is currently the director of the Milwaukee Children's Choir and continues to instill the love of singing in young people.

*Optional English lyrics

Progress Checkpoints

Observe students' progress in:

✓ Their ability to pronounce *alleluia* with tall vowel sounds.

✓ Their ability to sing parallel sixths.

✓ Their ability to pronounce the Spanish lyrics.

ENRICHMENT

The Psalms

The Psalms have long been a source of lyrics for composers. A Hebrew poetry collection, the Psalms are ancient prayers and songs used by the Jews. Scholars date the earliest psalms to around 500 B.C. Nothing is known, however, about how psalms were sung at that time. As a poetry collection, the Psalms are remarkable for the vast span of human emotions that are included.

2. Rehearse

Direct students to:

- Part by part, count the rhythms in Section A, measures 6–26. When rhythms are correct, add pitches part by part.
- Learn Section B by counting the rhythms. Notice phrases that repeat similar rhythmic patterns. *(measures 30–31 and 32–33, measures 34–35 and 36–37, 38–39, 40–41 and 42–43; measures 46–47 and 50–51)*
- Learn pitches when rhythms are accurate. Give particular focus to measures 50–55, which is the transition into the return of Section A.
- Identify measures 56–65 as the return of Section A and is a repetition of the themes learned earlier. Sight-sing measures 56–65.

40 Intermediate Mixed

TEACHING STRATEGY

Suspensions and Dissonances

Be sure to point out the suspensions, discussed in Lesson 4, in measure 20 of "Cantemos Alleluia." Ask students if they hear this harmonic interest in other places. *(measures 24, 30–31, 42–43, 59, 63, and 73)* Review how suspensions are created and have students find these examples in the music.

- Learn the descant that begins at measure 66, beginning with rhythms and then the pitches.
- Combine the melody with the descant from measure 66 to the end, giving focus to the ending that begins at measure 72.

Progress Checkpoints

Observe students' progress in:

✓ Their ability to perform accurate rhythms and pitches.
✓ Their ability to sing in clear harmony where three parts are notated.
✓ Their ability to sing parallel sixths between the outer voices in measures 30–32 and 40–43.
✓ Their ability to sing clearly the pitches slurred together in the descant.

TEACHING STRATEGY

Phrase Form

Understanding form is most important when trying to memorize music. The section form ABA is obvious to singers and listeners alike. The phrase form, or the poetic form, is also important to singers. Once the phrase form is analyzed and the repetitions are obvious, singing from memory is much easier.

3. Refine

Direct students to:

- Pronounce the English and Spanish with active and energetic diction and with tall vowel sounds.
- Accurately place syllables that begin a phrase off the beat, such as in measures 8, 11, 17, 30, and so on. Don't allow these to be late or rushed.
- Apply the dynamic markings as indicated, giving artistic shape to the whole composition.

MORE ABOUT...

Twentieth-Century Composers

Have students:

- Contact local arts agencies to learn the names of any composers in the community.
- Invite a local composer to visit the classroom. (You will need to screen choices for appropriateness.)
- Plan questions to ask about the art of composing music.
- Listen to some compositions by this composer. Plan a performance or video using the composer's piece.

Progress Checkpoints

Observe students' progress in:

- Their correct pronunciation of both the English and Spanish lyrics.
- Their correct application of the dynamic markings.

ASSESSMENT

Informal Assessment

In this lesson, students showed the ability to:

- Pronounce English and Spanish lyrics with tall vowel sounds.
- Sing parallel sixths.
- Recognize ABA form.

Student Self-Assessment

Have students evaluate their individual performances based on the following:

- Posture
- Breath Management
- Diction
- Spanish Pronunciation
- Accurate Rhythms

Have each student rate his/her performance of this song in the areas above on a scale of 1–5, 5 being the best.

MORE ABOUT...

Form

The form of a piece is shown in alphabetical order, with each new section being named by the next letter. The first section is always A, and any identical section will also be called A. If a section is nearly identical, it will become A' (A prime) The second section will be called B, the next C, and so on. Common forms are AB (verse-refrain), ABA (ternary), ABACA (rondo). These forms are frequently modified by the composer and may have introductions, interludes and codas as well.

To help students expand their music literacy, have them list the characteristics of the A and B sections of "Cantemos Alleluia." Compare the lists and discuss any contrast between the two sections.

Individual and Group Performance Evaluation

To further measure growth of musical skills presented in this lesson, direct students to complete the Evaluation section on page 37.

- Have students create movements to "Cantemos Alleluia" to demonstrate ABA form. Have them perform these movements in class. Evaluate their ability to understand ABA form.
- Each student should find an example of a parallel sixths in their music. Check their answers.
- Have students pair up and check each other's translation of the Spanish lyrics.

44 Intermediate Mixed

MORE ABOUT...

Spanish Music in Your Community

Have students:

- Search for performances of Spanish music within your community.
- Explore recordings of Spanish music available in the record store.
- Make plans to attend a live performance of Spanish music.
- Invite a Spanish music performer, composer, or other artist from the community to come to the class and discuss Spanish music with them.

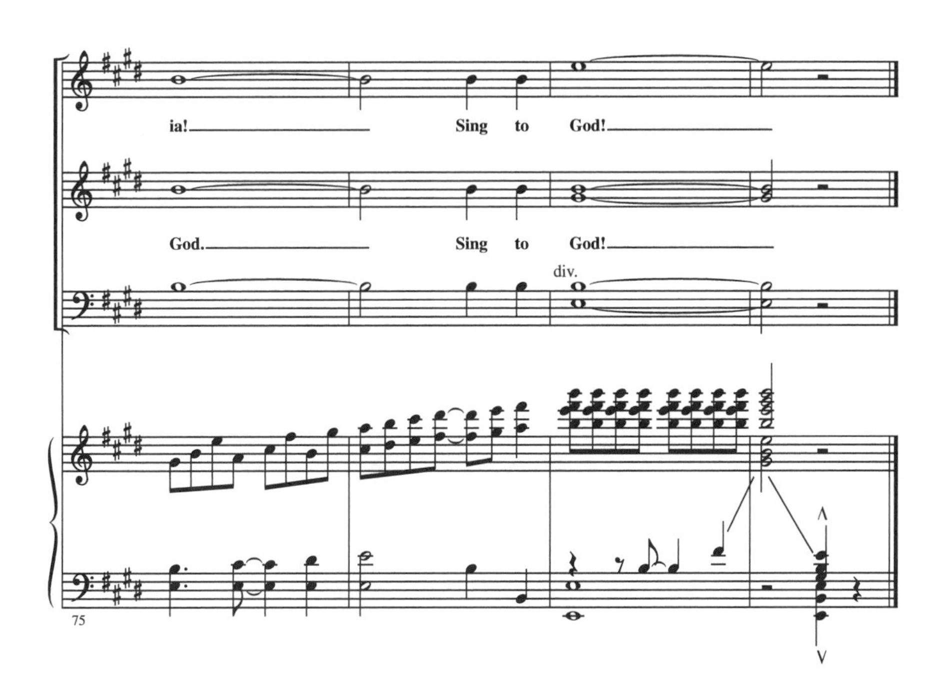

EXTENSION

Adding Percussion Instruments

The addition of Latin percussion instruments (maracas, clavès, or hand drums) can enhance or horribly detract from the performance of a concert piece. Limiting them to the introduction, interludes and the last two measures where there is only piano accompaniment or the final chord will make sure they do not cover the sound of the voices.

Music, Society and Culture

Have students perform additional songs representing diverse cultures, including American and Texas heritage. Go to **music.glencoe.com**, the Web site for Glencoe's choral music programs, for additional music selections students can perform.

Additional National Standards

The following National Standards are addressed through the Assessment, Extension, Enrichment and bottom-page activities:

1. Singing, alone and with others, a varied repertoire of music. **(a, b, c)**

6. Listening to, analyzing, and describing music. **(b)**

7. Evaluating music and music performances. **(a, b)**

9. Understanding music in relation to history and culture. **(a)**

Winter Storm (from *Windseasons*)

OVERVIEW

Composer: Audrey Snyder
Text: Audrey Snyder
Voicing: 3-Part Mixed
Key: D minor
Meter: 4/4 with two 3/4 measures
Form: ABCBC Coda
Style: Contemporary American Song
Accompaniment: Piano
Programming: Winter Concert

Vocal Ranges:

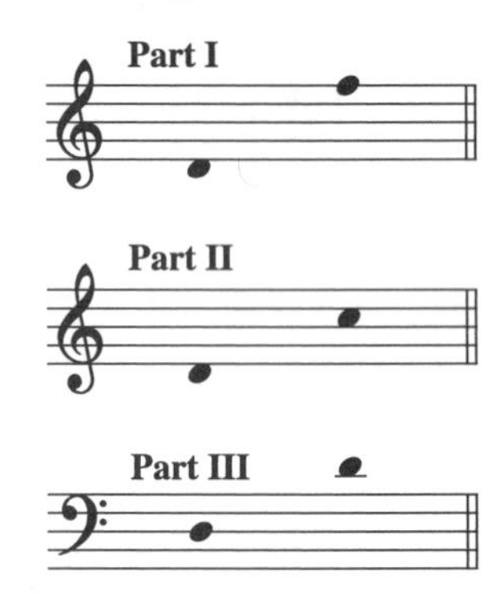

OBJECTIVES

After completing this lesson, students will be able to:

- Relate music to other subjects.
- Describe, write and perform syncopated rhythm patterns.
- Sing accurately and expressively in a percussive style.

VOCABULARY

Have students review vocabulary in student lesson. Introduce terms found in the music. A complete glossary of terms is found on page 240 of the student book.

LESSON 6

Winter Storm

Composer: Audrey Snyder
Text: Audrey Snyder
Voicing: 3-Part Mixed

VOCABULARY

chord
syncopation

Focus

- Relate music to other subjects.
- Use standard terminology to describe a chord.
- Read and perform syncopated rhythmic patterns.

SKILL BUILDERS

To learn more about the key of D minor, see Intermediate Sight-Singing, *page 52.*

Getting Started

Select one word to complete the following phrases.

1. *Who has seen the _______, neither you nor I, but when the leaves bow down their heads the _______ is passing by.*
2. The _______ chill factor today is a frigid -3°. Brrr!

The word is *wind*, the ubiquitous weather phenomenon present in every season. For such a small word, it can cause much havoc. Its strong force during a tornado or hurricane can destroy an entire house or region. In the winter, the wind can change a few inches of snow into a treacherous blizzard that paralyzes a community. *Wind*—a small word with a mighty punch.

◆ History and Culture

To prepare for this lesson, write an acrostic poem about the wind. An acrostic poem is one in which the first letter of each line, taken in order, forms a word. Write each letter of the word *wind* down the side of your paper. Then, compose a four-line poem with descriptive words that begin with each letter of the word *wind*. Study the example below to get started.

W *ailing and howling,*
I *ncessant and urgent,*
N *ovember winds blow*
D *ecember to calendar's end.*

RESOURCES

Intermediate Sight-Singing

Sight-Singing in D minor, pages 63–64 and 78–80

Reading Syncopations, pages 126–129

Teacher Resource Binder

Teaching Master 7, *Rhyming With "Winter Storm"*

Skill Builder 1, *Building Harmony*

Skill Builder 23, *Rhythm and Kodály*

Skill Builder 24, *Rhythm Challenge Using Syncopation*

Kodály 6, Music Reading: *Rhythm*

For additional resources, see TRB Table of Contents.

Links to Learning

◆ Vocal

Perform the following example to sing chords that are used in "Winter Storm." A **chord** is *a combination of three or more notes sung at the same time.*

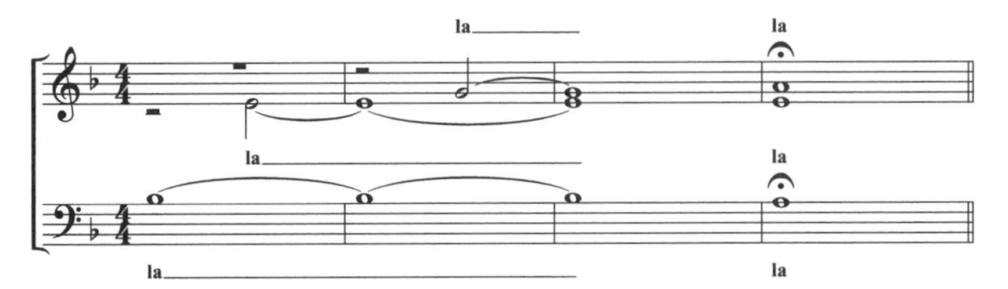

◆ Theory

Syncopation is *a rhythmic pattern in which the placement of accents is on a weak beat or a weak portion of the beat.* Copy the following rhythmic patterns on a sheet of paper. Perform by clapping, tapping or chanting. What makes these patterns syncopated?

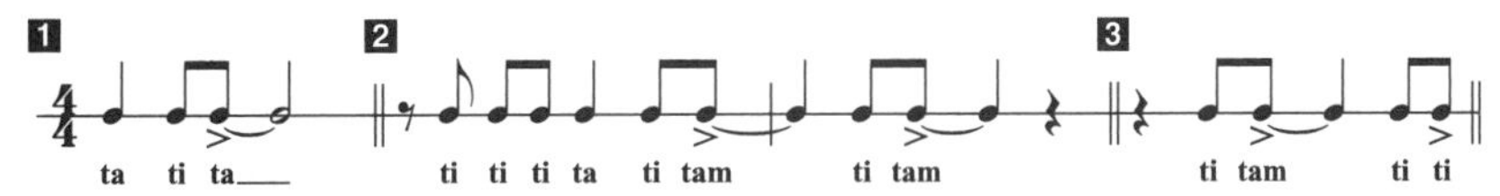

Evaluation

Demonstrate how well you have learned the skills and concepts featured in the lesson "Winter Storm" by completing the following:

- Share your acrostic poem with the class. Find places in the music that match the descriptive words you used in your poem.
- With a partner, perform measures 10–17 to show your ability to sing syncopated rhythms correctly. One partner will tap steady eighth notes while the other partner sings. Switch roles. How did you do?

LINKS TO LEARNING

Vocal

The Vocal section is designed to prepare students to sing chords, moving from suspension to resolution.

Have students:

- Learn their part of the vocal exercise and sing.
- Recognize the dissonance that builds and finally resolves at the fermata.

Theory

The Theory section is designed to prepare students to:

- Understand, identify and perform syncopated rhythms.
- Recognize major, minor and diminished chords found in "Winter Storm."

Have students:

- Read the definition of syncopation and circle each example of it in the exercise.
- Write in the beats of each pattern.
- Perform each rhythm example until it can be recited and clapped to a steady beat.

RESOURCES

Intermediate Mixed Rehearsal/Performance CD

CD 1:11 Voices
CD 1:12 Accompaniment Only
CD 3:6 Vocal Practice Track—Part I
CD 4:6 Vocal Practice Track—Part II
CD 6:6 Vocal Practice Track—Part III

National Standards

1. Singing, alone and with others, a varied repertoire of music. **(a, d, e)**
5. Reading and notating music. **(a, c)**
6. Listening to, analyzing, and describing music. **(a, c)**
8. Understanding relationships between music, the other arts, and disciplines outside the arts. **(a)**

LESSON PLAN

Suggested Teaching Sequence and Performance Tips

1. Introduce

Direct students to:

- Read and complete the activities presented in the Getting Started section on page 46. Have students use a winter-looking font or create an illustrated background for their acrostic poem.
- Practice singing three-part chords in the Vocal section on page 47.
- Practice and perform the pattern of the Theory exercise by clapping and chanting the counting at the same time.
- Write three different two-measure syncopated patterns in 4/4 meter using eighth rests and ties. Exchange patterns with a friend and sing and tap the patterns.
- Practice identifying and building major, minor and diminished chords. Choose one student to sing any pitch and challenge teams of students to build chords on that pitch.

Winter Storm

from *Windseasons*

For 3-Part Mixed and Piano

Words and Music by
AUDREY SNYDER

48 Intermediate Mixed

TEACHER 2 TEACHER

Most winter songs speak of gently falling snow and sparkling stars at night. But there is definitely another side to winter. So it is refreshing to come upon a winter song full of angular poetry, icy rhythms and jagged melodies. "Winter Storm" also provides an excellent vehicle for introducing syncopated patterns utilizing eighth rests and ties. Have your students listen to "Winter" from the *Four Seasons* by Antonio Vivaldi to set the mood for this song. This will be especially helpful if you begin learning "Winter Storm" in October, and it is a balmy 70° where you live!

- Listen and find any two measure syncopated patterns in the voice parts other than measures 10–11 that the teacher or accompanist plays on the piano. *(Suggested patterns to find: measures 16–17, 25–26, 28–29, 35–36, and 38–39.)*
- Sing measures 10-16 on solfège while keeping a steady tempo by tapping a subdivided beat.

Progress Checkpoints

Observe students' progress in:

✓ Their ability to maintain a steady beat.

✓ Their ability to discriminate between syncopated and nonsyncopated passages.

✓ Their ability to tune chords accurately.

MORE ABOUT...

Listen to Winter by Other Composers:

- Antonio Vivaldi: *The Four Seasons,* Concerto No. 4 F minor rv 297—"Winter"
- Peter Ilyich Tchaikovsky: *The Seasons*—A collection of short piano works written for each month of the year and intended to be published in the monthly magazine *The Novelist* during 1916.
- Franz Joseph Haydn: *The Seasons*—This is a choral drama that tells the story of a year in the life of a small rural community. The weather plays a very important part of the piece, such as "the fleecy clouds rise up sublime," and "flashes of livid flame dart through the air."

2. Rehearse

Direct students to:

- Chant the words to measures 10–26 while tapping a steady subdivided beat in a very icy staccato style. Then sing the words in the same style.
- Divide into small 3-part mixed groups. Assign each group one of the following phrases: measures 28–31, measures 32–34, and measures 35–39. Groups should write in the counting, clap or tap the notes while counting out loud, and then chant the words to rhythm. Allow groups to perform for and critique each other.
- Sing measures 28–39 on solfège syllables and then sing on words.

TEACHING STRATEGY

Related Minor Keys

Teaching the relationship of minor keys to major keys is not very hard if you use solfège. Merely relate the *do* scale to the *la* scale. In vocal warm-ups, have students sing scales in solfège starting on *do* first. Then move down to *la* and make it the home tone of the warm-up. Explain that minor scales have the same whole-step half-step pattern as found in the *la*-based scale. Students will respond to the minor tonality, which will set up the song "Winter Storm."

- Return to small groups to learn the slow introduction. This time, students should work out the rhythm, solfège and words in a sequential manner. Allow time for students to perform for and critique each other.
- Rehearse the entire piece section by section, all staccato, then all legato. Work to combine the two, creating a style that has the pointed quality of the staccato with the connection of the legato.

Progress Checkpoints

Observe students' progress in:

✓ Ability to work and accomplish tasks in small groups.

✓ Ability to listen and match tones with each other.

TEACHING STRATEGY

Tuning Chords

To help students listen to one another, have one student in each of three groups choose a pitch and hold it out until everyone in the group is singing the same pitch, using a neutral syllable such as "oo" or "ah." Point to one student from another group. That student changes the group pitch, and everyone must listen and move to that pitch. Continue to point to individual students in each of the three groups, waiting each time until the group has tuned to the new pitch. The chords will be very interesting, sometimes dissonant, which require even more careful listening. Encourage soft singing, and very careful listening within and among groups.

3. Refine

Direct students to:

- Rehearse the entire piece at different tempos, working for crisp articulation, clean releases and precise rhythms.
- Find and define all expressive and dynamic markings. Work in sectionals to perform all markings.
- Choose individual students to sing two measure solos during the unison sections (measures 10–23, 41–50) while each section performs the entire song for the class. Repeat and rotate solo measures and singers.
- Perform the entire song with different combinations of students singing the two-measure solo phrases.

Progress Checkpoints

Observe students' progress in:

✓ Ability to express the mood of the piece through facial energy.

✓ Vocal independence through solo singing.

ASSESSMENT

Informal Assessment

In this lesson, students showed the ability to:

- Independently learn a short phrase by sequentially addressing rhythm, pitch and text in a small group setting.
- Identify and sing major, minor and diminished chords

Student Self-Assessment

Have students evaluate their individual performances based on the following:

- Breath Management
- Diction
- Expressive Singing
- Intonation
- Correct Part-Singing

Have each student rate his/her performance of this song in the areas above on a scale of 1–5, 5 being the best.

MORE ABOUT...

Minor Sound

If students seem interested in the minor sound, place a staff on the board and write both the F major scale and the D minor scale. They both have the same key signature. Minor scales have three possibilities: natural, melodic and harmonic. There are also minor modes. Have the students find out more about minor scales and modes in a Theory text, then learn to play each one. They might improvise or compose short minor melodies using mostly stepwise motion.

Individual and Group Performance Evaluation

To further measure growth of musical skills presented in this lesson, direct students to complete the Evaluation section on page 47.

- After students share their acrostic poems with the class, have them find places in the music that match words used in their poems.
- Have students pair up and sing measures 10–17. One partner will sing while the other taps steady eighth notes. They should evaluate each other's ability to sing syncopated rhythms.

EXTENSION

- Have students compose music for the acrostic wind poetry using at least one major, minor and diminished chord.
- Have students learn the other pieces in the *Windseasons* cycle.

ENRICHMENT

- Have students create a travel brochure for an actual location for "Winter Storm," promoting the positive features of winter at that location.
- Have students collect recordings of winter music and design a radio program that combines the music with a short informative narrative about each piece.

54 Intermediate Mixed

Additional National Standards

The following National Standards are addressed through the Assessment, Extension, Enrichment and bottom-page activities:

4. Composing and arranging music within specific guidelines. **(a)**

7. Evaluating music and music performances. **(b)**

9. Understanding music in relation to history and culture. **(a, b)**

Vowels

The style of a given piece of music dictates how we should pronounce the words. If we are singing a more formal, classical piece, then we need to form taller vowels as in very proper English. If we are singing in a jazz or pop style, then we should pronounce the words in a more relaxed, conversational way. To get the feeling of taller vowels for classical singing, do the following:

- Let your jaw gently drop down and back as if it were on a hinge.
- Place your hands on your cheeks beside the corners of your mouth.
- Sigh on an *ah* [ɑ] vowel sound, but do not spread the corners of your mouth.
- Now sigh on other vowel sounds—*eh* [ɛ], *ee* [i], *oh* [o] and *oo* [u]—keeping the back of the tongue relaxed.
- As your voice goes from higher notes to lower notes, think of gently opening a tiny umbrella inside your mouth.

ee
[i]

eh or ā*
[ɛ] [e]

ah
[a]

oh
[o]

oo
[u]

Other vowel sounds used in singing are diphthongs. A **diphthong** is *a combination of two vowel sounds*. For example, the vowel *ay* consists of two sounds: *eh* [E] and *ee* [i]. To sing a diphthong correctly, stay on the first vowel sound for the entire length of the note, only lightly adding the second vowel sound as you move to another note or lift off the note.

I = *ah*________(ee) [ɑi]

boy = *oh*________(ee) [oi]

down = *ah*________(oo) [ɑu]

*Note: This is an Italian "ā," which is one sound, and not an American "ā," which is a diphthong, or two sounds.

Spotlight *Vowels* 55

RESOURCES

Teacher Resource Binder

Vocal Development 15, *Vowels*

Reference 16, *My Music Dictionary*

Reference 29, *Zeroing in on IPA*

National Standards

1. Singing, alone and with others. **(b)**

VOWELS

Objectives

- Demonstrate basic performance techniques through proper use of vowels.

Suggested Teaching Sequence

Direct students to:

- Read the Spotlight On Vowels on student page 55 and identify the importance of uniform vowels in singing.
- Practice the exercise as presented on page 55.
- Identify the five basic vowels. Practice speaking and singing each.
- Define *diphthong* and demonstrate the proper and improper way to sing a diphthong.
- Find examples of each of the five basic vowels and diphthongs in music they are currently studying.
- Compare the concept of uniform vowels to appropriate large- and small-ensemble performance techniques.

Progress Checkpoints

Observe students' progress in:

✓ Their ability to speak the five basic vowels properly and uniformly.

✓ Their ability to define *diphthong,* find examples in the music and sing them properly.

✓ Their ability to relate the importance of uniform vowels in ensemble singing.

Shalom Aleichem

OVERVIEW:

Composer: I. and S. E. Goldfarb, arranged by Gil Aldema, edited by J. Mark Dunn
Text: Traditional
Voicing: SAB
Key: A harmonic minor
Meter: 4/4
Form: ABBA
Style: Jewish Song
Accompaniment: a cappella
Programming: Multicultural Concert, Festival

Vocal Ranges:

OBJECTIVES

After completing this lesson, students will be able to:

- Sing music in a various articulation styles.
- Write and perform music in the key of A minor.
- Describe and perform Jewish music.

VOCABULARY

Have students review vocabulary in student lesson. Introduce terms found in the music. A complete glossary of terms is found on page 240 of the student book.

LESSON 7

Shalom Aleichem

Composer: I. and S. E. Goldfarb, arranged by Gil Aldema, edited by J. Mark Dunn
Text: Traditional
Voicing: SAB

VOCABULARY

- articulation
- staccato
- legato
- harmonic minor scale

Focus

- Sing music using various articulation styles.
- Write and perform music in the key of A minor.
- Perform music that represents the Jewish culture.

Getting Started

Match the following greetings with the correct country.

1. *bonjour*	**a.** Italy
2. *konnichi wa*	**b.** Spain
3. *ssalamu 'lekum*	**c.** Japan
4. *ciao*	**d.** Israel
5. *hola*	**e.** France
6. *shalom*	**f.** Morocco

It is not uncommon for greetings to have more than one meaning. For example, the Hebrew greeting *shalom* means "hello," "goodbye" and "peace."

SKILL BUILDERS

To learn more about the A harmonic minor scale, see Intermediate Sight-Singing, *page 68.*

◆ History and Culture

Shalom aleichem, (translated, "Peace be with you") is a traditional Hebrew greeting that Jewish families sing at Shabbat (Sabbath) on Friday evenings. The Hebrew words and Yiddish melody welcome the Shabbat angels to the dinner table and wish them a safe journey back home. Candles are always present at the Shabbat table, but there can also be fresh flowers, handmade paper decorations and challah—a special braided egg bread—to celebrate the peace and joy of the occasion.

The Shabbat spirit of togetherness is also reflected in this beautiful arrangement of "Shalom Aleichem." The vocal lines intertwine and complement each other with musical sensitivity. Listen carefully while you sing and decide how you can support the others in your choir by using dynamic contrast and expressive phrasing.

RESOURCES

Intermediate Sight-Singing

Sight-Singing in A Minor, pages 20–22, 33–35, and 68–72.

Reading Triplets and Duplets, pages 135–136.

Teacher Resource Binder

Teaching Master 8, *Pronunciation Guide for "Shalom Aleichem"*

Teaching Master 9, *Composing a Melody in A minor*

Skill Builder 13, *Constructing Minor Scales*

Vocal Development 8, *Articulation*

Kodály 5, *Music Reading: Pitch*

For additional resources, see TRB Table of Contents.

Links to Learning

◆ Vocal

Articulation is *the amount of separation or connection between notes.* Perform the following example **staccato** *(a short and detached style of singing).* Then, sing it again **legato** *(a connected and sustained style of singing)*, disregarding the staccato markings. When singing legato, use lots of breath support on the syllable "-lom" to avoid an aspirated "h" sound between pitches.

◆ Theory

"Shalom Aleichem" is loosely based on the harmonic minor scale. The **harmonic minor scale** is *a minor scale in which the* sol *(7th pitch) is raised a half step to* si. Sing the following A harmonic minor scale.

Evaluation

Demonstrate how well you have learned the skills and concepts featured in the lesson "Shalom Aleichem" by completing the following:

- Choose a four-measure phrase from "Shalom Aleichem" to sing for a classmate. Sing the phrase first in a staccato style and then in a legato style. Switch roles. Evaluate how well you were able to sing in both styles.
- Using the pitches found in the A harmonic minor scale, compose a four-measure melody in $\frac{4}{4}$ meter that begins and ends on *la* or A. Perform your melody for the class. Check your work for rhythmic and melodic accuracy.

RESOURCES

Intermediate Mixed Rehearsal/Performance CD

CD 1:13 Voices

CD 1:14 Accompaniment Only

CD 3:7 Vocal Practice Track—Soprano

CD 4:7 Vocal Practice Track—Alto

CD 6:7 Vocal Practice Track—Baritone

National Standards

1. Singing, alone and with others, a varied repertoire of music. **(a, b, c, d, e)**
5. Reading and notating music. **(a, b, c, d, e)**
6. Listening to, analyzing, and describing music. **(a, b, c)**
9. Understanding music in relation to history and culture. **(a)**

LINKS TO LEARNING

Vocal

The Vocal section is designed to prepare students to:

- Understand the term *articulation* and how to sing both legato and staccato phrases.
- Develop and use breath support strategies for singing legato phrases.

Have students:

- Read the definition of articulation.
- Practice singing the exercise in both staccato and then legato styles, making note that the exercise is in A minor.
- Sing as written.

Theory

The Theory section is designed to prepare students to sing melodic patterns from the harmonic minor scale.

Have students:

- Sing the exercise in both solfège and then pitch names. Make note of the altered *sol (si)* that creates a half step between the seventh and eighth scale tones.
- Practice the descending scale passage *la, si, fa* until it is properly tuned.

LESSON PLAN

Suggested Teaching Sequence and Performance Tips

1. Introduce

Direct students to:

- Read, discuss and complete the activities as outlined in the Getting Started section on the student page 56. Ask the students to share any other foreign language greetings they may know. Jewish students may want to contribute to the discussion of Shabbat (Sabbath).
- Sing any other Jewish/ Hebrew songs they may know. Start a list of similarities among the songs, such as tempo, language and tonality.
- Practice the articulation exercise as outlined in the Vocal section on page 57. Ask students to work with a partner. While one student sings, the other will listen for a smooth legato between the two pitches on the syllable "lom." Remind students to take a deep breath and sing "lom" with a rounded "oh" vowel and no tension in the jaw or throat.
- Chant or recite the solfège syllables for the Soprano line measures 1–8 at a slow, steady tempo. Working in groups of 4–8, ask each student to be responsible for one or two pitches from the Soprano line *(re, mi, fa, si, la, ti, do, re′, mi′)*. As a small group, sing measures 1–8 with each student singing only the pitches she/he is responsible for. Keep a steady tempo between singers. Ask students to create a legato line by holding their pitch until the next singer begins. Allow groups to sing for and critique each other.

Shalom Aleichem

For SAB, a cappella

Arranged by GIL ALDEMA
Edited by J. MARK DUNN

Music by
I. & S. E. GOLDFARB

TEACHER 2 TEACHER

Some students may know other traditional Jewish melodies for the text "Shalom Aleichem." Invite the students to share these with the class. This particular melody, with its initial ascending *mi* to *do* skip and harmonic minor character, is a challenging but beautiful technical study for all singers. Encourage students to learn all three parts and sing them interchangeably. This will be especially helpful for the students who cannot comfortably sing the wide range of the Bass part as written.

CONNECTING THE ARTS

Listening

Composer Leonard Bernstein (1918–1990) wrote "Chichester Psalms" for boy soprano, adult choir and orchestra. The lyrics are Hebrew and include various psalms from the Bible and the Torah. The beautiful and lyrical soprano solo is very accessible for intermediate treble voices.

- Learn their individual voice part for measures 1–8 using the strategies from above, working in voice groups. Allow sections to sing for each other.
- Learn measures 9–16 in a similar manner.

Progress Checkpoints

Observe students' progress in:

✓ Their ability to contribute productively to small group work.

✓ Their ability to sing a harmonic minor scale with accurate intonation.

✓ Their ability to distinguish between *sol* and *si*.

2. Rehearse

Direct students to:

- Follow their voice line as the song is played and sing only the correct pitches on all the dotted quarter notes. Repeat and sing only the eighth notes, then only the dotted half notes.
- Sing measures 1–16 in solfège at a steady tempo with accurate rhythm patterns.
- Write out the Hebrew text for measures 1–6, discuss pronunciation and speak in rhythm.
- As a class, sing measures 1–16 with the Hebrew text.
- Ask students to find similarities and differences between measures 18–25 and measures 1–16.
- A pronunciation guide can be found in the Teacher Resource binder, Teaching Master 8.
- Working in SAB ensembles of six to nine ask students to learn the notes, rhythms and text for measures 18–25. Allow students to perform for and critique each other.

Progress Checkpoints

Observe students' progress in:

✓ Their ability to sing in three parts.

✓ Their correct pronunciation of the gutteral"ch" consonant with a strong current of air.

3. Refine

Direct students to:

- Work in voice part sectionals, and find all syllables that are sung over two, three, or four pitches. Practice each of these syllables (vocal slurs) and work for a smooth, legato connection as demonstrated in the Vocal section on page 57. Give special attention to the syllables with large interval skips. *(Soprano measure 4, and measure 5; Bass measure 4; Alto measure 10)*
- Discuss the concept of four-measure phrasing. Brainstorm techniques that will enable the students' breath support to extend for four measures.

  For example: Slow and silent deep breathing, impeccable posture, starting each phrase *piano* and growing in intensity to the middle of the phrase. Ask students to demonstrate these ideas in sectional groups.

Progress Checkpoints

Observe students' progress in:

✓ Their ability to maintain a steady pulse.

✓ Their ability to crescendo and decrescendo of the phrase.

✓ Ability to bring out the moving parts of each vocal line.

60 Intermediate Mixed

CULTURAL CONNECTIONS

- Have students compile a list of foreign language greetings and use a different greeting in choir every day for a month.
- Have students learn to write "Shalom Aleichem" using Hebrew letters.

ASSESSMENT

Informal Assessment

In this lesson, students showed the ability to:

- Make technical decisions that lead to a legato style of singing.
- Read and sing with independence and accuracy 4/4 measure patterns in harmonic minor.

Student Self-Assessment

Have students evaluate their individual performances based on the following:

- Posture
- Phrasing
- Hebrew Language
- Accurate Pitches
- Correct Part-Singing

Have each student rate his/her performance of this song in the areas above on a scale of 1–5, 5 being the best.

MORE ABOUT...

Staggered Breathing

Legato style necessitates well-supported staggered breathing.

Have students:

- Practice holding out chord tones, each person breathing at a different time than either neighbor and then joining back in without any accent.
- Continue to hold the chord indefinitely, each section changing their pitch as indicated by the teacher, but sustaining the tone through staggered breathing.

Individual and Group Performance Evaluation

To further measure growth of musical skills presented in this lesson, direct students to complete the Evaluation section on page 57.

- After students pair up, have them select a phrase to sing for their partner. They should sing it first staccato and then legato. Evaluate and switch roles.
- After each student has composed a four-measure melody in A minor, ask for volunteers to play or sing their composition for the class. The class should evaluate. Did the student meet all the requirements of the assignment?

EXTENSION

- Using the library, music textbooks, recordings, or the Internet, have students find another version of "Shalom Aleichem" with a different melody. Learn and sing for the class.
- Using solfège syllables have students learn "Hine Ma Tov," "Shalom Chaverim," "Artza Alinu" or another Hebrew folk song. Add the text, sing for the class and incorporate this song into a performance with "Shalom Aleichem."

Additional National Standards

The following National Standards are addressed through the Assessment, Extension, Enrichment and bottom-page activities:

4. Composing and arranging music within specific guidelines. **(a)**

7. Evaluating music and music performances. **(a)**

8. Understanding relationships between music, the other arts, and disciplines outside the arts. **(a)**

9. Understanding music in relation to history and culture. **(b)**

Arranging

In music, an **arrangement** is *a composition in which a composer takes an existing melody and adds extra features or changes the melody in some way.* An **arranger** is *a composer who writes an arrangement by changing an existing melody to fit certain musical parameters.* The arranger has the following things to consider:

- Pitch—What is the range of the melody?
- Tempo—What is the speed of the beat?
- Instrumentation—Is the music for voices, instruments or both?
- Accompaniment—What will be used for accompaniment (piano, guitar, etc.), if anything?
- Harmony—What type of chords will be used for the harmony?
- Melody/Countermelody—Will harmony be added by use of a **countermelody** (*a separate vocal line that supports and contrasts the primary melody*)?

Read and perform the familiar melody "Hot Cross Buns."

Now you are ready to write your own arrangement. Using "Hot Cross Buns" as the existing melody, decide which element or elements you wish to change to compose your arrangement. You can try one or more of the ideas listed below:

- Pitch—Start the song higher or lower than currently written.
- Tempo—Alter the tempo in some manner (faster or slower).
- Instrumentation—Play the melody on different instruments.
- Accompaniment—Use a piano, guitar or other instrument to accompany your melody.
- Harmony—Add harmony notes from the chords and play them on an instrument or sing them with the melody.
- Melody/Countermelody—Compose a second melody or countermelody that fits musically with the existing melody.

ARRANGING

Objectives

- Arrange melodic and rhythmic phrases.

Suggested Teaching Sequence

Direct students to:

- Read the Spotlight On Arranging on student page 63 and discuss the difference between an arranger and an arrangement.
- Identify the six elements an arranger must consider in writing an arrangement.
- Sing "Hot Cross Buns," then write an arrangement of "Hot Cross Buns" following the guidelines listed on page 63.
- Perform the arrangement for the class.
- Compare an arrangement to an original composition and find examples of arrangements in this book.

Progress Checkpoints

Observe students' progress in:

✓ Their ability to identify the six components to consider in arranging.

✓ Their ability to write a simple arrangement of "Hot Cross Buns."

RESOURCES

Teacher Resource Binder

Teaching Master 10, *Arranging "Hot Cross Buns"*
Skill Builder 14, *8-line Staff Paper*
Reference 7, *Building a Musical Vocabulary*
Reference 16, *My Music Dictionary*

National Standards

4. Composing and arranging music within specific guidelines. **(b)**

Calypso Gloria

OVERVIEW

Composer: Emily Crocker
Text: Traditional Latin
Voicing: SATB
Key: E♭ Major
Meter: 4/4
Form: Two phrases repeated with varied textures
Style: Contemporary American Calypso
Accompaniment: Piano with optional Bass and Percussion
Programming: Concert, Contest or Festival

Vocal Ranges:

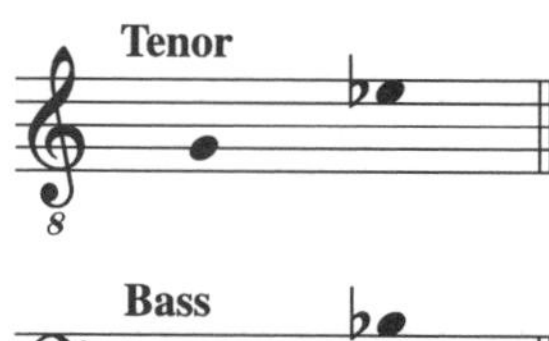

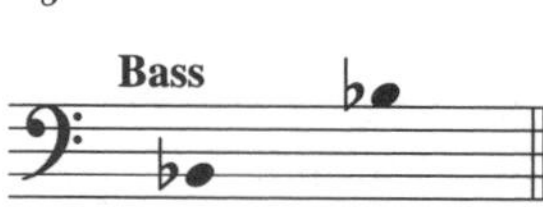

OBJECTIVES

After completing this lesson students will be able to:

- Perform expressively in Latin.
- Perform increasingly complex rhythmic phrases.
- Read music notation.

VOCABULARY

Have students review vocabulary in student lesson. Introduce terms found in the music. A complete glossary of terms is found on page 240 of the student book.

LESSON 8

Calypso Gloria

Composer: Emily Crocker
Text: Traditional Latin
Voicing: SATB

VOCABULARY
calypso
diction
syncopation

Focus

- Sing in Latin using tall, pure vowel sounds.
- Perform music that contains calypso rhythms.
- Create and perform rhythmic phrases.

Getting Started

Have you ever seen a parade? Maybe you have watched the Macy's Thanksgiving Day Parade from New York City, or the Rose Bowl Parade from Pasadena, California. At first, you can hear the music of the marching band long before you can see it. The sound is distant. As the band moves closer and closer, the sound gets louder and louder. Then, it passes by in full display. Soon the band marches on and the sound fades away. When you perform "Calypso Gloria," think of the passing band and the changing dynamics from beginning to end.

SPOTLIGHT

To learn more about diction, see page 25.

◆ History and Culture

Calypso is *a style of music that originated in the West Indies and which features syncopated rhythms.* Composer Emily Crocker has taken the syncopated rhythms associated with calypso music and used them in "Calypso Gloria." The calypso style of music can be traced back to the early slaves in the Caribbean islands of Trinidad and Tobago. During that time, slaves were forbidden to speak to one another. They developed a unique way of communicating through singing. From this the rhythms of calypso music emerged, a blend of African, Spanish and French influence.

The translation of the Latin text is as follows:

Gloria in excelsis deo. Et in terra pax hominibus bonae voluntatis.

Glory to God on high. And on earth peace to men of good will.

RESOURCES

Intermediate Sight-Singing

Sight-Singing in E♭ major, pages 141–143
Reading in Tied notes, pages 32 and 44
Reading in Syncopations, pages 126–129

Teacher Resource Binder

Teaching Master 11, *Pronunciation Guide for "Calypso Gloria"*
Teaching Master 12, *Creating Syncopated Phrases*
Evaluation Master 3, *Assessing Performing Syncopated Rhythms*
Evaluation Master 6, *Diction Checkup*
Vocal Development 9, *Diction*
For additional resources, see TRB Table of Contents.

Links to Learning

Vocal

As you perform the example below, let your jaw gently drop down and back as if it were on a hinge. Place your hands on your cheeks beside the corners of your mouth. Sing this example at a very slow tempo. **Diction,** or *the pronunciation of words while singing,* includes both tall, pure vowels and crisp consonants.

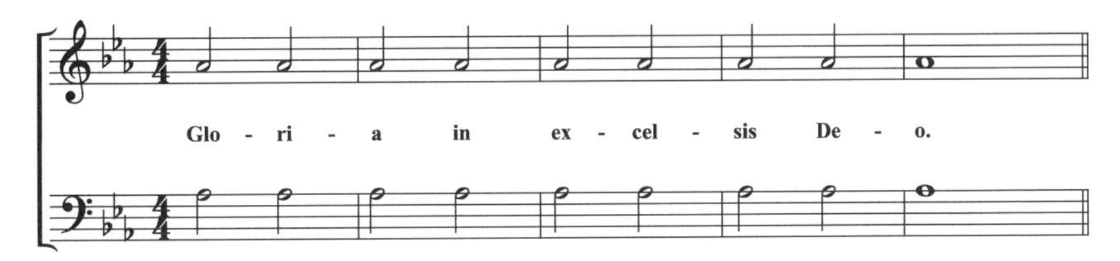

Theory

Syncopation is *a rhythmic pattern that places the accents on a weak beat or a weak portion of the beat.* Read and perform the following examples to practice placing the accents off the beat.

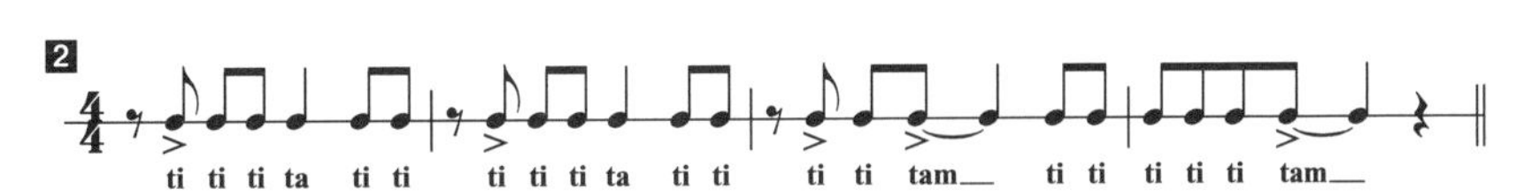

Artistic Expression

To develop artistry through movement, clap the rhythmic patterns in the Theory section above while stepping the steady beat. For a super challenge, clap the steady beat while you step the syncopated rhythms!

Evaluation

Demonstrate how well you have learned the skills and concepts featured in the lesson "Calypso Gloria" by completing the following:

- Record yourself as you sing measures 29–36. Listen carefully to the recording and evaluate how well you were able to sing with pure, tall vowel sounds.
- Accompany your choir as they sing "Calypso Gloria." Play Example 1 from the Theory section above using hand percussion instruments such as finger cymbals, a guiro, rhythm sticks, a tambourine or a hand drum.
- Write an original four-measure rhythmic phrase that contains syncopation. Perform your phrase for another student. Check your work for rhythmic accuracy and the correct notation for syncopation.

LINKS TO LEARNING

Vocal

The Vocal section is designed to prepare students to:

- Understand diction
- Sing with a relaxed jaw using tall, pure vowels and crisp consonants.

Have students:

- Sing the exercise using tall, pure vowels and with a dropped, relaxed jaw.
- Sing the exercise slowly and without diphthongs.

Theory

The Theory section is designed to prepare students to:

- Understand syncopation.
- Read, perform, and notate syncopated rhythms using eighths, quarters, and rests.

Have students:

- Tap or clap the quarter note pulse.
- Speak the rhythm pattern accenting the syncopated beats, while continuing to tap the quarter-note pulse.
- Speak the rhythm pattern while director conducts in 4/4, while feeling the quarter-note pulse inside.

RESOURCES

Intermediate Mixed Rehearsal/Performance CD

CD 1:15 Voices
CD 1:16 Accompaniment Only
CD 3:8 Vocal Practice Track—Soprano
CD 4:8 Vocal Practice Track—Alto
CD 5:1 Vocal Practice Track—Tenor
CD 6:8 Vocal Practice Track—Bass

National Standards

1. Singing, alone and with others, a varied repertoire of music. **(a, d)**
4. Composing and arranging music within specific guidelines. **(a)**
9. Understanding music in relation to history and culture. **(a, d)**

Artistic Expression:

The Artistic Expression section is designed to prepare students to be able to:

- Kinesthetically apply rhythms in a flowing, eurhythmic, manner.
- Develop artistry through movement.
- Step the steady beat, while clapping the rhythm patterns in the Theory section.
- Clap the steady beat, while stepping the syncopated rhythms.

LESSON PLAN

Suggested Teaching Sequence and Performance Tips

1. Introduce

Direct students to:

- Read and discuss the information found in the Getting Started section on the student page 64.
- Practice the rhythm patterns in the Theory section on page 65.

Calypso Gloria

For SATB and Piano with Optional Bass and Percussion*

Traditional Latin

Music by EMILY CROCKER

* *Pizz. bass may double piano LH*

TEACHER 2 TEACHER

This Caribbean-like setting of the "Gloria" is rhythmically buoyant and full of fun. The arrangement is harmonically diatonic and rhythmically syncopated in the style of a typical calypso. The tessitura falls well within each section's midrange. The rhythmic component is by far the most compelling aspect of the whole piece and affords the opportunity to accompany with claves, rhythm sticks or other hand-held percussion instruments. "Calypso Gloria" provides a wonderful opportunity for your choir to vocally project the joy of Christmas with rhythmic "bounce."

- Discriminate between syncopated and nonsyncopated passages as they listen to the music.
- Discuss social and cultural environment from which this music arises. Talk about the African-European cultural mix as described in the Getting Started section and how this genre of music (calypso) arose out of it.
- Practice having rhythmic precision regarding the clapping of each pattern. In the very beginning the movement should be at least "errhythmic" (regular and mechanically correct).

Progress Checkpoints

Observe students' progress in:

✓ Reading and singing each phrase with a eurhythmic sense of musical line.

✓ Performing syncopations with power and accuracy.

TEACHING STRATEGY

Adding Percussion Instruments

When adding percussion parts it is sometimes easier for young players if they have a chant or something physical to assist them. Try reciting "in ex-cel-sis" to the eighth-note pattern for the shaker rhythm. The clavès rhythm is harder but reciting "Glo-ri (rest rest) De-o" to the suggested rhythm should give the player something to aid in playing the part.

2. Rehearse

Direct students to:

- Analyze the musical score identifying measures containing the rhythms identical or similar to those given in the Theory section on page 65.
- Divide into two groups. Have half the choir clap or play the steady beat while the other half sings the alto line in measures 5–8.
- Reverse roles.
- Face a partner. Partner 1 will pat and sing measures 5–9 with his/her right hand into the left hand of partner 2. Partner 2 does the same but only pats quarter notes.
- Switch roles.
- Do the above steps again. This time partner 2 will sing and pat the Bass line of measures 21–24 against the Alto main theme.

TEACHING STRATEGY

Unified Vowels

Vowels are the fundamental building blocks of tone production, intonation and blend. A pure vowel is one that does not change when sung. When the pure vowels (*ee, ay, ah, oh,* and *oo*) are sung identically by all singers, there is a magical musical resonance and blend that can occur.

Why is it important? The unity of vowels when sung by a chorus is the key to resonance and blend. The choral instrument should sound as one voice, and even one voice in a hundred singing a different sounding vowel can destroy the resonance and blend of the artistic choral tone. Try singing identical vowels and have one or more singers sing the same vowel slightly differently. Ask: Can you hear the difference?

- Combine the two parts of measures 13–16 in this fashion (yes, even the males will learn the females' parts!).

Progress Checkpoints

Observe students' progress in:

✓ Identifying syncopated rhythms.

✓ Accurate and expressive clapping and stepping. The claps should all occur on the beat.

MORE ABOUT...

Unified Vowels

Have students listen to the recording of "Calypso Gloria" as found on the CDs in the Teacher Resource Binder. Have them listen carefully to the vowel sounds they hear on the recording. Then sing the piece live, comparing the two sounds.

3. Refine

Direct students to:

- Sing entire song one part at a time while moving to the rhythm in a eurhythmic manner. Try performing the entire piece while stepping the steady beat.
- Sing until measure 36 in four parts while moving in four circles. Sopranos and Altos can move clockwise. Basses and Tenors can move inside of the trebles and move counter-clockwise. There will be four circles, one inside the other in this order:
  - Outside circle: Soprano
  - Inside sopranos: Altos
  - Inside altos: Tenors
  - Inside tenors: Basses
- Rotate circles until the best blend is discovered.

Progress Checkpoints

Observe students' progress in:

✓ Moving with precision.

✓ Their ability to maintain perfect focus and concentration in the midst of the other two parts.

✓ Their ability to experience the happy mood of the occasion while stepping any of the parts.

TEACHING STRATEGY

More on Unified Vowels

Each vowel has a different shape in the mouth. Warm-ups and vocal exercises should focus on the shape and sound of each individual vowel and change from one vowel to another. The key is listening carefully to the vocal model and to the surrounding singers to adjust and blend the vowel tone. Connecting the vowel to breath support is another crucial feature of unified vowels. Lowered larynx, raised soft palate and open throat also contribute to the unity of the vowel sounds. Singing in another language introduces singers to new sounds that are unhindered by local, American dialectical problems such as regional diphthongs. Latin is ideal for teaching pure vowel sounds.

ASSESSMENT

Informal Assessment

In this students showed the ability to:

- Maintain a steady beat in 4/4 meter.
- Experience each part while performing and moving the other part.
- Read, perform and identify each of the four rhythms given in the Theory section.
- Experience the difference between rhythms that occur on the beat and off the beat.

MORE ABOUT...

History of Calypso Music

Calypso music is probably derived from the carnival folk music in Trinidad, West Indies. Song themes are usually stories of local interest. Originally, the only music accompaniment to calypso songs might have been a guitar, maracas or a combination of instruments. Around 1945, singers in calypso bands began to include a steel drum, now characteristic of calypso music. A vocal characteristic of calypso music is the shifting of emphasis, or putting emphasis on the unexpected syllables of words. American singer, actor and civil rights activist Harry Belafonte made calypso music popular in the United States.

Student Self-Assessment

Have students evaluate their individual performances based on the following:

- Posture
- Phrasing
- Dynamics
- Accurate Pitches
- Accurate Rhythms

Have each student rate his/her performance of this song in the areas above on a scale of 1–5, 5 being the best.

Individual and Group Performance Evaluation

To further measure growth of musical skills presented in this lesson, direct students to complete the Evaluation section on page 65.

- After recording themselves singing measures 29–36, students should listen to the recording and evaluate their ability to sing pure, tall vowels.
- Have selected students play rhythm instruments to accompany this piece, using the rhythm patterns in the Theory section. Ask, "Do these instruments enhance the performance?"
- After each student has written a rhythmic phrase with syncopation, have students pair up and evaluate each other's work.

EXTENSION

- Have students improvise gestures that coincide with the words.
- Teach the conducting pattern of 4/4. Using neutral syllables such as *ta* and *ti* ask students to intone rhythmic passages both from Links to Learning and from the piece itself while conducting. Be sure it is eurhythmic and not errhythmic.
- Compose a rhythmic phrase of 4–6 measures in length using values that have been learned. Have students notate and step their compositions.

Online

MUSIC, SOCIETY AND CULTURE

Have students perform additional songs representing diverse cultures, including American and Texas heritage. Go to **music.glencoe.com**, the Web site for Glencoe's choral music programs, for additional music selections students can perform.

Additional National Standards

The following National Standards are addressed through the Assessment, Extension, Enrichment and bottom-page activities:

1. Singing, alone and with others, a varied repertoire of music. **(b, c)**

4. Composing and arranging music within specific guidelines. **(a)**

6. Listening to, analyzing and describing music. **(a)**

7. Evaluating music and music performances. **(b)**

8. Understanding relationships between music, the other arts, and disciplines outside the arts **(a, b)**

Pitch Matching

As you begin to learn how to read music, you must learn not only how to identify the notes on the printed page, but also how to sing the notes you read in tune. Accurate pitch matching requires that you hear the note in your head before you sing it instead of trying to find the note with your voice. Learning to sing from one note to another in scale patterns will help you hear the notes in your head before you sing them. Perform the scale below first using note names, then numbers, and finally solfège syllables.

To help you sing the following examples on the correct pitch, hear the notes in your head before you sing them. If you cannot hear the interval skip in your head before you sing it, mentally sing the first note followed by all the notes in between until you come to the right note. Then, begin again and sing the pattern as written.

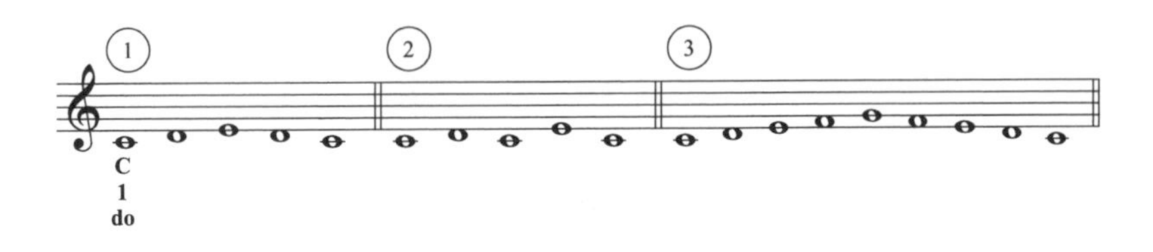

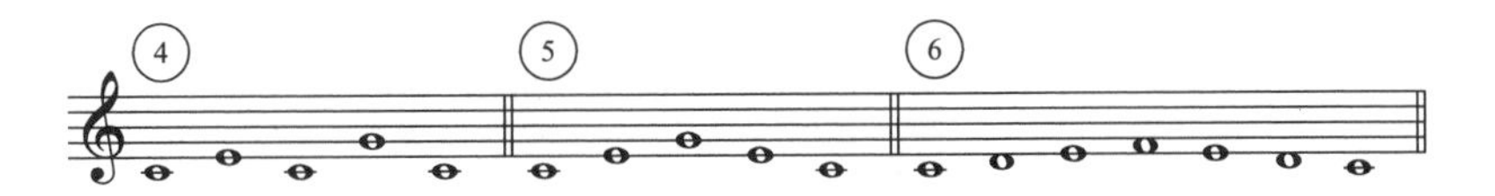

RESOURCES

Teacher Resource Binder

Skill Builder 20, *Naming Intervals*
Skill Builder 21, *Pitch and Kodály*
Kodály 5, *Music Reading: Pitch*
Reference 16, *My Music Dictionary*
Reference 29, *Zeroing in on IPA*

National Standards

1. Singing, alone and with others. **(b)**

PITCH MATCHING

Objectives

- Perform independently with accurate intonation.

Suggested Teaching Sequence

Direct students to:

- Read the Spotlight On Pitch Matching on student page 77 and identify the importance of hearing a pitch in their heads before singing it.
- Sing the C major scale as presented on page 77.
- Chant the pitch names for exercise 1, then sing the exercise, repeating as many times necessary to sing in tune securely.
- Repeat the same process for each exercise.
- Sing exercises 1–9 straight through. Check constantly for accurate intonation.

Progress Checkpoints

Observe students' progress in:

✓ Their ability to sing the C major scale in tune.
✓ Their ability to sing intervals found in the C major scale in tune.
✓ Their ability to read and sing simple melodic passages on solfège syllables.

Innsbruck, ich muss dich lassen

OVERVIEW

Composer: Heinrich Isaac (c. 1450–1517), edited by John Leavitt
Text: Heinrich Isaac
Voicing: SATB
Key: G major
Meter: 3/2, 2/2
Form: Through-composed
Style: Dutch Renaissance Chanson
Accompaniment: a cappella
Programming: Festival, Contest, Small Ensemble

Vocal Ranges:

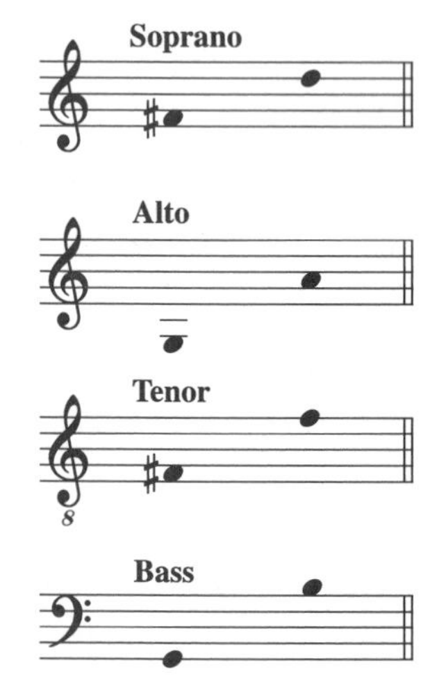

OBJECTIVES

After completing this lesson, students will be able to:

- Perform a varied repertoire of music representing styles from diverse cultures.
- Perform independently with accurate rhythm.

VOCABULARY

Have students review vocabulary in student lesson. Introduce terms found in the music. A complete glossary of terms is found on page 240 of the student book.

Innsbruck, ich muss dich lassen

Composer: Heinrich Isaac (c. 1450–1517), edited by John Leavitt
Text: Heinrich Isaac
Voicing: SATB

VOCABULARY

Renaissance period
motet
madrigal
$\frac{3}{2}$ meter
$\frac{2}{2}$ meter

Focus

- Describe and perform music from the Renaissance period.
- Read and write music in $\frac{3}{2}$ meter and $\frac{2}{2}$ meter.

Getting Started

If composer Heinrich Isaac lived today, he would probably take skis and a snowboard to Innsbruck, because this beautiful Austrian town is nestled among the snow-capped Alps. When Isaac arrived in Innsbruck around 1500, however, he probably brought musical instruments, parchment and feather pens. That's because Maximilian I, the Holy Roman Emperor, had persuaded Isaac to leave Florence, Italy, and come to Innsbruck to serve as an imperial diplomat and court composer. Isaac is best remembered for his German song "Innsbruck, ich muss dich lassen."

MUSIC & HISTORY

To learn more about the Renaissance period, see page 108.

History and Culture

Heinrich Isaac (c. 1450–1517) lived during the **Renaissance period** *(1430–1600).* Vocal music flourished during the Renaissance. The short pieces that composers wrote for singers fall into two categories, the motet and the madrigal. A **motet** is *a short, sacred choral piece with Latin text that is used in religious services but is not a part of the regular mass.* A **madrigal** is *a short, secular choral piece of the Renaissance period with text in the common language.* The joys and sorrows of love are common themes for madrigals, as are stories of country life. As a rule, most motets and madrigals are unaccompanied. Although "Innsbruck, ich muss dich lassen" ("Innsbruck, I Now Must Leave You") has a German text, Isaac used several characteristics of the Italian madrigal in this piece.

RESOURCES

Intermediate Sight-Singing

Sight-Singing in G Major, pages 82–85, 89–90

Reading Rhythms in 2/2 Meter and Cut Time, page 140

Reading Tied Notes, pages 32, 44

Teacher Resource Binder

Teaching Master 13, *Pronunciation Guide for "Innsbruck, ich muss dich lassen"*

Teaching Master 14, *Composing a Rhythmic Pattern in 3/2 or 2/2 Meter*

Music and History 1, *Characteristics of Renaissance Music: 1430–1600*

Music and History 4, *Heinrich Isaac, a "Renaissance" Composer*

For additional resources, see TRB Table of Contents.

Links to Learning

◆ Vocal

"Innsbruck, ich muss dich lassen" is in the key of G major and is based on the G major scale. To locate "G" on the keyboard, find any set of three black keys. "G" is the white key just to the left of the middle black key. This scale uses the notes G, A, B, C, D, E, F#, G. Using the keyboard as a guide, play the G major scale.

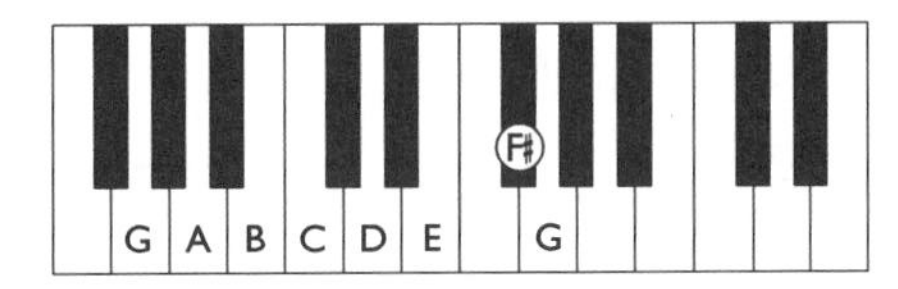

Sing the G major scale.

◆ Theory

This song is written in $\frac{3}{2}$ **meter** *(a time signature in which there are three beats per measure and the half note receives the beat)* and in $\frac{2}{2}$ **meter** *(a time signature in which there are two beats per measure and the half note receives the beat)*. Perform the following example to practice reading rhythmic patterns in both of these meters.

Evaluation

Demonstrate how well you have learned the skills and concepts featured in the lesson "Innsbruck, ich muss dich lassen" by completing the following:

- Discuss the musical characteristics of the Renaissance period.
- Using the music as a guide, compose a four-measure rhythmic pattern in $\frac{3}{2}$ or $\frac{2}{2}$ meter. Play your pattern on a rhythm instrument for the class. Check your work for correct use of notation and rhythms in $\frac{3}{2}$ or $\frac{2}{2}$ meter.

RESOURCES

Intermediate Mixed Rehearsal/Performance CD

CD 1:17 Voices
CD 1:18 Accompaniment Only
CD 3:9 Vocal Practice Track—Soprano
CD 4:9 Vocal Practice Track—Alto
CD 5:2 Vocal Practice Track—Tenor
CD 6:9 Vocal Practice Track—Bass

National Standards

1. Singing, alone and with others, a varied repertoire of music. **(b, c)**
9. Understanding music in relation to history and culture. **(a, b)**

LINKS TO LEARNING

Vocal

The Vocal section is designed to prepare students to:

- Understand the meaning of scale and major scale.
- Sing the G major scale with accuracy.

Have students:

- Play the G major scale on the keyboard. If selected students will play the scale on the keyboard, others should follow closely on the keyboard printed on page 79.
- Sing the G major scale on note names.
- Sing the G major scale on solfège.

Theory

The Theory section is designed to prepare students to:

- Read rhythms in 3/2 and 2/2 meters.
- Read and perform half notes and rests and quarter notes and rests in 3/2 and 2/2 meter.

Have students:

- Clap or tap the half note pulse.
- Clap or tap the rhythm in the exercise.
- Speak the rhythm in the exercise using rhythm syllables.

LESSON PLAN

Suggested Teaching Sequence and Performance Tips

Direct students to:

- Read the information in the Getting Started section on page 78. Discuss any other general information the students know about the Renaissance, 16th century music, Innsbruck or Austria.
- Practice singing the ascending and descending pitches of the G major scales in the Vocal section on page 79. Relate the scale to the key of the song.
- Practice clapping the exercise in the Theory section of page 79. Note that these two meters are used in the song.
- As a choir, determine the key signature *(G major)* and sing only *do* and *re* in all four voice parts. Have the entire choir sing each voice part.
- Divide into three groups. Group One will sing the *do* and *re's,* Group Two the *mi* and *fa's,* Group Three the *sol, la* and *ti's.* Sing each voice part in this manner. Repeat and exchange pitches.
- Sing all of the pitches using solfège syllables for measures 1–6 in each of the voice parts.
- Learn the notes for measures 7–18 in the same manner.
- Recite the German text in rhythm for each of the voice parts. A pronunciation guide can be found in the Teacher Resource Binder, Teaching Master 13.

Innsbruck, ich muss dich lassen

(Innsbruck, I Now Must Leave You)

For SATB, a cappella

Edited with English text by
JOHN LEAVITT

HEINRICH ISAAC
(c. 1450–1517)

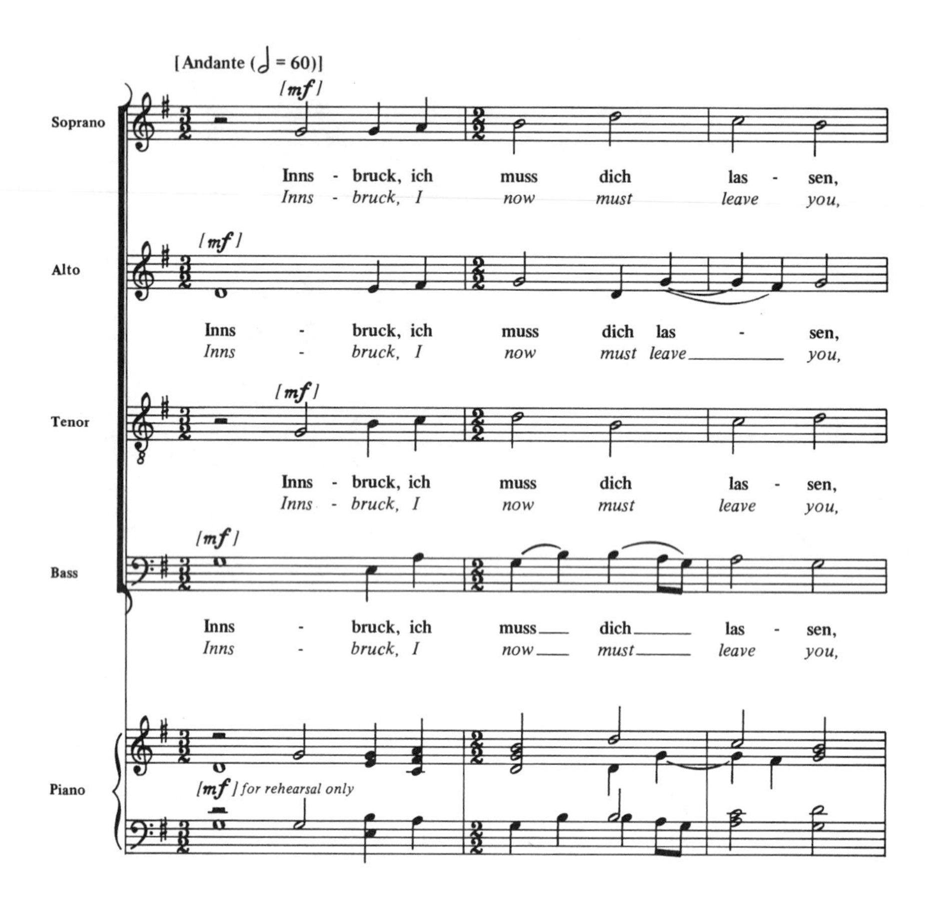

TEACHER 2 TEACHER

Despite its brevity, there is a multitude of teachable topics within "Innsbruck, ich muss dich lassen." Consider revisiting this piece throughout the year, each time with a different focus. These might include a cappella singing, count singing, quartet singing, German text, Renaissance style and historical connections. As the students' skill and maturity grow throughout the year, they will gain more satisfaction and a sense of accomplishment from this legendary Renaissance gem.

- Work in sectionals and sing each individual voice part with the German text. Repeat until students feel secure.
- Discuss legato phrasing. Sing the entire song, breathing only at the rests. Have students work in sectionals and choose one note, syllable or word to be the focal point of each phrase. Allow each section to perform for the class. Ask the class to identify each focal point.
- Sing "Innsbruck, ich muss dich lassen" in English several times to emphasize the meaning of the text.
- Perform "Innsbruck, ich muss dich lassen" a cappella in German with all necessary phrasing and dynamic markings. Allow students to compliment and critique the performance.

Progress Checkpoints

Observe students' progress in:

✓ Singing rhythms accurately.
✓ Their ability to read musical notation.
✓ Their use of correct German pronunciation of the vowels.
✓ Their ability to sing single measures with independence.
✓ Their ability to maintain a steady pulse while count-singing.
✓ Their ability to express mood of piece through facial expression.

CURRICULUM CONNECTIONS

Renaissance Life

Have students:

- Make an illustrated, abbreviated chart about the art, philosophy, politics, music, science and daily life of Europe from 1450–1550.
- Choose a famous person from the sixteenth century to portray. Research the life and accomplishments of that person. With a small group of friends improvise a scene in which all the famous people meet each other at a roadway inn and have a conversation over dinner.

ASSESSMENT

Informal Assessment

In this lesson, students showed the ability to:

- Sing intervals accurately while using solfège syllables in the key of G major.
- Sing expressively in German with an understanding of the text.

Student Self-Assessment

Have students evaluate their individual performances based on the following:

- Diction
- Foreign Language
- Expressive Singing
- Intonation
- Correct Part-Singing

Have each student rate his/her performance of this song in the areas above on a scale of 1–5, 5 being the best.

Individual and Group Performance Evaluation

To further measure growth of musical skills presented in this lesson, direct students to complete the Evaluation section on page 79.

- After discussing musical characteristics of the Renaissance period, write a one-page report on those characteristics found in "Innsbruck, ich muss dich lassen."
- After playing the four-measure rhythm patterns for the class, combine the patterns and play them one after another without stopping.

82 Intermediate Mixed

Additional National Standards

The following National Standards are addressed through the Assessment, Extension, Enrichment and bottom-page activities:

4. Composing and arranging music within specific guidelines. **(a)**

5. Reading and notating music. **(b)**

6. Listening to, analyzing, and describing music. **(b)**

8. Understanding relationships between music, the other arts, and disciplines outside the arts. **(b)**

9. Understanding music in relation to history and culture. **(b)**

Breath Management

Vocal sound is produced by air flowing between the vocal cords; therefore, correct breathing is important for good singing. Good breath management provides you with the support needed to sing expressively and for longer periods of time.

To experience, explore and establish proper breathing for singing, try the following:

- Put your hands on your waist at the bottom of your rib cage.
- Take in an easy breath for four counts, as if through a straw, without lifting your chest or shoulders.
- Feel your waist and rib cage expand all the way around like an inflating inner tube.
- Let your breath out slowly on "sss," feeling your "inner tube" deflating as if it has a slow leak.
- Remember to keep your chest up the entire time.
- Take in another easy breath for four counts before your "inner tube" has completely deflated, then let your air out on "sss" for eight counts.
- Repeat this step several times, taking in an easy breath for four counts and gradually increasing the number of counts to let your air out to sixteen counts.

Sometimes in singing it is necessary to take a quick or "catch" breath.

- Look out the window and imagine seeing something wonderful for the first time, like snow.
- Point your finger at the imaginary something and let in a quick, silent breath that expresses your wonderment and surprise.
- A quick breath is not a gasping breath, but rather a silent breath.

RESOURCES

Teacher Resource Binder

Vocal Development 13, *Posture & Breathing*

Evaluation Master 4, *Checking Out Phrasing*

Reference 16, *My Music Dictionary*

National Standards

1. Singing, alone and with others. **(b)**

BREATH MANAGEMENT

Objectives

- Sing accurately with good breath control.

Suggested Teaching Sequence

Direct students to:

- Read the Spotlight On Breath Management on student page 83 and identify the importance of breath management when singing.
- Perform the exercise described on page 83.
- Practice a "catch" breath as described at the bottom of page 83.
- Compare the concept of proper breath management to effective performance practices.

Progress Checkpoints

Observe students' progress in:

✓ Their ability to perform the breathing exercises described on page 83.

✓ Their ability to discuss the importance of proper breath management when singing.

Come Joyfully Sing

OVERVIEW

Composer: George Frideric Handel (1685-1759), edited by Patrick M. Liebergen
Text: English Text by Patrick M. Liebergen
Voicing: SAB
Key: B♭ major
Meter: 3/4
Form: IntroAABCBCACoda
Style: German Baroque Anthem
Accompaniment: Piano
Programming: Seasonal Concert

Vocal Ranges:

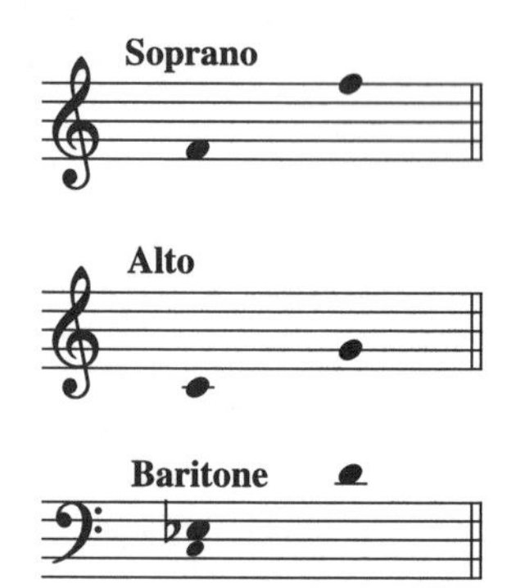

OBJECTIVES

After completing this lesson, students will be able to:

- Classify aurally presented music representing diverse periods.
- While performing, demonstrate fundamental skills.
- Perform independently with accurate rhythm.

VOCABULARY

Have students review vocabulary in student lesson. Introduce terms found in the music. A complete glossary of terms is found on page 240 of the student book.

LESSON 10

Come Joyfully Sing

Composer: George Frideric Handel (1685–1759), edited by Patrick M. Liebergen
Text: English Text by Patrick M. Liebergen
Voicing: SAB

VOCABULARY

Baroque period
oratorio
serenata
dynamics
conductor

Focus

- Describe and perform music from the Baroque period.
- Perform music with accurate dynamics.
- Read and conduct rhythmic patterns in $\frac{3}{4}$ meter.

Getting Started

If you attended a wedding in 1708, you might have heard "Come Joyfully Sing," instead of "Here Comes the Bride." That is because "Come Joyfully Sing" was written for a wedding celebration. During the eighteenth century, it was not uncommon for composers to write music for special occasions such as weddings and birthdays for members of the royal family.

MUSIC & HISTORY

To learn more about the Baroque period, see page 112.

◆ History and Culture

George Frideric Handel (1685–1759) is one of the most famous composers from the **Baroque period** *(1600–1750).* Born in Germany, he studied harpsichord, oboe, organ and violin and began composing at a young age. As an adult, he lived and worked in Italy and England, where he composed operas and other works. One of his most famous compositions is the "Hallelujah Chorus" from an **oratorio** *(a dramatic work for solo voices, chorus and orchestra presented without theatrical action)* called the *Messiah.*

"Come Joyfully Sing" was composed in 1708 and is from a larger work called a **serenata,** *a dramatic cantata or semi-opera written for a special occasion.* A serenata differs from a full-scale opera in that the singers are stationary and do not move about the stage. "Come Joyfully Sing" is from Handel's serenata *Acis, Galatea, e Polifemo* that tells the mythological tale of Acis (a shepherd), Galatea (a sea nymph), and Polifemo (a cyclops). Serenatas were very popular during the Baroque period.

RESOURCES

Intermediate Sight-Singing

Sight-Singing in B♭ Major, pages 121–129
Reading Rhythms in 3/4 Meter, pages 17–22
Reading Eighth Notes and Rests, pages 26–27
Reading Dotted Notes, pages 45, 48, 49

Teacher Resource Binder

Teaching Master 15, *Conducting with a Difference*
Skill Builder 7, *Conducting: an Introduction*
Skill Builder 9, *Conducting in 3/4 Meter*
Music and History 6, *Characteristics of Baroque Music: 1600–1750*
Music and History 9, *George Frideric Handel, a "Baroque" Composer*
For additional resources, see TRB Table of Contents.

Links to Learning

◆ Vocal

Using solfege syllables, perform the following example to practice good intonation in the key of B♭ major. Notice the contrasting **dynamics,** or *symbols that indicate how loud or soft to sing,* and follow these as you sing.

◆ Theory

Conducting is an important part of musical performance. A **conductor** is *a person who uses hand and arm gestures to interpret the expressive elements of music for singers and instrumentalists.*

Read and perform the following examples to practice rhythmic patterns in 3/4 meter. Conduct the 3/4 pattern as you count the patterns below. Start with a moderate to slow tempo. Repeat the pattern several times, each time using a different tempo. As the tempo increases, you will start feeling the beat in one rather than in three.

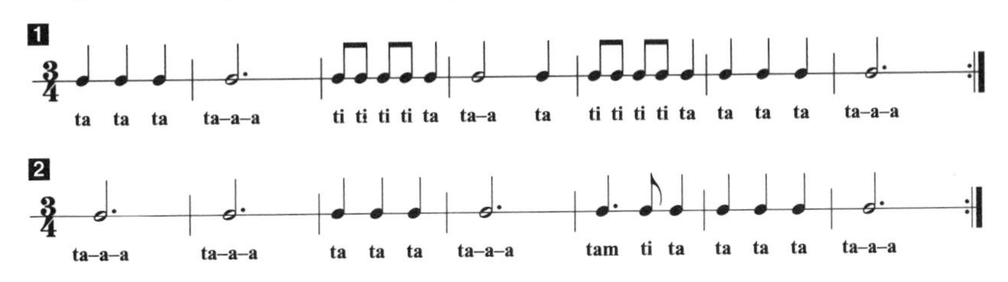

Evaluation

Demonstrate how well you have learned the skills and concepts featured in the lesson "Come Joyfully Sing" by completing the following:

- Discuss the musical characteristics of the Baroque period.
- Sing measures 30–45 in a group of six (two to a part), accurately following all dynamics. Discuss as a group how well you were able to show the varied dynamics.
- Be a conductor! Conduct the choir singing measures 1–13 of "Come Joyfully Sing." First, establish a moderate tempo and appropriate conducting pattern. Then, repeat at the performance tempo with the correct conducting pattern. Can you successfully conduct in patterns of one and three?

RESOURCES

Intermediate Mixed Rehearsal/Performance CD

CD 1:19 Voices
CD 1:20 Accompaniment Only
CD 3:10 Vocal Practice Track—Part I
CD 4:10 Vocal Practice Track—Part II
CD 6:10 Vocal Practice Track—Part III

National Standards

1. Singing, alone and with others, a varied repertoire of music. **(b)**
6. Listening to, analyzing, and describing music. **(b)**

LINKS TO LEARNING

Vocal

The Vocal sections is designed to prepare students to:

- Develop pitch accuracy within B♭ major, the key of the song.
- Establish an understanding of the dynamics that contrast in "Come Joyfully Sing."

Have students:

- Sing the Vocal exercise using solfège syllables.
- Vary the dynamics by singing the exercise loudly *(f)* the first time and medium soft *(mp)* the second.

Theory

The Theory section is designed to prepare students to:

- Read rhythms in 3/4 meter.
- Conduct in 3/4 meter at various tempos.

Have students:

- Clap or tap the quarter note pulse in 3/4 meter.
- Clap or tap the rhythm in exercise 1.
- Speak the rhythm in exercise 1 using the rhythm syllables below the staff.
- Clap or tap the rhythm in exercise 2.
- Speak the rhythm in exercise 2 using the rhythm syllable below the staff.
- Perform the exercises as a selected student conducts in 3/4 meter at various tempos. Eventually, as the tempo increases he/she should use the conducting pattern in one.

LESSON PLAN

Suggested Teaching Sequence and Performance Tips

1. Introduce

Direct students to:

- Sight-sing measures 5–13 using solfège syllables.
- Sing measures 5–13 again on the neutral syllable "doo" with students emphasizing an accented downbeat on every measure.
- Sing measures 5–13 with text and dynamics as written.
- Sight-sing measures 14–29 on the neutral syllable "doo."

Come Joyfully Sing

For SAB and Piano

Arranged with English Text by
PATRICK M. LIEBERGEN

GEORGE FRIDERIC HANDEL
(1685–1759)

TEACHER 2 TEACHER

The joyful, exuberant message of "Come Joyfully Sing" is a great way to start a school year, a rehearsal or a performance. This light, buoyant tune will inspire and uplift your singers.

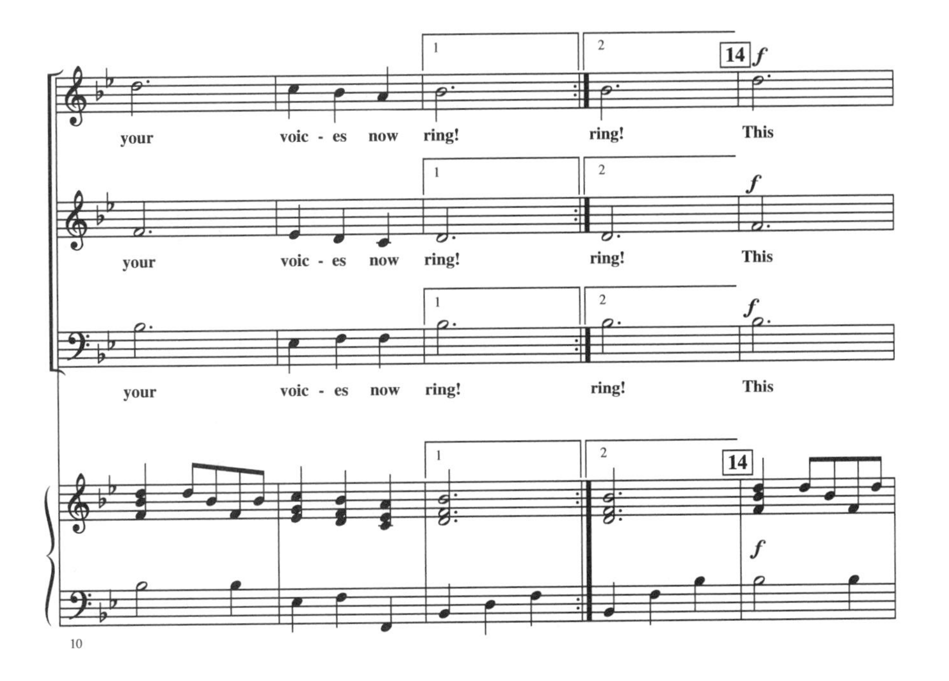

- Add text and work individual parts in measures 14–29 as needed.
- Have students listen to measures 30–45 and determine if this section is the same, similar or different from any previously learned portion of the song. *(measures 30–45 are the same as measures 14–29 with the exception of the dynamic markings. Note: measure 14 = f; measure 30 = mp; measure 38 = cresc. and measure 42 = f).*

Progress Checkpoints

Observe students' progress in:

✓ Establishing pitch accuracy in individual parts.

✓ Choral balance and intonation in chord building.

✓ Observing and performing true dynamic contrasts.

EXTENSION

Conducting

An effective conductor will enhance the expressive choral experience and not hinder it. Have the students further explore their conducting experience through other known repertoire. Dynamics and tempo are good places for an inexperienced conductor to begin to explore the power in their leadership skills. Have the students choose one of these elements and first explore the extremes (e.g., largo and presto tempos) in leading the choir. Then they should eventually come to an appropriate tempo for the selected repertoire.

2. Rehearse

Direct students to:

- Review all parts from the beginning, bringing out the moving eighth-note patterns in each voice in the C section.
- Sight-sing measures 46–end with text.
- Locate and discuss the dynamics indicated in measures 46 to the end.
- Practice measures 46–end with appropriate use of dynamics.
- Return to the beginning of the piece and locate and discuss the metronome marking.

88 Intermediate Mixed

TEACHING STRATEGY

3/4 Meter and Dotted Rhythms

If students are not familiar with either the meter or dotted quarter-eighth note rhythms, have them:

- Clap a rhythm challenge in 3/4 meter that you write on the board until they are comfortable with the elements found in "Come Joyfully Sing."
- Learn the conducting pattern for 3/4 meter and conduct as they sing to feel the meter more securely.

- Play on a metronome or clap a steady beat and ask students to listen to and then identify a variety to tempo settings.
- Choose three different tempos and sing "Come Joyfully Sing" at each of these tempos.
- Discuss which tempos felt awkward and inappropriate and which felt natural and effective for the piece.

Progress Checkpoints

Observe students' progress in:

✓ Bringing out moving eighth-note patterns in measures 25–29 with clear, clean articulation.

✓ Singing with a light, buoyant choral sound.

✓ Determining a tempo that allows for clear articulation of the text and effective dynamics while maintaining buoyant, joyful tone.

MORE ABOUT...

Arranger Patrick M. Liebergen

Patrick Liebergen is the Director of Choral Activities at the University of Wisconsin (Stout) and Director of the Chancel Choir at United Methodist Church in Menomonie, Wisconsin. With music degrees from St. Norbert College in DePere, Wisconsin, the University of Wisconsin (Madison), and the University of Colorado, Dr. Liebergen frequently appears throughout the country as an adjudicator and clinician. His choral editions, arrangements, and original works are widely performed. Dr. Liebergen was the 1988 winner of the Wisconsin Choral Directors Association Composition Competition and the 1990 winner of the anthem contest sponsored by the Twin Cities Church Musicians Association.

3. Refine

Direct students to:

- Compare and sing four-measure phrases with everyone breathing together, to eight-measure phrases with staggered breathing.
- Conduct while singing. Practice both four-measure and eight-measure phrasing.
- Memorize the piece.
- Work toward a pleasant performance by emphasizing facial expressions and posture that exhibit and invitation to light-heartedness.

Progress Checkpoints

Observe students' progress in:

✓ Establishing an effective tempo and maintaining a steady beat throughout the piece.

✓ Reacting to dynamics as indicated through student and teacher conducting techniques.

✓ Using effective body and facial expression to convey the text and joy of the music.

ASSESSMENT

Informal Assessment

In this lesson, students showed the ability to:

- Interpret various conducting movements referring to dynamics.
- Interpret and perform various conducting patterns referring to tempo.
- Conduct in 3/4 meter at various tempos.
- Demonstrate the ability to sing in three parts in the choral setting while maintaining accurate pitch and intonation.

90 Intermediate Mixed

CURRICULUM CONNECTIONS

The Baroque Style

Have students:

- Research the social and musical characteristics of the Renaissance and Baroque periods.
- Identify characteristics of this piece that make it an example of Renaissance music.
- Identify the characteristics of this piece that make it an example of Baroque music.
- Find examples of art, architecture, poetry, drama or dance that reflect any or all of the characteristics identified in the piece.

Student Self-Assessment

Have students evaluate their individual performances based on the following:

- Breath Management
- Phrasing
- Expressive Singing
- Intonation
- Correct Part-Singing

Have each student rate his/her performance of this song in the areas above on a scale of 1–5, 5 being the best.

Individual and Group Performance Evaluation

To further measure growth of musical skills presented in this lesson, direct students to complete the Evaluation section on page 85.

- After discussing musical characteristics of the Baroque period, write a one-page report on those characteristics found in "Come Joyfully Sing."
- After singing measures 30–45 in groups of six, evaluate the performances by asking, "How obvious were the varied dynamics?"
- After students have conducted measures 1–13 in patterns of one and three, review each example by asking, "How clear was each conductor? Could we follow the tempos when he/she used conducting patterns of one and three?"

Additional National Standards

The following National Standards are addressed through the Assessment, Extension, Enrichment and bottom-page activities:

5. Reading and notating music. **(a)**
8. Understanding relationships between music, the other arts, and disciplines outside the arts. **(a)**
9. Understanding music in relation to history and culture. **(b)**

Bless The Lord, O My Soul

OVERVIEW

Composer: Mikhail Ippolitov-Ivanov (1859–1935), edited by Joyce Eilers
Text: Psalm 103
Voicing: 3-Part Mixed
Key: E♭ major
Meter: 4/4
Form: AA'A"BA'"
Style: Russian Romantic Anthem
Accompaniment: a cappella
Programming: Contest, Large and Small Ensemble

Vocal Ranges:

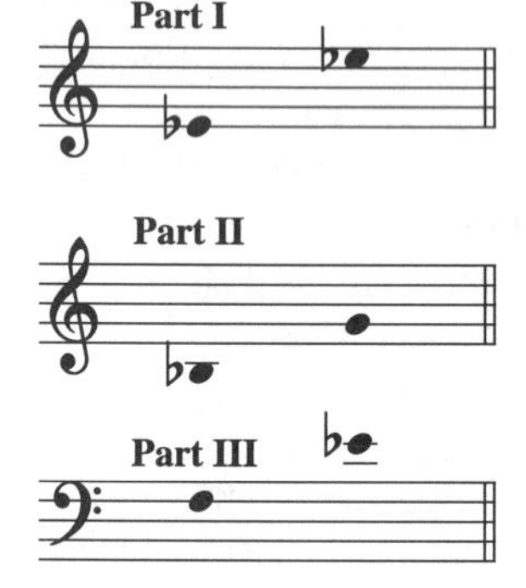

OBJECTIVES

After completing this lesson, students will be able to:

- Perform independently with accurate rhythm.
- Perform independently with accurate intonation.
- Perform a varied repertoire of music representing styles from diverse cultures.

VOCABULARY

Have students review vocabulary in student lesson. Introduce terms found in the music. A complete glossary of terms is found on page 240 of the student book.

LESSON 11

Bless The Lord, O My Soul

Composer: Mikhail Ippolitov-Ivanov (1859–1935), edited by Joyce Eilers
Text: Psalm 103
Voicing: 3-Part Mixed

VOCABULARY

syncopation
Romantic period
dynamic markings
tempo markings

Focus

- Read, write and perform rhythmic patterns with syncopation.
- Read and perform music in the key of E♭ major.
- Describe and perform music from the Romantic period.

Getting Started

Composers often show the importance of different words in a song's text with clever notation tactics. Often, various dynamics and rhythms are used to accomplish this. In "Bless The Lord, O My Soul," both are used extensively. The song features many contrasts in dynamics. **Syncopation,** or *the intentional placement of an accent on a weak beat or weak portion of the beat*, is used throughout this song to emphasize words of importance. Notice how the composer rhythmically places the word *bless* in the text. As you learn "Bless The Lord, O My Soul," challenge yourself to perform this song freely and expressively.

MUSIC & HISTORY

To learn more about the Romantic period, see page 120.

◆ History and Culture

Mikhail Ippolitov-Ivanov (1859–1935) was a composer and teacher. Born in Russia, he lived and worked during the **Romantic period** *(1820–1900).* He studied music at the St. Petersburg Conservatory and later in life taught at the Moscow Conservatory. In addition, he was the director of the Russian Choral Society.

Though primarily a composer of orchestral music and operas, Ippolitov-Ivanov wrote a variety of short choral pieces. "Bless The Lord, O My Soul" is one of these works. With its singable melody and full sound, this song is an example of the choral music of the Romantic period.

RESOURCES

Intermediate Sight-Singing

- Sight-singing in E♭ Major, pages 141-143
- Reading Rhythms in 4/4 Meter, pages 2–6
- Reading Eighth Notes and Rests, pages 26–27
- Reading Syncopation, pages 126–129

Teacher Resource Binder

- Teaching Master 17, *The Changing Accent with Syncopation*
- Music and History 16, *Characteristics of Romantic Music: 1820–1900*
- Music and History 19, *Mikhail Ippolitov-Ivanov, a "Romantic" Composer*
- Music and History 20, *Fine Art Teaching Strategy: Romantic*
- For additional resources, see TRB Table of Contents.

Links to Learning

◆ Vocal

"Bless The Lord, O My Soul" is in the key of E♭ major and is based on the E♭ major scale. To locate "E♭" on the piano, find any set of two black keys. "E♭" is the black key on the right. This scale uses the notes E♭, F, G, A♭, B♭, C, D, E♭. Using the keyboard below as a guide, play the E♭ major scale.

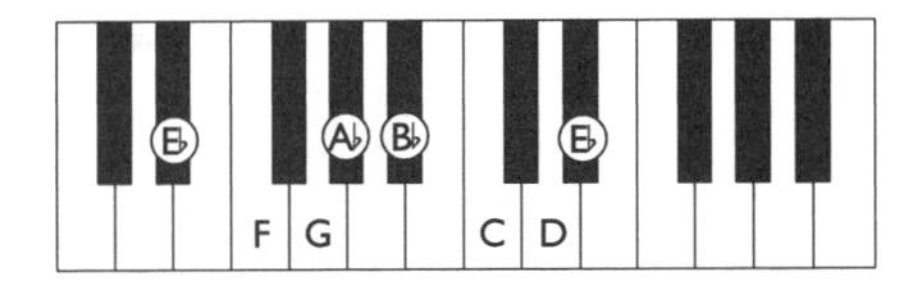

Sing the E♭ major scale.

◆ Theory

Read and perform the following examples to practice rhythmic patterns that use syncopation.

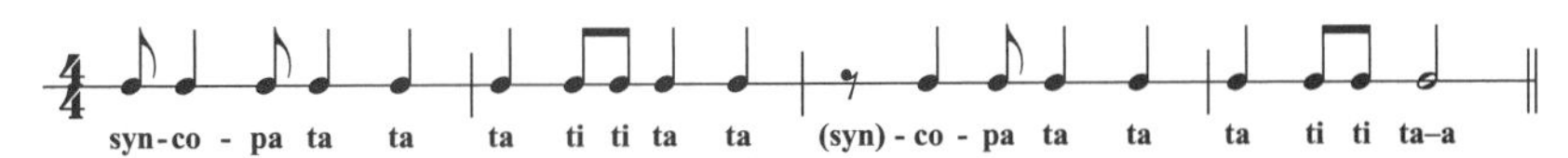

◆ Artistic Expression

By adhering to the **dynamic markings** *(symbols in music that indicate how loud or soft to sing)* and the **tempo markings** *(terms in music that indicate how fast or slow to sing)* found in the score of the music, you will add artistic expression to your performance.

Evaluation

Demonstrate how well you have learned the skills and concepts featured in the lesson "Bless The Lord, O My Soul" by completing the following:

- Compose a four-measure rhythmic phrase that uses syncopation. You may want to use your music as a guide. Perform your phrase for the class.
- Sight-sing measures 25–32 to show your ability to read music in the key of E♭ major.

RESOURCES

Intermediate Mixed Rehearsal/Performance CD

CD 1:21 Voices
CD 1:22 Accompaniment Only
CD 3:11 Vocal Practice Track—Part I
CD 4:11 Vocal Practice Track—Part II
CD 6:11 Vocal Practice Track—Part III

National Standards

1. Singing, alone and with others, a varied repertoire of music. **(b, c)**

LINKS TO LEARNING

Vocal

The Vocal section is designed to prepare students to:

- Understand the meaning of scale and major scale.
- Sing the E♭ major scale with accuracy.

Have students:

- Play the E♭ major scale on the keyboard. If selected students will play the scale on the keyboard, others should follow closely on the keyboard printed on page 93.
- Sing the E♭ major scale on note names.
- Sing the E♭ major scale using solfège syllables.

Theory

The Theory section is designed to prepare students to:

- Read rhythms in 4/4 meter.
- Read and perform syncopated rhythms.

Have students:

- Clap or tap the quarter note pulse in 4/4 meter.
- Clap or tap the rhythm in the Theory exercise.
- Speak the rhythm in the exercise using the rhythm syllables below the staff.

Artistic Expression

The Artistic Expression section is designed to prepare students to:

- Observe dynamic markings used in a song.
- Observe tempo markings used in a song.

Have students:

- Locate the first dynamic mark *(p)* in "Bless The Lord, O My Soul" and describe its meaning *(sing softly)*.
- Locate the first place in "Bless The Lord, O My Soul" where the tempo is to change *(measure 23)* and what is to happen *(rit. = becoming gradually slower)*.

LESSON PLAN

Suggested Teaching Sequence and Performance Tips

1. Introduce

Direct students to:

- Read and discuss the information found in the Getting Started section on page 92.
- Practice singing the ascending and descending scale in the Vocal section on page 93. Relate the scale to the key of the song.
- Chant the rhythmic example in the Theory section on page 93. Have the students locate similar patterns in the music and chant the text.
- Extract each dynamic marking from the piece and generate a worksheet/study sheet with the symbol and definition of each marking.

Bless The Lord, O My Soul

For 3-Part Mixed, a cappella

From Psalm 103
Edited by JOYCE EILERS

MIKHAIL IPPOLITOV-IVANOV
(1859–1935)

*Use for rehearsal purposes only, to reinforce tonality.

TEACHER 2 TEACHER

"Bless The Lord, O My Soul" offers many teaching opportunities for introducing your students to musical characteristics from the Romantic period. Different shades of dynamics are used throughout as well as fluctuating tempos. Work on all of these variables to create an expressive musical experience.

Progress Checkpoints

Observe students' progress in:

✓ Singing the pitches of the E♭ major scale.

✓ Their ability to discriminate between syncopated and nonsyncopated passages.

✓ Their ability to interpret each dynamic marking found in the piece.

2. Rehearse

Direct students to:

- Learn pitches and rhythms to the entire piece in phrases that are approximately four measures in length, so that students rehearse appropriate breath control and support.
- Practice singing those same phrases with marked dynamics.

Progress Checkpoints

Observe students' progress in:

✓ Singing with pitch and rhythmic accuracy. Modify and/or adjust reinforcement of appropriate breath control with phrasing.

✓ Singing each phrase with the correct interpretation of the dynamic marking.

TEACHING STRATEGY

Maintaining a Steady Tempo

Have students:

- Pat the beat almost inaudibly as they sing.
- Sing with a metronome on occasion.
- Listen to recorded performances when they are inclined to rush, describe the problem and suggest solutions.

Understand that students who are struggling with tempo cannot hold back the group alone; they will only split the ensemble. It must be something the group feels together.

3. Refine

Direct students to:

- Sing the text in phrases with accurate diction and unified vowel sounds.
- Add word stress based upon markings and nature of the text.

Progress Checkpoints

Observe students' progress in:

✓ Their ability to demonstrate dynamic contrast.

✓ Their use of phrase markings and proper articulation (i.e., legato phrases, accented words).

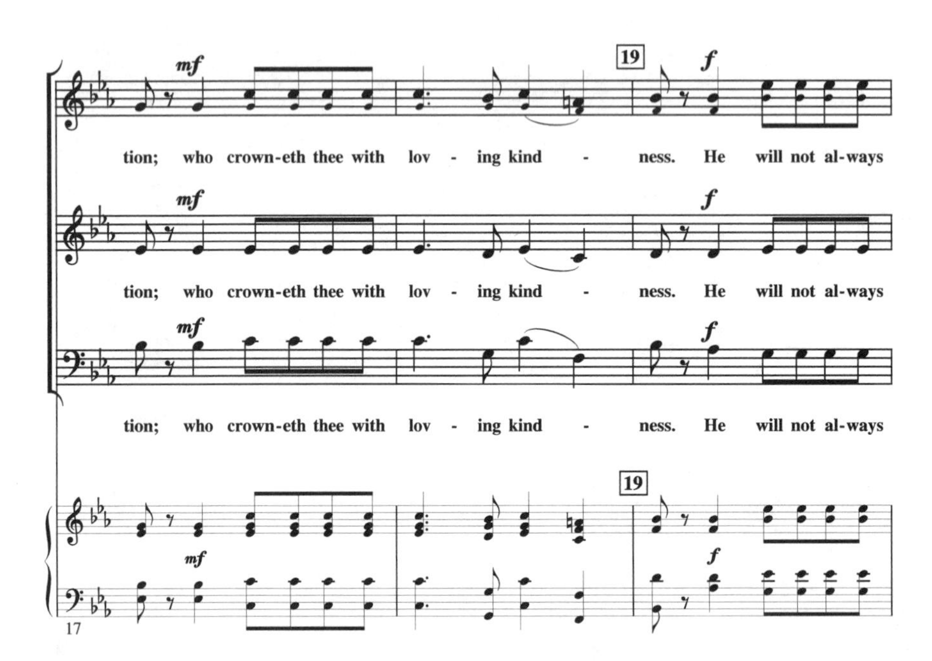

96 Intermediate Mixed

MUSIC LITERACY

Dynamics and Shaping Phrases

To help students expand their music literacy, have them:

- Review the parts of a phrase—beginning, peak, and end.
- Discuss how to shape phrases using dynamics, with a crescendo from the beginning to the peak, and then a release to the end.
- Recall that the dynamic marking at the beginning of a phrase may indicate the overall average dynamic for the entire phrase.

Lesson 11 *Bless The Lord, O My Soul* 97

MORE ABOUT...

Arranger Joyce Eilers

Joyce Eilers' compositions are consistent favorites of teachers and students across the nation, and while her teaching experience spans all levels, she is particularly well known for her work with elementary and junior high singers. Her guidelines for and writing of the 3-Part Mixed idiom revolutionized the middle school/junior high choral experience. Many of her compositions are standards for this age group, including "Dreamer," "Brighten My Soul With Sunshine" and "Send Down The Rain." She is the co-author of *The Choral Approach to Sight-Singing* and *Patterns Of Sound,* both sight-singing methods for the beginning part singer, as well as the choral textbook *Essential Elements for Choir.*

ASSESSMENT

Informal Assessment

In this lesson, students showed the ability to:

- Sing musical phrases based upon dynamic markings by observing the dynamic marks.
- Sing the text expressively by reflecting its meaning in the performance.

Student Self-Assessment

Have students evaluate their individual performances based on the following:

- Breath Management
- Phrasing
- Expressive Singing
- Intonation
- Correct Part-Singing

Have each student rate his/her performance of this song in the areas above on a scale of 1–5, 5 being the best.

Individual and Group Performance Evaluation

To further measure growth of musical skills presented in this lesson, direct students to complete the Evaluation section on page 93.

- After composing a four-measure rhythmic phrase that uses syncopation, perform it on an unpitched rhythm instrument. Evaluate the performance by asking, "Did the example include syncopation? Was it rhythmically correct for the chosen meter?"
- After sight-singing measures 25–32, have a friend review your performance by asking, "How accurate were the pitches and rhythms? How could the performance be improved?"

EXTENSION

Ensemble Performances

Design specific criteria of the expressive qualities desired for the performance of this piece. Divide students into small ensembles. From the performances, select leaders for each ensemble that exhibit the criteria for expressing the text. Have each group rehearse with their leader. Monitor and videotape each group's progress. Have each group perform for the class. Videotape the performances. Ask students to write an evaluation of each ensemble and determine the one that most accurately displays the set criteria. Consider adding their performance to the next concert. Use the videotape as an instructional tool and/or an observable lesson for your administrative supervisor.

Music, Society and Culture

Have students perform additional songs representing diverse cultures, including American and Texas heritage. Go to **music.glencoe.com**, the Web site for Glencoe's choral music programs, for additional music selections students can perform.

Additional National Standards

The following National Standards are addressed through the Assessment, Extension, Enrichment and bottom-page activities:

1. Singing, alone and with others, a varied repertoire of music. **(a)**

4. Composing and arranging music within specific guidelines. **(a)**

5. Reading and notating music. **(a)**

7. Evaluating music and music performances. **(b)**

Concert Etiquette

The term **concert etiquette** describes *how we are expected to behave in formal musical performances.* Understanding appropriate concert etiquette allows you to be considerate of others, including audience members and performers. It also helps everyone attending to enjoy the performance.

Different types of musical performances dictate certain behavior guidelines. How one shows excitement at a rock concert is certainly worlds apart from the appropriate behavior at a formal concert or theater production. Understanding these differences allows audience members to behave in a manner that shows consideration and respect for everyone involved.

What are the expectations of a good audience member at a formal musical presentation?

- Arrive on time. If you arrive after the performance has begun, wait outside the auditorium until a break in the music to enter the hall.
- Remain quiet and still during the performance. Talking and moving around prevent others from hearing and enjoying the performance.
- Leave the auditorium only in case of an emergency. Try to leave during a break in the musical selections.
- Sing or clap along only when invited to do so by the performers or the conductor.
- Applaud at the end of a composition or when the conductor's arms are lowered at the conclusion of a performance. It is customary to not applaud between movements or sections of a major work.
- Save shouting, whistling and dancing for rock concerts or athletic events. These are never appropriate at formal musical performances.

Remembering these important behavior guidelines will ensure that everyone enjoys the show!

RESOURCES

Teacher Resource Binder

Evaluation Master 5, *Concert Etiquette Quiz*

Reference 16, *My Music Dictionary*

National Standards

7. Evaluating music and musical performances. **(a, b)**

CONCERT ETIQUETTE

Objective

- Apply concert etiquette in a variety of settings.

Suggested Teaching Sequence

Direct students to:

- Read the Spotlight On Concert Etiquette on student page 99 and discuss the importance of concert etiquette in respecting the efforts of others.
- Identify the six elements that constitute proper concert etiquette.
- Compare the elements of concert etiquette to appropriate performance practices. In what ways are they related to one another?
- Apply concert etiquette during live performances in a variety of settings such as school concerts and assemblies, professional symphony and/or opera performances and solo recitals.
- Divide the class into small groups and assign each group one concert venue. Ask each group to make a list of five appropriate and five inappropriate behavior expectations for the assigned venue. Share findings with the class.

Progress Checkpoints

Observe students' progress in:

✓ Their ability to identify the elements of concert etiquette.

✓ Their ability to understand the importance of concert etiquette.

✓ Their ability to apply concert etiquette in a variety of settings.

Sing To The Lord

OVERVIEW

Composer: Noel Goemanne (b. 1927)
Text: Based on the Psalms
Voicing: SATB
Key: Modal (Hypo-Mixolydian Mode)
Meter: Mixed Meter
Form: Through-composed
Style: Contemporary American Anthem
Accompaniment: Piano
Programming: Concert or Festival Opener

Vocal Ranges:

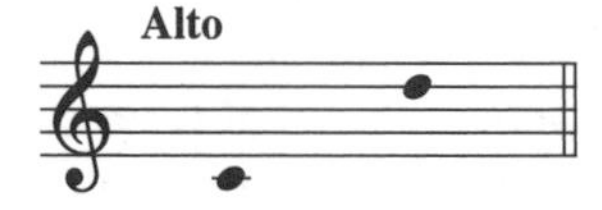

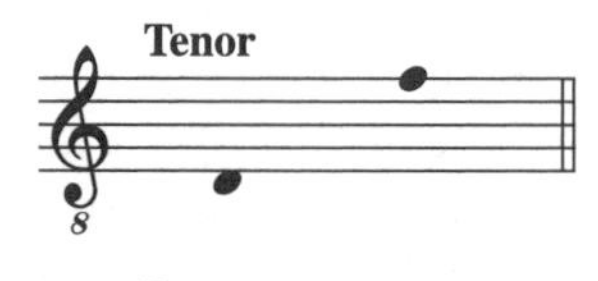

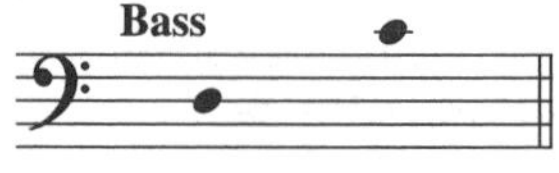

OBJECTIVES

After completing this lesson, students will be able to:

- Perform independently with accurate rhythm.
- Read music notation.
- Perform a varied repertoire of music representing styles from diverse cultures.

VOCABULARY

Have students review vocabulary in student lesson. Introduce terms found in the music. A complete glossary of terms is found on page 240 of the student book.

LESSON 12

Sing To The Lord

Composer: Noel Goemanne (b. 1927)
Text: Based on the Psalms
Voicing: SATB

VOCABULARY

Contemporary period
mixed meter
sempre accel.
accent

Focus

- Perform music in mixed meter.
- Identify musical symbols.
- Perform music that represents the Contemporary period.

Getting Started

For centuries, composers have used unusual rhythmic patterns to make a piece of music come alive for the singer and for the audience. In "Sing To The Lord," composer Noel Goemanne frequently changes from $\frac{3}{8}$ meter to $\frac{3}{4}$ meter to generate an energetic and dancelike style. "Sing To The Lord" is from his set of songs called *Three Meditations.*

MUSIC & HISTORY

To learn more about the Contemporary period, see page 124.

◆ History and Culture

"Sing To The Lord" is a musical composition from the **Contemporary period** *(1900–present).* One common practice in this period was to compose music in **mixed meter,** *a technique in which the time signature changes frequently within a piece.* Look at the music. How many different time signatures can you find?

Noel Goemanne (b. 1927) was born and raised in Belgium, where his name is pronounced "Whoo-MAHN." Following more study in Europe, he migrated to the United States and settled in Dallas, Texas. There he continued his musical career with an extensive church music ministry and the publication of over three hundred compositions. In 1987, in honor of the Pope's visit to Texas, Goemanne was commissioned to compose the processional for the Papal Mass. *Fanfare and Concertato on "All Creatures of Our God and King"* was the result.

RESOURCES

Intermediate Sight-Singing

Sight-Singing Modes, pages 168-170
Reading Rhythms in 3/4 Meter, pages 17-22
Reading Rhythms in Mixed Meter, page 97

Teacher Resource Binder

Teaching Master 18, *Composing in Mixed Meter*
Music and History 21, *Characteristics of Contemporary Music*
Music and History 24, *Noel Goemanne, a "Contemporary" Composer*
Music and History 25, *Fine Art Teaching Strategy: Contemporary*
For additional resources, see TRB Table of Contents.

Links to Learning

◆ Vocal

To communicate well while singing, you must not only form your vowels correctly, but also voice your consonants as clearly and cleanly as possible with accurate and precise pitch. Perform the following exercise to develop crisp diction by singing first on "loo," and then on words.

◆ Theory

The rhythmic challenges found in this piece can be easily mastered by maintaining an even eighth-note pulse. Divide each quarter note into two steady eighth-note pulses. This technique will help you with the changes in meter. Keep the eighth note constant throughout the example. Stress the syllables indicated with an accent mark.

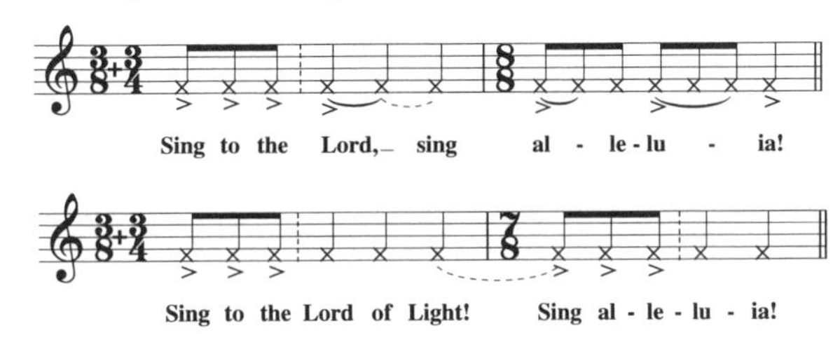

◆ Artistic Expression

In "Sing To The Lord," the term **sempre accel. (accelerando)** is *a marking that indicates to gradually get faster* and is used to bring the piece to an energetic closing. **Accents,** the *symbols placed above or below notes to indicate that those notes should receive extra emphasis or stress,* are also used. Find accents in the music and apply them to your performance.

Evaluation

Demonstrate how well you have learned the skills and concepts featured in the lesson "Sing To The Lord" by completing the following:

- Alone or in a small group, sing page 104 of the music to demonstrate rhythmic precision in mixed meter. Evaluate how well you did.
- Chant the last three measures of "Sing To The Lord" in rhythm and include the application of accents and sempre accel. as indicated. Were you able to demonstrate both while singing?

RESOURCES

Intermediate Mixed Rehearsal/Performance CD

CD 2:21 Voices
CD 2:22 Accompaniment Only
CD 3:23 Vocal Practice Track—Soprano
CD 4:22 Vocal Practice Track—Alto
CD 6:23 Vocal Practice Track—Baritone

National Standards

1. Singing, alone and with others, a varied repertoire of music. **(b, c)**
5. Reading and notating music. **(a)**

LINKS TO LEARNING

Vocal

The Vocal section is designed to prepare students to:

- Sing an exercise in mixed meter.
- Sing an exercise to develop crisp diction.

Have students:

- Sing the Vocal exercise using the neutral syllable "dah."
- Sing the exercise with the text using crisp consonants.

Theory

The Theory section is designed to prepare students to perform a rhythmic exercise in mixed meter.

Have students:

- Say the rhythm using the text in the Theory exercise without accenting any syllables.
- Add the accents by stressing the syllables where the accents appear.

Artistic Expression

The Artistic Expression section is designed to prepare students to:

- Interpret *sempre accel.*, which means to gradually get faster.
- Recognize accents and apply them when performing.

Have students:

- Identify the placement of *sempre accel.* in "Sing To The Lord" *(measure 41)* and adjust the tempo accordingly when performing it.
- Locate several examples of accents in "Sing To The Lord." Say the text in rhythm and stress the syllables where accents are indicated.

Sing To The Lord

from *Three Meditations*

For SATB and Piano

Based on the Psalms

Music by NOEL GOEMANNE

LESSON PLAN

Suggested Teaching Sequence and Performance Tips

1. Introduce

Direct students to:

- Read and discuss the information found in the Getting Started section on page 100.
- Practice singing the exercise in mixed meter in the Vocal section on page 101. Locate the melody in the score *(measures 9–10)*.
- Practice saying the rhythmic examples in the Theory section on Page 101. Observe the accents by stressing the syllables where they are indicated.
- Discuss the definitions of *sempre accel.* and locate it in the score *(measure 41)*. Have students say the text for measures 41–43 and gradually get faster.

Progress Checkpoints

Observe students' progress in:

✓ Their ability to read and perform compound meter and mixed meter.

✓ Their ability to observe accents and perform accordingly.

✓ Successfully performing at increasing tempos.

TEACHER 2 TEACHER

The driving accompaniment, changing meters and dramatic ending of "Sing To The Lord" combine to make it a tried and proven concert or festival closer.

2. Rehearse

Direct students to:

- Count the rhythms for Soprano and Alto parts in measures 9–16. When accurate, add pitches and text.
- Count the rhythms for all parts in measures 24–27 making special note of the measure in 8/8 meter *(measure 25)* for Tenors and Basses. When accurate, add pitches and text.
- Rehearse Sopranos and Tenors, then Altos and Basses, in measures 28–31 noting the exact call and response of pitches and rhythms.
- Chant the rhythms in measures 32–35 taking special care with the 7/8 measure *(measure 35)*. Keep the eighth note constant throughout. When rhythm is correct, add text and pitches.
- Rehearse all parts in measures 36–43 separately. When all are secure, put together and practice at a steady tempo.
- Practice slowly increasing the tempo, driving to the end of the piece. Make sure the students are in the habit of watching the conductor for all tempo variations.

Progress Checkpoints

Observe students' progress in:

✓ Performing with correct rhythmic precision on all mixed meter figures.

✓ Singing similar and contrasting intervals correctly in all four parts.

✓ Their ability to recognize a "call-and-response" section in music.

✓ Their ability to follow the conductor for all tempos.

CURRICULUM CONNECTIONS

Social Studies

Although this song was written in the twentieth century, the modal scale that it is based on was developed in the Middle Ages. Have a class discussion on the world events of that time period.

3. Refine

Direct students to:

- Apply the dynamic markings in the score to achieve a full and healthy *forte.*
- Sing accents as noted by making unaccented syllables less important.
- Work to gently release the final syllable of "Allelu-ia" so that it becomes unaccented in the word stress throughout the song.
- Practice closing to the "ng" on the final word while continuing the breath and healthy vocal production through the *sforzando.*
- Work to perfect the accelerando in the final page without sacrificing any of the accented notes.

Progress Checkpoints

Observe students' progress in:

✓ Performing with accuracy accented and unaccented text.

✓ Using proper vocal technique and tone production on all dynamics noted in the score.

✓ Singing with their unified vowels and word stress on final syllables.

✓ Articulating the final "ng" and *sforzando* of the song.

✓ Their unified accelerando of the final section of the piece.

104 Intermediate Mixed

TEACHING STRATEGY

Composing Music

For students to experience composing, direct student to:

1. Select a meter (simple meter, compound meter, asymmetric meter).
2. Write a four-measure simple or complex rhythmic pattern in that meter.
3. Select a key (major, minor, pentatonic, modal).
4. Using the newly composed rhythmic pattern, write a melody based on the selected key.
5. Exchange compositions with a classmate. Check each other's work for rhythmic and melodic accuracy.
6. Make changes and corrections as necessary, and then perform the compositions for the class.

MORE ABOUT...

Modes

The eight modes (sometimes called church modes or ecclesiastical modes to distinguish them from the rhythmic modes) were defined through a combination of range and final (the final is the note on which a melody ends). If melodies were consistently above the final, they were in an authentic mode; if they ranged both above and below the final, they were in a plagal mode. In medieval theory, there were only four appropriate final pitches: D, E, F and G. In the Renaissance, theorists added modes on A and C.

ASSESSMENT

Informal Assessment

In this lesson, students showed the ability to:

- Read and perform mixed meter rhythms with a constant eighth note.
- Accurately perform four-part harmony with healthy vocal production.
- Watch the conductor for all tempo modifications.

Student Self-Assessment

Have students evaluate their individual performances based on the following:

- Phrasing
- Diction
- Accurate Pitches
- Accurate Rhythms
- Correct Part-Singing

Have each student rate his/her performance of this song in the areas above on a scale of 1–5, 5 being the best.

Individual and Group Performance Evaluation

To further measure growth of musical skills presented in this lesson, direct students to complete the Evaluation section on page 101.

- After singing page 104 alone or in a small group, evaluate the performance by asking, "How precise were the rhythms? Did the soloist (or group) gradually get faster at the same rate?"
- Record the choir singing the last three measures of "Sing To The Lord." Review the performance by asking, "Was there a uniformity of rhythms, vowels and tempo? How could the performance improve? Which section of the choir was the most together?"

EXTENSION

Composing with Modes

Try writing a well-known tune (e.g., "Twinkle, Twinkle Little Star") in one of the medieval modes. It will sound a bit different than what you are used to. How is it similar? How is it different?

Music, Society and Culture

Have students perform additional songs representing diverse cultures, including American and Texas heritage. Go to **music.glencoe.com**, the Web site for Glencoe's choral music programs, for additional music selections students can perform.

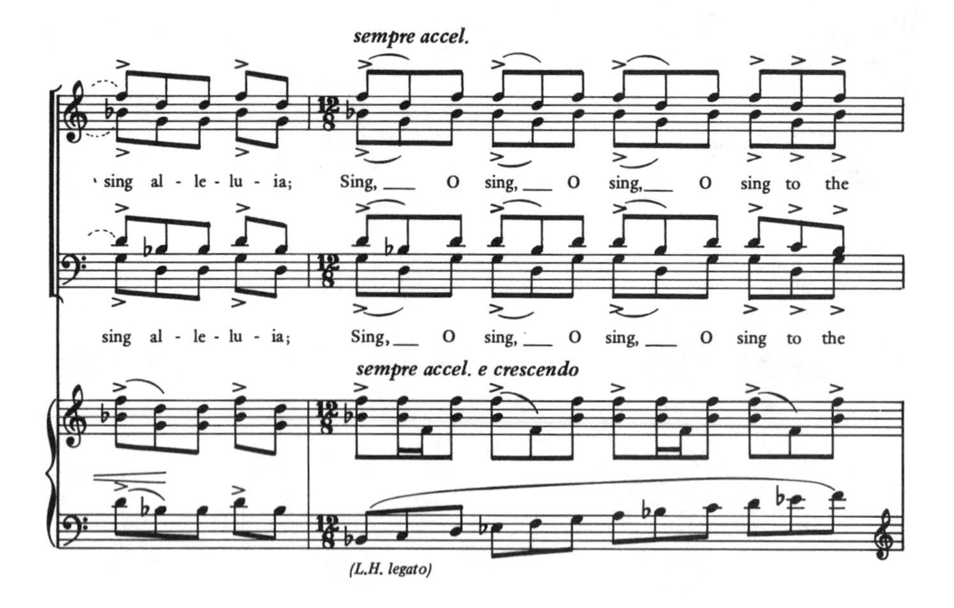

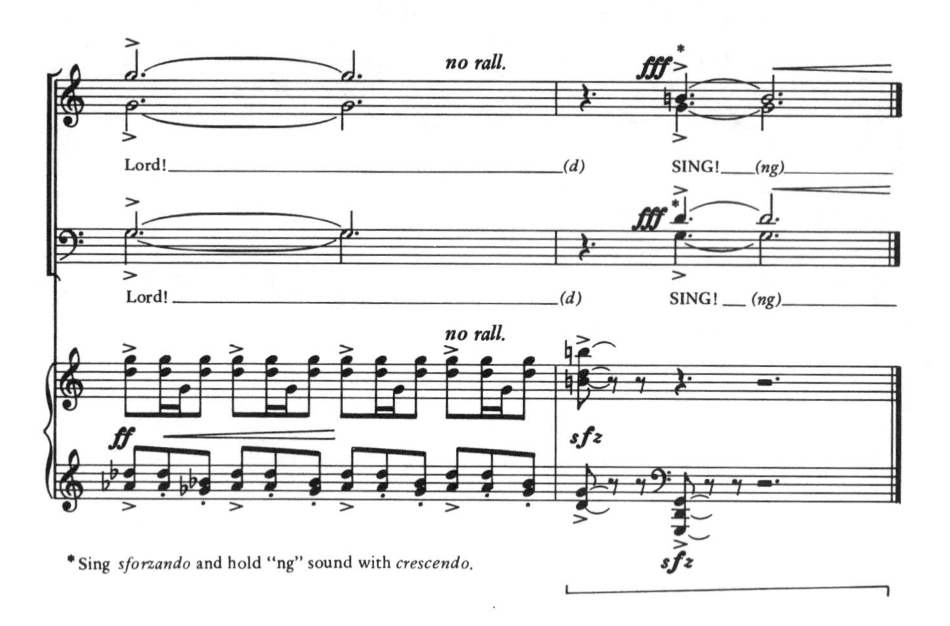

* Sing *sforzando* and hold "ng" sound with *crescendo*.

Additional National Standards

The following National Standards are addressed through the Assessment, Extension, Enrichment and bottom-page activities:

4. Composing and arranging music within specific guidelines. **(b)**

5. Reading and notating music. **(b)**

7. Evaluating music and music performances. **(a)**

Music & History

Links to Music

RENAISSANCE

OVERVIEW

Objectives

After completing this lesson, students will be able to:

- Describe the Renaissance period, including important developments.
- Describe characteristics of Renaissance music.

VOCABULARY

Have students review vocabulary in student lesson. A complete glossary of terms is found on page 240 of the student book.

Introduce the Renaissance period through visual art. Analyze the painting by Sandro Botticelli on page 108. Direct students to discuss Renaissance interest in religious subjects, as depicted in *The Adoration of the Magi.*

Sandro Botticelli (1445–1510) was an Italian painter who lived and worked in Florence, Italy, during the Renaissance. *The Adoration of the Magi* reflects the Renaissance interest in religious subjects. Framing the central figures within the strong geometric pillars emphasized those figures over others. Botticelli was also commissioned by the Pope to paint frescoes in the Sistine Chapel in the Vatican.

Sandro Botticelli. *The Adoration of the Magi.* c. 1480. Tempera and oil on panel. 70.2 x 104.2 cm (27 5/8 x 41"). National Gallery of Art, Washington, D. C. Andrew W. Mellon Collection.

RESOURCES

Teacher Resource Binder

Music and History 1, *Renaissance Music*

Music and History 4, *Heinrich Isaac*

Transparency 1, *The Adoration of the Magi*, Sandro Botticelli

Music and History 5, *Fine Art Teaching Strategy*

For additional resources, see Music and History section.

Listening Selections CD

(found in the Teacher Resource Binder)

Track 1 "As Vesta Was Descending"

Track 2 "Three Voltas" from *Terpsichore*

RENAISSANCE c. 1430–1600

Focus

- Describe the Renaissance period, including important developments.
- Describe characteristics of Renaissance music.

The Renaissance—A Time of Exploration

The **Renaissance period** *(1430–1600)* was a time during the fifteenth and sixteenth centuries of rapid development in exploration, science, art and music. This period could be called the beginning of modern history and the beginning of Western civilization as we know it now.

The development and use of the compass as a navigational aid in China made it possible for explorers to travel to new continents and to discover other cultures. Renaissance sailors first took to the seas to supply Europeans with Asian spices such as peppercorns, nutmeg and cinnamon. Also from the East came precious jewels and fine silk, a fabric especially valued for women's clothing.

Sailors also brought back information and customs from other cultures. This new information, along with a revived interest in writings from the ancient Greek and Roman cultures, was quickly spread across Europe, thanks to the invention of the printing press and mass-produced books. The invention of the printing press, credited to Johann Gutenberg, was one of the most significant developments of the Renaissance. As books became more available and less expensive, more people learned to read and began to consider new ideas.

A major change in the Christian religion occurred at this time. During the Protestant Reformation, various groups of Christians left the Catholic Church and formed some of the present-day Protestant denominations. Many Protestant groups translated Bibles from the Catholic Church's language of Latin to the language spoken by the people.

Remarkable advances were made in the arts and sciences by:

- Thomas Weelkes—English composer
- Gerardus Mercator—German mapmaker
- Vasco da Gama—Portuguese explorer who rounded the Horn of Africa and went on to India

COMPOSERS

Josquin des Prez (c. 1450–1521)

Andrea Gabrieli (c. 1510–1586)

Michael Praetorius (1571–1621)

Thomas Weelkes (c. 1576–1623)

ARTISTS

Gentile Bellini (1429–1507)

Sandro Botticelli (1445–1510)

Leonardo da Vinci (1452–1519)

Michelangelo (1475–1564)

Raphael (1483–1520)

AUTHORS

Martin Luther (1483–1546)

William Shakespeare (1565–1616)

VOCABULARY

Renaissance period
sacred music
mass
motet
secular music
lute
polyphony
a cappella
madrigal
word painting

National Standards

6. Listening to, analyzing, and describing music. **(a, b, c, e, f)**
8. Understanding relationships between music, the other arts, and disciplines outside the arts. **(a, b, c, d, e)**
9. Understanding music in relation to history and culture. **(a, c, d, e)**

LESSON PLAN

Suggested Teaching Sequence

1. Examine the Renaissance period in a historical perspective.

Direct students to:

- Read and discuss the information found on student page 109.
- Turn to the time line on pages 110–111 and read the citations.
- Discuss why these are considered important dates during the Renaissance period.
- Identify specific accomplishments that were made during the Renaissance period and the people associated with those accomplishments.
- Compare each of these events to what occurred after the Renaissance period.

2. Define the musical aspects of Renaissance music.

Direct students to:

- Read and discuss information on Renaissance music found on student page 110.
- Describe the difference between sacred and secular music.
- Define *polyphony*, *mass* and *motet*.

3. Discuss the performance guidelines of Renaissance music.

Direct students to:

- Read the Performance Links found on student page 110.
- Discuss the performance guidelines.

LISTENING LESSONS

This feature is designed to expand students' appreciation of choral and instrumental music of the Renaissance period.

1. Choral Selection:

"As Vesta Was Descending" by Thomas Weelkes

Direct students to:

- Read the information on student page 111 to learn more about Thomas Weelkes and "As Vesta Was Descending."
- Review the meaning of the musical style of the madrigal.
- Define *word painting*.
- After listening to the recorded performance, identify the word painting techniques used (*descending*—all the voices move downward, *ascending*—all the voices move upward, *running down amain*—the voices vigorously "run" downward separately, *two by two*—groups of two voices sing together, *three by three*—groups of three voices sing together, *all alone*—one solo voice). At the end of the piece, "Long live fair Oriana" is repeated over and over (52 times) to honor and gain the favor of Oriana, a common nickname for Queen Elizabeth I of England.

2. Instrumental Selection:

"Three Voltas" from *Terpsichore* by Michael Praetorius

Direct students to:

- Read the information on student page 111 to learn more about Michael Praetorius and "Three Voltas" from *Terpsichore*.
- After the first listening, discuss the ancient instruments that are heard.

Renaissance Music

During the Renaissance, the Catholic Church gradually lost some of its influence over the daily lives of people. Much of the important music of the period, however, was still **sacred music**, or *music associated with religious services and themes*. In music, a **mass** is *a religious service of prayers and ceremonies*. A **motet** is *a shorter choral work, also set to a Latin text and used in religious services, but not part of the regular mass*. These two types of compositions were the most important forms of sacred Renaissance music. In Protestant churches, sacred music was composed and sung in the languages of the worshippers.

Like sacred music, **secular music**, or *music not associated with religious services or themes*, flourished during the Renaissance period. The center of musical activity gradually began to shift from churches to castles and towns. Music became an important form of entertainment for members of the emerging middle class. Social dancing became more widespread. Dance music of this period was written for **lute**, *an early form of the guitar*, and other instruments.

The Renaissance period is often referred to as the "golden age of polyphony." **Polyphony**, which literally means "many-sounding," is *a type of music in which there are two or more different melodic lines being sung or played at the same time*. Much of the choral music of the time was polyphonic, with as many as sixteen different vocal parts. Instruments were sometimes used to accompany and echo the voices.

Performance Links

When performing music of the Renaissance period, it is important to apply the following guidelines:

- Sing with clarity and purity of tone.
- Balance the vocal lines with equal importance.
- In polyphonic music, sing the rhythms accurately and with precision.
- When designated by the composer, sing **a cappella** *(unaccompanied or without instruments)*.

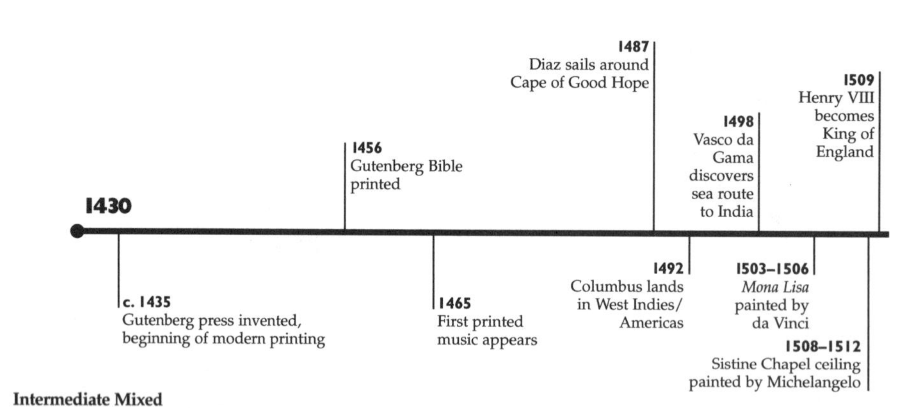

MORE ABOUT

Renaissance Painting

During the Renaissance, the styles, subjects and even art materials of painters changed. Painting became more realistic; human figures appeared more lifelike. Painters were able to use perspective and to give three-dimensional quality. Many paintings still depicted religious subjects, especially scenes from the Bible. Other artists began to show nonreligious subjects in their works. Oil paints, which were first used during the early 1400s, made it possible for painters to revise and refine their ideas as they worked.

Listening Links

CHORAL SELECTION

"As Vesta Was Descending" by Thomas Weelkes (c.1576–1623)

Thomas Weelkes was an important English composer and organist. "As Vesta Was Descending" is an outstanding example of a **madrigal**, *a musical setting of a poem in three or more parts*. Generally, a madrigal has a secular text and is sung a cappella. This madrigal was written in honor of Queen Elizabeth I of England. This piece is an excellent example of **word painting**, *a technique in which the music reflects the meaning of the words*. Listen carefully to discover what occurs in the music on the following words: "descending," "ascending," "running down amain," "two by two," "three by three," and "all alone." Why do you think Weelkes chose to use the repeated text at the end?

INSTRUMENTAL SELECTION

"Three Voltas" from *Terpsichore* by Michael Praetorius (1571–1621)

During the Renaissance, a favorite type of composition involved a combination of dances in changing tempos and meters. Some of the dance music developed into stylized pieces for listening, which were not intended for actual dancing. *Terpsichore*, by German composer Michael Praetorius, is a collection of 312 short dance pieces, written in four, five or six parts, with no particular instrumentation specified.

You will hear authentic early instruments in this recording. By listening carefully, guess which modern-day instruments are descended from these early ones.

Check Your Understanding

1. List three major nonmusical changes that took place during the Renaissance period.
2. Describe polyphony as heard in "As Vesta Was Descending."
3. Describe how music from the Renaissance is different from music of today.

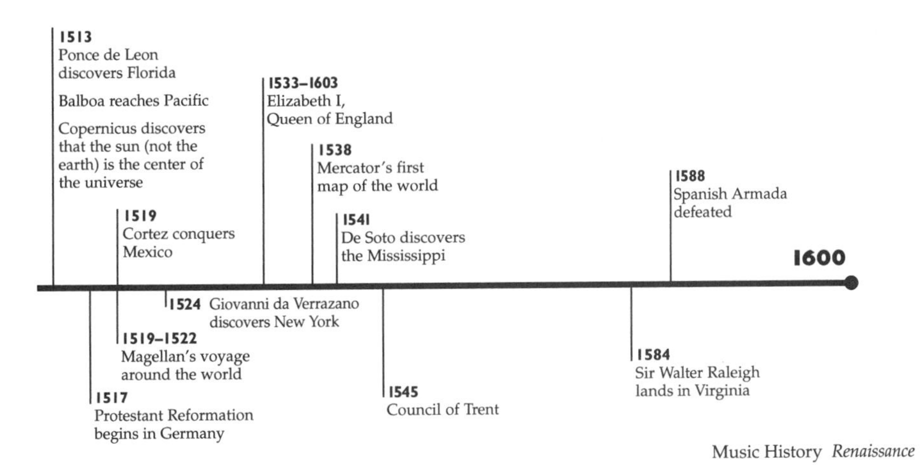

Answers to Check Your Understanding

1. Answers will vary. For example, the use of the compass made it possible to explore new continents. The invention of the printing press and mass-produced books helped information spread rapidly. The Protestant Reformation led to the formation of many of the world's present-day Protestant denominations.
2. Polyphony is when two or more melodic lines begin at different places and act independently of each other. In "As Vesta Was Descending," polyphony can be heard throughout the piece, in contrast to the sections sung all together.
3. Answers will vary. For example, now we use many different instruments to provide interesting accompaniments for songs—then, they were sung a cappella or with simple instruments that echoed the voice lines. One thing the two styles have in common is a frequent use of dissonance.

- After the second listening, discuss which modern day instruments are descended from these early ones. *(The first Volta features a cornett, three sackbuts, drum and tabor. The second Volta is performed on pommer, three sackbuts and tabor. The third Volta features three recorders, pommer, three sackbuts, two violins, viola, violoncello, lute, drum and tabor. The cornett was the most highly prized instrument of the sixteenth century, but has no modern descendent. It was made of wood and had finger holes like a recorder, but was played with a mouthpiece similar to a trumpet's. A sackbut is the ancestor of the modern trombone. The tabor is a type of drum. The pommer, or shawm, was the double-reed forefather of the oboe.)*

ASSESSMENT

Informal Assessment

In this lesson, students showed the ability to:

- Share what they know about the Renaissance period.
- Describe musical characteristics, styles and forms found in Renaissance music.
- Describe some characteristics of Renaissance art.

Student Self-Assessment

Direct students to:

- Review the questions in Check Your Understanding on page 111.
- Write a paragraph answering each of the three questions about music during the Renaissance period.

BAROQUE

OVERVIEW

Objectives

After completing this lesson, students will be able to:

- Describe Baroque period including important developments.
- Describe characteristics of Baroque music.

VOCABULARY

Have students review vocabulary in student lesson. A complete glossary of terms is found on page 240 of the student book.

Introduce the Baroque period through visual art. Analyze the painting by Orazio Gentileschi on student page 112. Direct students to discuss the technique of placing the subjects in sharp relief before a dark background. Note the small table pipe organ.

The work of the Italian painter Orazio Gentileschi (1563–1639) was influenced by the innovative style of Caravaggio. In later years, Orazio's works tend to place a single figure or a restricted figure group in sharp relief before a dark background. The subject of this painting, St. Cecilia, is often referred to as the patron saint of music. She is playing a small table pipe organ.

Orazio Gentileschi. *Saint Cecilia and an Angel.* c. 1610. Oil on canvas. 87.8 x 108.1 cm (34 5/8 x 42 1/2"). National Gallery of Art, Washington, D. C. Samuel H. Kress Collection.

RESOURCES

Teacher Resource Binder

Music and History 6, *Baroque Music*

Music and History 9, *George Frideric Handel*

Transparency 3, *Saint Cecilia and an Angel*, Orazio Gentileschi

Music and History 10, *Fine Art Teaching Strategy*

For additional resources, see Music and History section.

Listening Selections CD

(found in the Teacher Resource Binder)

Track 3 "Gloria in excelsis Deo" from *Gloria in D Major*

Track 4 "The Arrival of the Queen of Sheba" from *Solomon*

BAROQUE 1600–1750

Focus

- Describe the Baroque period, including important developments.
- Describe characteristics of Baroque music.

The Baroque Period—A Time of Elaboration

The **Baroque period** *(1600–1750)* was a time of powerful kings and their courts. In Europe, elaborate clothing, hats and hairstyles for the wealthy men and women matched the decorated buildings, gardens, furniture and paintings of this period. The term *baroque* comes from a French word for "imperfect or irregular pearls." Often, pearls were used as decorations on clothing.

There was a great interest in science and exploration. During the Baroque period, Galileo perfected the telescope by 1610, providing the means for greater exploration of the universe. Sir Isaac Newton identified gravity and formulated principles of physics and mathematics. Bartolomeo Cristofori developed the modern pianoforte in which hammers strike the strings. Exploration of new worlds continued, and colonization of places discovered during the Renaissance increased.

Most paintings and sculptures of the time were characterized by their large scale and dramatic details. Artwork celebrated the splendor of royal rulers. For example, the Palace at Versailles near Paris, was built and decorated as a magnificent setting for King Louis XIV of France. It features notably elaborate architecture, paintings, sculptures and gardens.

The Baroque period was a time of great changes brought about through the work of extraordinary people such as:

- Johann Sebastian Bach—German composer
- Orazio Gentileschi—Italian painter
- Alexander Pope—English poet
- Galileo Galilei—Italian mathematician who used his new telescope to prove that the Milky Way is made up of individual stars

COMPOSERS

Johann Pachelbel (1653–1706)
Antonio Vivaldi (1678–1741)
Johann Sebastian Bach (1685–1750)
George Frideric Handel (1685–1759)

ARTISTS

El Greco (1541–1614)
Orazio Gentileschi (1563–1639)
Peter Paul Rubens (1577–1640)
Rembrandt van Rijn (1606–1669)
Jan Steen (1626–1679)
Jan Vermeer (1632–1675)

AUTHORS

Ben Jonson (1572–1637)
René Descartes (1596–1650)
John Milton (1608–1674)
Molière (1622–1673)
Alexander Pope (1688–1744)
Samuel Johnson (1709–1784)

VOCABULARY

Baroque period
basso continuo
opera
oratorio
concerto grosso

National Standards

6. Listening to, analyzing, and describing music. **(a, b, c, e, f)**
8. Understanding relationships between music, the other arts, and disciplines outside the arts. **(a, b, c, d, e)**
9. Understanding music in relation to history and culture. **(a, c, d, e)**

LESSON PLAN

Suggested Teaching Sequence

1. Examine the Baroque period in a historical perspective

Direct students to:

- Read and discuss the information found on student page 113.
- Turn to the time line on pages 114–115 and read the citations.
- Discuss why these are considered important dates during the Baroque period.
- Identify specific accomplishments that were made during the Baroque period and the people associated with those accomplishments.
- Compare each of these events to what occurred before and after the Baroque period.

2. Define the musical aspects of Baroque music.

Direct students to:

- Read and discuss information on Baroque music found on student page 114.
- Discuss instruments used during this period.
- Define *basso continuo, oratorio, opera* and *concerto grosso.*

3. Discuss the performance guidelines of Baroque music.

Direct students to:

- Read the Performance Links found on student page 114.
- Discuss the performance guidelines.

LISTENING LESSONS

This feature is designed to expand students' appreciation of choral and instrumental music of the Baroque period.

1. Choral Selection:

"Gloria in excelsis Deo" from *Gloria in D Major* by Antonio Vivaldi

Direct students to:

- Read the information on student page 115 to learn more about Antonio Vivaldi and "Gloria in excelsis Deo" from *Gloria in D Major*.
- Listen to the recorded performance to enjoy the energy and emotion of this piece.
- After listening again, discuss the use of ornamentation. *(A great amount of ornamentation is used in the accompaniment. The vocal line fits with this elaborate accompaniment by providing contrast with long tones and silences that allow the accompaniment to be heard.)*

2. Instrumental Selection:

"The Arrival of the Queen of Sheba" from *Solomon* by George Frideric Handel

Direct students to:

- Read the information on student page 115 to learn more about George Frideric Handel and "The Arrival of the Queen of Sheba" from *Solomon*.
- Review the meaning of *oratorio*.
- Listen to the recorded performance to identify the two instruments that perform a duet. *(Oboes)*
- Identify the instrument family to which they belong. *(Woodwind)*

Baroque Music

The music of the Baroque period shows the same kind of dramatic flair that characterized the clothing, architecture and art of the time. Most of the compositions of that period have a strong sense of movement, often including a **basso continuo**, or *a continually moving bass line.*

The Baroque period brought about a great interest in instrumental music. Keyboard instruments were refined, including the clavichord, harpsichord and organ. The modern string family of instruments were now used, and the trumpet became a favorite melody instrument in orchestras.

During the Baroque period, a number of new forms of music were developed. **Opera**, *a combination of singing, instrumental music, dancing and drama that tells a story*, was created beginning with *Orfeo*, by Claudio Monteverdi (1567–1643). The **oratorio**, *a large-scale work for solo voices, chorus and orchestra based on a literary or religious theme*, was also developed. In 1741, George Frideric Handel (1685–1759) composed the *Messiah*, one of the most famous oratorios still performed today. The **concerto grosso** *(a multi-movement Baroque piece for a group of soloists and an orchestra)* was also made popular with Antonio Vivaldi's (1678–1741) *The Four Seasons* and Johann Sebastian Bach's (1685–1750) *Brandenberg Concertos*.

Performance Links

When performing music of the Baroque period, it is important to apply the following guidelines:

- Sing with accurate pitch.
- Be conscious of who has the dominant theme and make sure the accompanying part or parts do not overshadow the melody.
- Keep a steady, unrelenting pulse in most pieces. Precision of dotted rhythms is especially important.
- When dynamic level changes occur, all vocal lines need to change together.

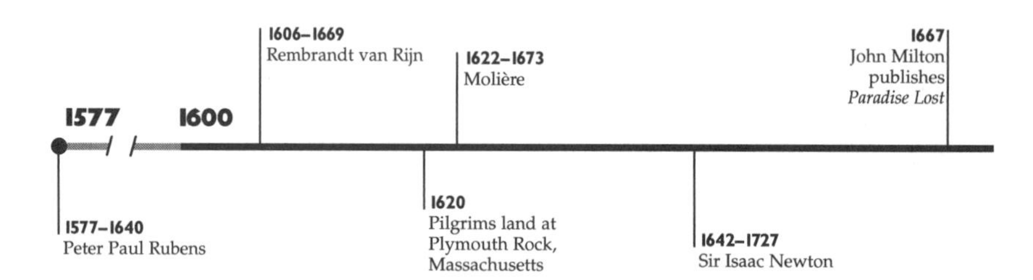

MORE ABOUT

Baroque Painting

The Baroque period was a time of reaction to the reserved, restrained attitudes of the Renaissance. Baroque art became more and more emotional and excessive, with an emphasis on opulence, ornamentation and gaudy elegance. The aristocracy was still in power and commissioned even grander art to impress themselves and others.

Listening Links

CHORAL SELECTION

"Gloria in excelsis Deo" from *Gloria in D Major* by Antonio Vivaldi (1678–1741)

Antonio Vivaldi was one of the greatest composers and violinists of his time. He wrote operas and concertos, as well as sacred works (oratorios, motets and masses) for chorus, soloists and orchestra. One of his most popular choral works is the *Gloria in D Major* mass. "Gloria in excelsis Deo" is a magnificent choral piece. It is full of energy and emotion that is expressed with great drama. It was composed for three solo voices and chorus, and is accompanied by a variety of instruments. Does ornamentation occur in the vocal parts, in the accompaniment, or both?

INSTRUMENTAL SELECTION

"The Arrival of the Queen of Sheba" from *Solomon* by George Frideric Handel (1685–1759)

George Frideric Handel was a German-born composer who lived in England for most of his life. The oratorio *Solomon* tells the story of King Solomon, of tenth-century Israel. Solomon was known for his great wisdom. Sheba, the Queen of Ethiopia, came to visit and challenge Solomon, but he wisely answered all her questions, and she left as an ally. *Solomon* was written for two choruses, five soloists, a chamber orchestra and a harpsichord. Two instruments are featured playing a duet in this piece. What is the name of these instruments, and to what instrument family do they belong?

Check Your Understanding

1. List three major nonmusical developments that took place during the Baroque period.
2. How would the performance of the oratorio *Solomon* differ from the performance of an opera?
3. Describe how music from the Baroque period is different from music of the Renaissance.

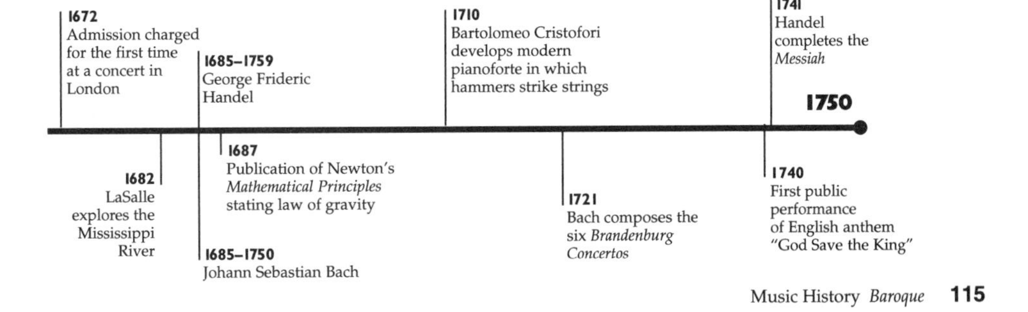

Answers to Check Your Understanding

1. Answers will vary. For example, invention of the telescope, discovery of the law of gravity, exploration and colonization, pilgrims land at Plymouth Rock.
2. Opera and oratorios are both written for solo voices, chorus and orchestra. They both tell a story. Operas, however, are designed to be performed on stage with dancing, costuming and scenery. Oratorios like *Solomon* are composed to be sung in a church or concert setting.
3. Music in the Baroque period can be described as large scale with complex details and dramatic elaborations. In contrast, music of the Renaissance period emphasized smaller groups performing, often unaccompanied, with an emphasis on polyphony.

ASSESSMENT

Informal Assessment

In this lesson, students showed the ability to:

- Share what they know about the Baroque period.
- Describe musical characteristics, styles and forms found in Baroque music.
- Describe some characteristics of Baroque art.

Student Self-Assessment

Direct students to:

- Review the questions in Check Your Understanding on page 115.
- Write a paragraph answering each of the three questions about the Baroque period.

ENRICHMENT

Research Project

As a small group activity, assign each group one of the following important figures of the Baroque period: J. S. Bach, George Frideric Handel, Antonio Vivaldi, Orazio Gentileschi, Alexander Pope, Galileo Galilei, Sir Isaac Newton, and Bartolomeo Cristofori. Have each group do research on the contributions of each, and then present findings to the rest of the class.

CLASSICAL

OVERVIEW

Objectives

After completing this lesson, students will be able to:

- Describe the Classical period, including important developments.
- Describe characteristics of Classical music.

VOCABULARY

Have students review vocabulary in student lesson. A complete glossary of terms is found on page 240 of the student book.

Introduce the Classical period through visual art. Analyze the painting by Elisabeth Vigeé-LeBrun on student page 116. Direct students to discuss how this painting expresses friendship and maternal love. Review background information of Vigeé-LeBrun's *The Marquise de Pezé and the Marquise de Rouget with Her Two Children* on page 116.

French artist Elisabeth Vigée-LeBrun (1755–1842) lived and worked in Paris during the time of the French Revolution and was forced to flee the city in disguise in 1789. A majority of Vigeé-LeBrun paintings are portraits of women and children. This painting expresses friendship and maternal love.

Elisabeth Vigée-LeBrun. *The Marquise de Pezé and the Marquise de Rouget with Her Two Children.* 1787. Oil on canvas, 123.4 x 155.9 cm (48 5/8 x 61 3/8"). National Gallery of Art, Washington, D. C. Gift of the Bay Foundation in memory of Josephine Bay and Ambassador Charles Ulrick Bay.

RESOURCES

Teacher Resource Binder

Music and History 11, *Classical Music*

Music and History 14, *Michael Haydn*

Transparency 5, *The Marquise de Pezé and the Marquise de Rouget with Her Two Children,* Elisabeth Vigeé-LeBrun

Music and History 15, *Fine Art Teaching Strategy*

For additional resources, see Music and History section.

Listening Selections CD

(found in the Teacher Resource Binder)

Track 5 "The Heavens Are Telling" from *Creation*

Track 6 *Eine Kleine Nachtmusik*, First Movement

Focus

- Describe the Classical period, including important developments.
- Describe characteristics of Classical music.

The Classical Period—A Time of Balance, Clarity and Simplicity

The **Classical period** *(1750–1820)* was a time when people became influenced by the early Greeks and Romans for examples of order and ways of living life. Travelers of the period visited the ruins of ancient Egypt, Rome and Greece and brought the ideas of the ancients to the art and architecture of the time. As a result, the calm beauty and simplicity of this classical art from the past inspired artists and musicians to move away from the overly decorated styles of the Baroque period. The music, art and architecture reflected a new emphasis on emotional restraint and simplicity.

In the intellectual world, there was increasing emphasis on individual reason and enlightenment. Writers such as Voltaire and Thomas Jefferson suggested that through science and democracy, rather than mystery and monarchy, people could choose their own fate. Such thinking, brought on by the enlarging middle class and the excesses of the wealthy royal class, was the beginning of important political changes in society. In many parts of Europe, the power and authority of royalty were attacked, and members of the middle class struggled for their rights. There was a revolution against England by the American colonies, which resulted in the establishment of the United States. In France, the monarchy was overthrown, and the king and most of his court were beheaded.

Some of the most important contributors of the time were:

- Wolfgang Amadeus Mozart—Austrian composer
- Elisabeth Vigée-Lebrun—French painter
- Ben Franklin—American writer, inventor, diplomat
- Joseph Priestley—English chemist who discovered oxygen
- Robert Fulton—American inventor who produced the

COMPOSERS

Carl Philipp Emanuel Bach (1714–1788)
Johann Christian Bach (1735–1762)
Franz Joseph Haydn (1732–1809)
Wolfgang Amadeus Mozart (1756–1791)
Ludwig van Beethoven (1770–1827)

ARTISTS

Louis de Carmontelle (1717–1806)
Thomas Gainsborough (1727–1788)
Francisco Göya (1746–1828)
Jacques-Louis David (1748–1825)
Elisabeth Vigée-Lebrun (1755–1842)

AUTHORS

Voltaire (1694–1778)
Benjamin Franklin (1706–1790)
William Wordsworth (1770–1850)
Jane Austen (1775–1817)

VOCABULARY

Classical period
chamber music
symphony
crescendo
decrescendo
sonata-allegro form

National Standards

6. Listening to, analyzing, and describing music. **(a, b, c, e, f)**
8. Understanding relationships between music, the other arts, and disciplines outside the arts. **(a, b, c, d, e)**
9. Understanding music in relation to history and culture. **(a, c, d, e)**

LESSON PLAN

Suggested Teaching Sequence

1. Examine the Classical period in a historical perspective

Direct students to:

- Read and discuss the information found on student page 117.
- Turn to the time line on pages 118–119 and read the citations.
- Discuss why these are considered important dates during the Classical period.
- Identify specific accomplishments that were made during the Classical period and the people associated with those accomplishments.
- Compare each of these events to what occurred before and after the Classical period.

2. Define the musical aspects of Classical music.

Direct students to:

- Read and discuss information on Classical music found on student page 118.
- Define *chamber music* and *symphony*.
- Identify two major composers of the Classical period.

3. Discuss the performance guidelines of Classical music.

Direct students to:

- Read the Performance Links found on student page 118.
- Discuss the performance guidelines.

LISTENING LESSONS

This feature is designed to expand students' appreciation of choral and instrumental music of the Classical period.

Choral Selection:

"The Heavens Are Telling" from *Creation* by Franz Joseph Haydn

Direct students to:

- Read the information on student page 119 to learn more about Franz Joseph Haydn and "The Heavens Are Telling" from *Creation.*
- Listen to the recorded performance to identify the sections sung by the full chorus and those sung by the trio of soloists.
- While listening again, identify the imitative section, and list the order of the voice parts as they enter with the words "With wonders of His work." *(Bass, Tenor, Soprano, Alto)*

Instrumental Selection:

***Eine Kleine Nachtmusik,* First Movement by Wolfgang Amadeus Mozart**

Direct students to:

- Read the information on student page 118 to learn more about Wolfgang Amadeus Mozart and *Eine Kleine Nachtmusik,* First Movement.
- Read the definition of *sonata-allegro form.*
- Listen to the recorded performance to identify the three large sections.
- While listening again, write down Exposition, Development and Recapitulation as each section begins.

Music of the Classical Period

The music of the Classical period was based on balance, clarity and simplicity. Like the architecture of ancient Greece, music was fit together in "building blocks" by balancing one four-bar phrase against another. Classical music was more restrained than the music of the Baroque period, when flamboyant embellishments were common.

The piano replaced the harpsichord and became a favorite instrument of composers. Many concertos were written for the piano. The string quartet was a popular form of **chamber music** *(music performed by a small instrumental ensemble, generally with one instrument per part)*. The **symphony** *(a large-scale work for orchestra)* was also a common type of music during this period. Orchestras continued to develop and expand into four families: brass, percussion, strings and woodwinds. Other forms, such as the opera, mass and oratorio, continued to develop as well.

Two major composers associated with the Classical period are Franz Joseph Haydn (1732–1809) and Wolfgang Amadeus Mozart (1756–1791). A third major composer, Ludwig van Beethoven (1770–1827), began composing during this period. Beethoven's works bridge the gap between the Classical and Romantic periods, and are discussed in the next period.

Performance Links

When performing music of the Classical period, it is important to apply the following guidelines:

- Listen for the melody line so the accompaniment parts do not overshadow it.
- Sing chords in tune.
- Make dynamic level changes that move smoothly through each **crescendo** *(a dynamic marking that indicates to gradually sing or play louder)* and **decrescendo** *(a dynamic marking that indicates to gradually sing or play softer).*
- Keep phrases flowing and connected.

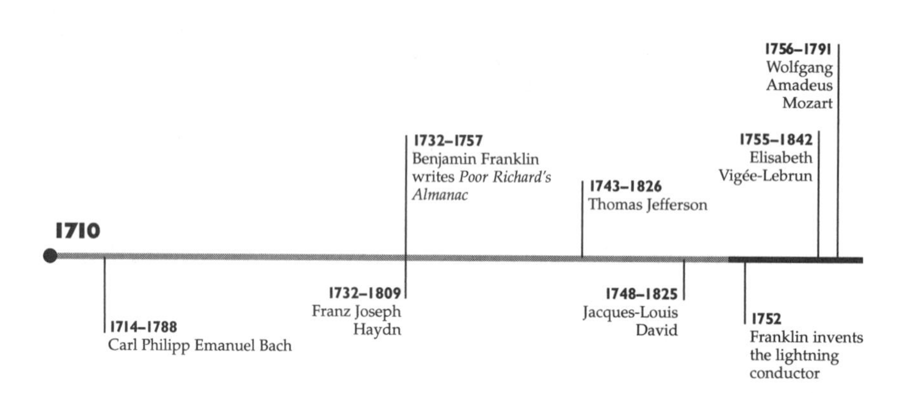

MORE ABOUT

Classical Painting

The styles developed by painters, sculptors and architects during the Classical period were largely a reaction against the excessive detail and embellishment of artworks produced during the late Baroque period. A prominent art historian of the time, Johann Wienckelmann, urged artists to imitate "the noble simplicity and calm grandeur" of the Greeks. Structures such as the Brandenburg Gate in Berlin and Jefferson's home, Monticello, are clear indications that artists responded. Painters and sculptors also worked toward balance, simplicity and clarity.

Listening Links

CHORAL SELECTION

"The Heavens Are Telling" from *Creation* by Franz Joseph Haydn (1732–1809)

Franz Joseph Haydn was an Austrian composer who was Beethoven's teacher, and Mozart's friend. The *Creation* is an oratorio based on a poem from John Milton's *Paradise Lost* and the first chapters of the book of Genesis from the Bible. The angels Gabriel, Uriel and Raphael are portrayed by three soloists, and they describe events of each day of the creation. "The Heavens Are Telling" is a grand celebration of praise that alternates between the full chorus and the trio of soloists. List the order of the choral voice parts in the imitative section as they enter with the words, "With wonders of His work."

INSTRUMENTAL SELECTION

Eine Kleine Nachtmusik, First Movement by Wolfgang Amadeus Mozart (1756–1791)

Wolfgang Amadeus Mozart, another Austrian composer, began his musical career at an extremely early age. By the time he was four years old, Mozart had already mastered the keyboard, and by age five, he had written his first composition. Considered one of the greatest composers of all time, he composed 600 musical works.

The first movement of *Eine Kleine Nachtmusik* is written in **sonata-allegro form**, *a large ABA form consisting of three sections: exposition, development and recapitulation.* The Exposition (section A) presents two themes: (a) and (b). Next comes the Development section (section B). The Recapitulation is a return to the original theme (a). Listen to this selection and write down the name for each section of the sonata-allegro form as you hear it.

Check Your Understanding

1. List three major nonmusical changes that took place during the Classical period.
2. Describe the characteristics of Classical music heard in *Eine Kleine Nachtmusik*.
3. Describe how music from the Classical period is different from music of the Baroque period.

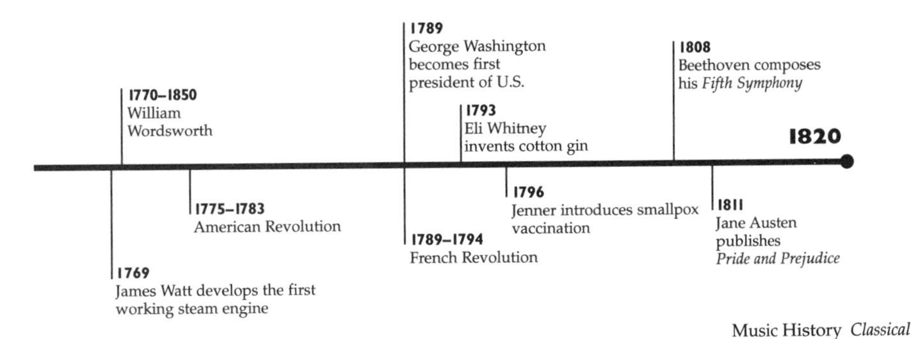

Answers to Check Your Understanding

1. Answers will vary. Revolutions in the American colonies and in France that produced new governments and new social structures; oxygen was discovered; the first submarine was produced.
2. The classical musical characteristics found in *Eine Kleine Nachtmusik*, First Movement, are: the music is based on balance, clarity and simplicity; it is written in *sonata-allegro* form.
3. Answers will vary. The music of the Classical period left the exaggerated embellishments and the use of improvisation behind; it emphasized precision and balance.

ASSESSMENT

Informal Assessment

In this lesson, students showed the ability to:

- Share what they know about the Classical period.
- Describe musical characteristics, styles and forms found in Classical music.
- Describe some characteristics of Classical art.

Student Self-Assessment

Direct students to:

- Review the questions in Check Your Understanding on page 119.
- Write a paragraph answering each of the three questions about the Classical period.

ENRICHMENT

Research Project

As a small group project, ask students to list two or more vocal selections from different time periods and cultures that might have been influenced by historical themes, such as political protest, homecoming of military personnel, and patriotism. Have students share their lists in a creative form with the entire class. (For example, poster, power point, chart, rap song, illustration, and so forth.)

ROMANTIC

OVERVIEW

Objectives

After completing this lesson, students will be able to:

- Describe the Romantic period, including important developments.
- Describe characteristics of Romantic music.

VOCABULARY

Have students review vocabulary in student lesson. A complete glossary of terms is found on page 240 of the student book.

Introduce the Romantic period through visual art. Analyze the painting by George Caleb Bingham on student page 120. Direct students to discuss the instruments being played. What kind of music might have been performed? Is there a story in the picture? Review background information on Bingham's *The Jolly Flatboatmen* on page 120.

MUSIC & ART

The American artist George Caleb Bingham (1811–1879) was born in Virginia and raised in Missouri. He became known for his river scenes, often of boatmen bringing cargo to the American West along the Missouri and Mississippi rivers. The scene here is a group of boatmen on a flatboat amusing themselves with their own music and dancing.

George Caleb Bingham. *The Jolly Flatboatmen*. 1846. Oil on canvas. 96.9 x 123.2 cm (38 1/8 x 48 1/2"). National Gallery of Art, Washington, D. C. Private Collection.

120 Intermediate Mixed

RESOURCES

Teacher Resource Binder

Music and History 16, *Romantic Music*

Music and History 19, *Mikhail Ippolitov-Ivanov*

Transparency 7, *The Jolly Flatboatmen*, George Caleb Bingham

Music and History 20, *Fine Art Teaching Strategy*

For additional resources, see Music and History section.

Listening Selections CD

(found in the Teacher Resource Binder)

Track 7 "Toreador Chorus" from *Carmen*

Track 8 "The Moldau"

ROMANTIC c. 1820–1900

Focus

- Describe the Romantic period, including important developments.
- Describe characteristics of Romantic music.

The Romantic Period—A Time of Drama

A new sense of political and artistic freedom emerged during the **Romantic period** *(1820–1900)*. The period began in the middle of the Industrial Revolution, a time when manufacturing became mechanized and many people left farm life to work and live in cities where the manufacturing plants were located. Scientific and mechanical achievements were made in the development of railroads, steamboats, the telegraph and telephone, photography, and sound recordings.

The Industrial Revolution caused a major change in the economic and social life of the common people and also produced a wealthy middle class. More people were able to take part in cultural activities, such as attending music performances and going to art museums. Musicians and artists experienced greater freedom to express their individual creative ideas. This was because they were able to support themselves by ticket sales or sales of their art, instead of relying on the patronage of royalty or the church.

As people moved into the cities, nature and life in the country became the inspiration for many artists. The paintings of William Turner expressed the feelings suggested by nature. Later, French Impressionistic painters, including Claude Monet and Pierre-Auguste Renoir, developed new techniques bringing nature and natural light alive for the viewer.

Some of the most prominent thinkers and creators of this period were:

- Georges Bizet—French composer
- George Caleb Bingham—American painter
- Charles Dickens—English author
- Samuel F. B. Morse—American inventor who developed the telegraph

COMPOSERS

Ludwig van Beethoven (1770–1827)
Franz Schubert (1797–1828)
Felix Mendelssohn (1809–1847)
Frédéric Chopin (1810–1849)
Franz Lizst (1811–1886)
Richard Wagner (1813–1883)
Giuseppe Verdi (1813–1901)
Bedrich Smetana (1824–1884)
Johannes Brahms (1833–1897)
Georges Bizet (1838–1875)
Peter Ilyich Tchaikovsky (1840–1893)
Antonín Dvorák (1841–1904)
Claude Debussy (1862–1918)

ARTISTS

George Caleb Bingham (1811–1879)
Edgar Degas (1834–1917)
Paul Cezanne (1839–1906)
Auguste Rodin (1840–1917)
Claude Monet (1840–1926)
Pierre-Auguste Renoir (1841–1919)
Mary Cassatt (1845–1926)
Paul Gauguin (1848–1903)
Vincent van Gogh (1853–1890)

AUTHORS

Alexandre Dumas (1802–1870)
Henry Wadsworth Longfellow (1807–1882)
Charles Dickens (1812–1870)
Jules Verne (1828–1905)
Louisa May Alcott (1832–1884)
Mark Twain (1835–1910)
Rudyard Kipling (1865–1905)

VOCABULARY

Romantic period
music critic
overture
symphonic poem

National Standards

6. Listening to, analyzing, and describing music. **(a, b, c, e, f)**
8. Understanding relationships between music, the other arts, and disciplines outside the arts. **(a, b, c, d, e)**
9. Understanding music in relation to history and culture. **(a, c, d, e)**

LESSON PLAN

Suggested Teaching Sequence

1. Examine the Romantic period in a historical perspective

Direct students to:

- Read and discuss the information found on student page 121.
- Share what they know about the composers, artists and authors listed on this page.
- Turn to the time line on pages 122–123 and read the citations.
- Discuss why these are considered important dates during the Romantic period.
- Identify specific accomplishments that were made during the Romantic period and the people associated with those accomplishments.
- Compare each of these events to what occurred before and after the Romantic period.

2. Define the musical aspects of Romantic music.

Direct students to:

- Read and discuss information on Romantic music found on student page 122.
- Name several important Romantic composers.
- Define *music critic, overture* and *symphonic poem.*

3. Discuss the performance guidelines of Romantic music.

Direct students to:

- Read the Performance Links found on student page 122.
- Discuss the performance guidelines.

LISTENING LESSONS

This feature is designed to expand students' appreciation of choral and instrumental music of the Romantic period.

Choral Selection:

"Toreador Chorus" from *Carmen* by Georges Bizet

Direct students to:

- Read the information on student page 123 to learn more about Georges Bizet and "Toreador Chorus" from *Carmen.*
- Review the definition of *opera.*
- Listen to the recorded performance to identify the mood created by this chorus.
- After listening again, write two or three sentences to describe this procession of the bullfighters scene from *Carmen.*

Instrumental Selection:

"The Moldau" by Bedrich Smetana

Direct students to:

- Read the information on student page 123 to learn more about Bedrich Smetana and "The Moldau."
- Review the definition of *symphonic poem.*
- Listen to the recorded performance to identify the story being told in the music about the Moldau River. *(For example, its beginning as a stream in the mountains, becoming a wide river, passing by hunters in the forest, and so forth.)*

Music of the Romantic Period

Music of the Romantic period focused on both the heights and depths of human emotion. The new musical ideas were expressed through larger works with complex vocal melodies and colorful harmonies. During this time, most of the brass and woodwind instruments developed into what they are today, and these instruments were used to add more tone and depth to the music.

Composers began to think about selling their music to the new audiences of middle-class people. Two types of music that appealed to these audiences were the extravagant spectacles of opera and the boldness of grand symphonic music. As music became public, it became subject to public scrutiny, particularly by music critics. A **music critic** is *a writer who gives an evaluation of a musical performance.*

Much of the music of the time was related to literature, such as Felix Mendelssohn's (1809–1847) *A Midsummer Night's Dream,* which was based on the play by William Shakespeare. A well-known section of this work is the **overture**, or *a piece for orchestra that serves as an introduction to an opera or other dramatic work.* The **symphonic poem** is *a single-movement work for orchestra, inspired by a painting, play or other literary or visual work.* Franz Liszt (1811–1886) was a prominent composer of this style of music. The Romantic period was also a time of nationalism, which was reflected in works such as Liszt's *Hungarian Dances,* Richard Wagner's focus on Germanic music, and the tributes to Italy found in Giuseppe Verdi's operas.

Performance Links

When performing music of the Romantic period, it is important to apply the following guidelines:

- Understand the relation of the text to the melody and harmony.
- Concentrate on phrasing, and maintain a clear, beautiful melodic line.
- Perform accurately the wide range of dynamics and tempos.
- Sing confidently in foreign languages to reflect nationalism in music.

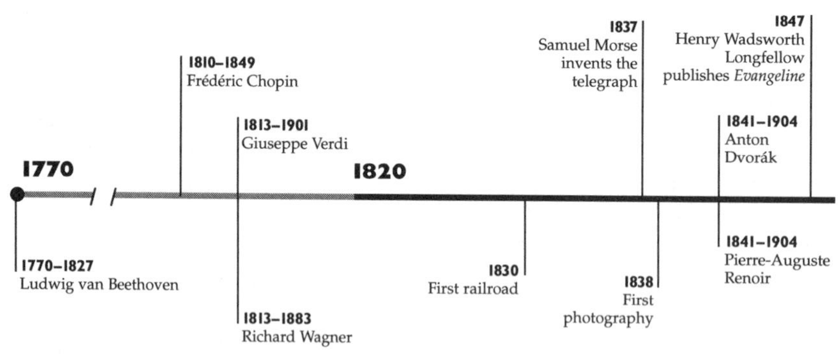

MORE ABOUT

Romantic Painting

Emotional response is the significant feature of many Romantic paintings. Interest in exploring feelings and reaction, rather than formal structure, is typical of visual arts and music during the Romantic period.

Point out the details in *The Jolly Flatboatmen.* Ask: In which ways does this painter use the elements and principals of art differently than artists of other periods studied?

Listening Links

CHORAL SELECTION

"Toreador Chorus" from *Carmen* by Georges Bizet (1838–1875)

Carmen, by French composer Georges Bizet, is considered to be one of the most popular operas ever written. The opera tells the story of a gypsy girl who is arrested when she gets into a fight. Placed in the custody of the soldier Don Jose, Carmen soon entices him into a love affair. She then meets Escamilio, a toreador (bullfighter), and tries to get rid of Don Jose. Jilted, Don Jose stabs Carmen and kills himself. The "Toreador Chorus" is heard during the Procession of the Bullfighters. As you listen to the music, write two or three sentences to describe this procession scene in the opera as you think it would look.

INSTRUMENTAL SELECTION

"The Moldau" by Bedrich Smetana (1824–1884)

Bedrich Smetana was a prominent Czech composer. Smetana had a passion for music and composed in spite of his father's desire for him to become a lawyer. His musical efforts were focused mainly on trying to produce Czech national music based on the folk songs and dances that already existed. Smetana awoke one morning to find himself totally deaf. This created a depression that stayed with him through the remainder of his life. "The Moldau" represents Smetana's deep feeling about the beauty and significance of the river that flows through the city of Prague.

Check Your Understanding

1. List three major nonmusical changes that took place during the Romantic period.
2. Describe how "The Moldau" reflects nationalism in music of the Romantic period.
3. Describe how music of the Romantic period is different from music of another period.

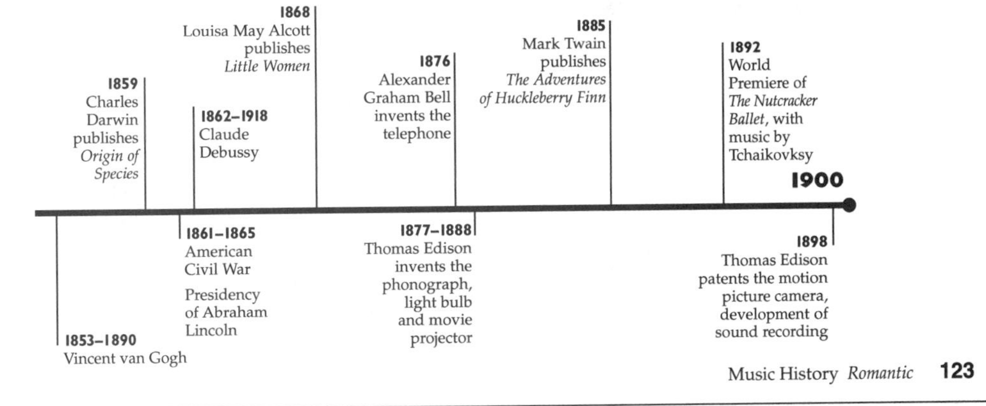

Answers to Check Your Understanding

1. Answers will vary. For example, Industrial Revolution, development of railroads, steamboats, the telegraph and telephone, photography and sound recordings are few choices they might use.
2. Smetana focused this composition on the major river that runs through his country of Czechoslovakia (now the Czech Republic), the Moldau River. He uses Czech folk songs and dance music in the piece to show his patriotism and pride in his country.
3. Answers will vary. For example, music of the Classical period was structured, less emotional, and emphasized clarity, repose and balance. Music of the Romantic period was full of emotion and less structured than music of the Classical period. Nationalism was an important element in Romantic music.

ASSESSMENT

Informal Assessment

In this lesson, students showed the ability to:

- Share what they know about the Romantic period.
- Describe musical characteristics, styles and forms found in Romantic music.
- Describe some characteristics of Romantic art.

Student Self-Assessment

Direct students to:

- Review the questions in Check Your Understanding on page 123.
- Write a paragraph answering each of the three questions about the Romantic period.

ENRICHMENT

Research Project

Have students:

- Write a paragraph that describes the Romantic period, based on research of one of the events in the time line. *(For example, the inventions of the telegraph and motion pictures were a result of the Industrial Revolution. New musical instruments were made as well.)*
- Write an additional paragraph that tells how this Romantic period time line event is related to the students' world. *(For example, new electronic sound devices, such as synthesizers, influence the sound of pop music today.)*

CONTEMPORARY

OVERVIEW

Objectives

After completing this lesson, students will be able to:

- Describe the Contemporary period, including important developments.
- Describe characteristics of Contemporary music.

VOCABULARY

Have students review vocabulary in student lesson. A complete glossary of terms is found on page 240 of the student book.

MUSIC & ART

Introduce the Contemporary period through art. Analyze the painting by Romare Howard Bearden on student page 124. Direct students to discuss the art form of collage. Review background information on Bearden's *The Piano Lesson (Homage to Mary Lou)* on page 124.

African American artist Romare Howard Bearden (1911–1988) is recognized as one of the most creative visual artists of the twentieth century. He experimented with many different styles and mediums but found a unique form of expression in collage. He had a great interest in literature, history, music, mathematics and the performing arts.

Romare Bearden. *The Piano Lesson (Homage to Mary Lou).* 1983. Color lithograph on paper. 75.2 x 52.3 cm (29 1/2 x 20 1/2"). The Pennsylvania Academy of the Fine Arts, Philadelphia, Pennsylvania. The Harold A. and Ann R. Sorgenti Collection of Contemporary African American Art.

RESOURCES

Teacher Resource Binder

Music and History 21, *Contemporary Music*

Music and History 24, *Noel Goemanne*

Transparency 9, *The Piano Lesson (Homage to Mary Lou)*, Romare Howard Bearden

Music and History 25, *Fine Art Teaching Strategy*

For additional resources, see Music and History section.

Listening Selections CD

(found in the Teacher Resource Binder)

Track 9 "The Battle of Jericho"

Track 10 "Infernal Dance of King Kaschei" from *The Firebird*

Focus

- Describe the Contemporary period, including important developments.
- Describe characteristics of Contemporary music.

The Contemporary Period— The Search for Originality

Nothing characterizes the **Contemporary period** *(1900–present)* better than technology. Many technological advances began on October 4, 1957, when the Soviet Union successfully launched *Sputnik I*, the world's first artificial satellite. While the Sputnik launch was a single event, it marked the start of the Space Age and began many new political, military, technological and scientific developments.

Isolation was greatly reduced worldwide by developments in travel (rail, sea and air) and communication (telephone, radio, television and the Internet). It was also reduced as countries came together during World War I and World War II. Elements of cultures merged as people moved from their countries to various parts of the world for economic, political or social reasons. It no longer seems strange, for example, to see Chinese or Mexican restaurants in most communities in the United States or McDonald's® restaurants in Europe and Asia.

Some of the noteworthy leaders of this period have been:

- Igor Stravinsky—Russian/American composer
- Romare Bearden—American artist
- Robert Frost—American poet
- Wilbur and Orville Wright—American inventors who designed and flew the first airplane
- Albert Einstein—German/American scientist who formulated theories of relativity

COMPOSERS

Sergei Rachmaninoff (1873–1943)
Arnold Schoenberg (1874–1951)
Béla Bartók (1881–1945)
Igor Stravinsky (1882–1971)
Sergey Prokofiev (1891–1953)
Carl Orff (1895–1982)
Aaron Copland (1900–1990)
Benjamin Britten (1913–1976)
Leonard Bernstein (1918–1990)
Moses Hogan (1957–2003)

ARTISTS

Henri Matisse (1869–1954)
Pablo Picasso (1881–1973)
Wassily Kandinsky (1866–1944)
Marc Chagall (1887–1985)
Georgia O'Keeffe (1887–1986)
Romare Howard Bearden (1911–1988)
Andy Warhol (1930–1987)

AUTHORS

Robert Frost (1874–1963)
Virginia Woolf (1882–1941)
Ernest Hemingway (1899–1961)
Rachel Carson (1907–1964)
James Baldwin (1924–1997)
JK Rowling (b. 1965)

VOCABULARY

Contemporary period
synthesizer
twelve-tone music
aleatory music
fusion

National Standards

6. Listening to, analyzing, and describing music. **(a, b, c, e, f)**
8. Understanding relationships between music, the other arts, and disciplines outside the arts. **(a, b, c, d, e)**
9. Understanding music in relation to history and culture. **(a, c, d, e)**

LESSON PLAN

Suggested Teaching Sequence

1. Examine the Contemporary period in a historical perspective

Direct students to:

- Read and discuss the information found on student page 125.
- Share what they know about the composers, artists and authors listed on this page.
- Turn to the time line on pages 126–127 and read the citations.
- Discuss why these are considered important dates during the Contemporary period.
- Identify specific accomplishments that were made during the Contemporary period and the people associated with those accomplishments.
- Compare each of these events to what occurred before the Contemporary period.

2. Define the musical aspects of Contemporary music.

Direct students to:

- Read and discuss information on Contemporary music found on student page 126.
- Name several important Contemporary composers.
- Identify the influences of technology on music of the Contemporary period.
- Define *synthesizer, twelve-tone music, aleatory music* and *fusion*.

3. Discuss the performance guidelines of Contemporary music.

Direct students to:

- Read the Performance Links found on student page 126.
- Discuss the performance guidelines.

LISTENING LESSONS

This feature is designed to expand students' appreciation of choral and instrumental music of the Contemporary period.

Choral Selection:

"The Battle of Jericho," Traditional Spiritual, arranged by Moses George Hogan

Direct students to:

- Read the information on student page 127 to learn more about Moses George Hogan and "The Battle of Jericho."
- Listen to the recorded performance to identify specific musical effects added by the arranger, Moses Hogan.
- List these musical effects. *(The men's voices add energetic rhythmic effects to the harmonized melody in the women's voices. Word painting is used several times, especially at the end, for the words "come a tumbalin' down.")*

Instrumental Selection:

"Infernal Dance of King Kaschei" from *The Firebird* by Igor Stravinsky

Direct students to:

- Read the information on student page 127 to learn more about Igor Stravinsky and "Infernal Dance of King Kaschei" from *The Firebird*.
- Listen to the recorded performance to enjoy the energy and drama of this ballet selection.
- Listen again to the first section of the piece to count the loud shrieks of the firebird in that section. *(7)*

Music of the Contemporary Period

Technology has had a large influence on Contemporary music. Most people have access to music via radio, television and recordings. Technology has also influenced the music itself. The invention of electrified and electronic instruments led many composers to experiment with the new sounds. One of the most important new instruments was the **synthesizer,** *a musical instrument that produces sounds electronically, rather than by the physical vibrations of an acoustic instrument.*

The Contemporary period has witnessed a number of musical styles. Maurice Ravel (1875–1937) and Claude Debussy (1862–1918), for example, wrote music in the Impressionist style, often describing an impression of nature. Some of the music of Igor Stravinsky (1882–1971) and others was written in a neo-Classical (or "new" classical) style. Other music was considered avant-garde (or unorthodox or experimental); this included Arnold Schoenberg's (1874–1951) **twelve-tone music,** *a type of music that uses all twelve tones of the scale equally.* Composers experimented with **aleatory music,** or *a type of music in which certain aspects are performed randomly and left to chance.*

In addition, composers began using the rhythms, melodies and texts of other cultures in their compositions in a trend called **fusion,** or *the act of combining various types and cultural influences of music into a new style.*

Performance Links

When performing music of the Contemporary period, it is important to apply the following guidelines:

- Sing on pitch, even in extreme parts of your range.
- Tune intervals carefully in the skips found in many melodic lines.
- Sing changing meters and unusual rhythm patterns precisely.
- Perform accurately the wide range of dynamics and tempos.

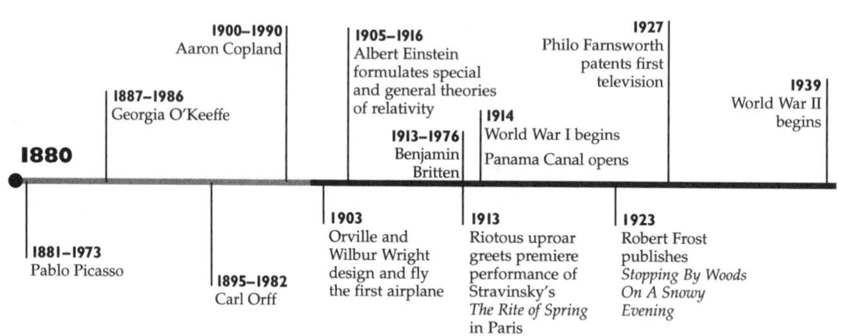

MORE ABOUT

Contemporary Art

The word that best describes the art of the Contemporary period is *diversity*. Today's artists make even greater use of new materials and techniques to express their ideas, beliefs and feelings. Many of these artists are moving away from traditional styles of art. Art movements of the past have given way to an astonishing array of individual art styles. Some of these styles reflect the influence of earlier artists while others reject entirely any reference to historical models.

Listening Links

CHORAL SELECTION

"The Battle of Jericho," Traditional Spiritual, arranged by Moses George Hogan (1957–2003)

Moses Hogan, born in New Orleans, Louisiana, was a pianist, conductor and arranger. He has been one of the most influential arrangers of our time in the revitalization of the songs of our forebearer. His contemporary settings of African American spirituals have been revered by audiences and praised by critics. He had a unique talent for expanding the harmonies and rhythms while preserving the traditional essence of these spirituals. Hogan's arrangements have become staples in the repertoires of choirs worldwide. What specific musical effects did Hogan add in his arrangement of "The Battle of Jericho"?

INSTRUMENTAL SELECTION

"Infernal Dance of King Kaschei" from *The Firebird* by Igor Stravinsky (1882–1971)

Igor Stravinsky was born in Russia, but lived the last twenty-five years of his life in California. *The Firebird* is a ballet that begins when Prince Ivan gives a magical golden bird with wings of fire its freedom in return for a feather. With the help of the magic feather, Ivan conquers an evil king and frees the princesses and prisoners that the king had held captive. Prince Ivan falls in love with a princess and they live happily ever after.

In the first section of this piece, you can hear the loud shrieks of the firebird. How many times did you hear this sudden loud sound?

Check Your Understanding

1. List three major nonmusical changes that took place during the Contemporary period.
2. Discuss the differences between a composer and an arranger.
3. Describe how music of the Contemporary period is different from music of the Romantic period.

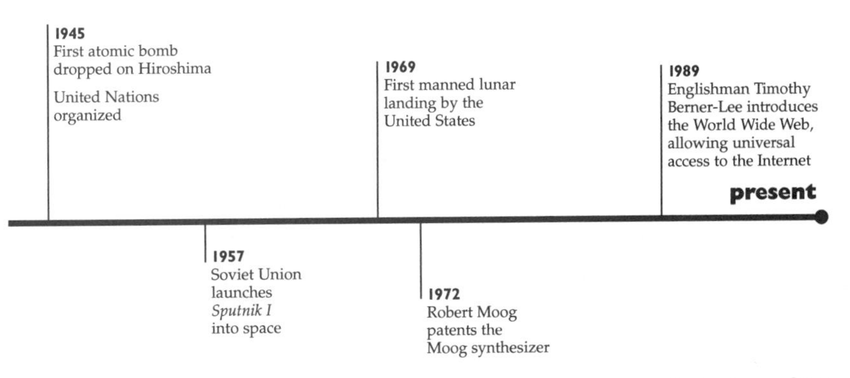

Answers to Check Your Understanding

1. Answers will vary. For example, Space Age/*Sputnik*; developments in travel and communication; WWI and WWII; theory of relativity
2. An arranger is a musician who adapts a composition or folk music for particular voices or instruments, or for another style of performance. A composer creates a piece of music as an original work.
3. Answers will vary. Music of the Romantic period focuses on the heights and depths of human emotion. Nationalism is reflected in many musical works. Music of the Contemporary period is marked by change and experimentation—new forms, new instruments, music written with no tonal center, music featuring a fusion of musical styles, and so forth.

ASSESSMENT

Informal Assessment

In this lesson, students showed the ability to:

- Share what they know about the Contemporary period.
- Describe musical characteristics, styles and forms found in Contemporary music.
- Describe some characteristics of Contemporary art.

Student Self-Assessment

Direct students to:

- Review the questions in Check Your Understanding on page 127.
- Write a paragraph answering each of the three questions about the Contemporary period.

ENRICHMENT

Research Project

The technology boom of the 1990s has brought so many possibilities for expansion of the arts, and also made arts production accessible and affordable to everyone. However, some people feel that there is a danger that the standards for excellence in the arts will be lost because now everyone is capable of making it. At the same time, each field of art may be taken to a level never imagined before. Have students:

- Discuss the advantages and disadvantages of technology as it applies to art and music.
- Have small groups do research on the specifics of each, and then present findings to the rest of the class.

CAREERS IN MUSIC

Objective

- Describe music-related vocations and avocations.

Suggested Teaching Sequence

Direct students to:

- Read the Spotlight on Careers in Music on page 128 and identify the many teaching opportunities in music.
- Divide into small groups and brainstorm on the many different teaching careers available in music. Make a list and share findings with the class. Why are these jobs important?
- Share personal experiences of music teachers that have influenced their lives in a positive way. If possible, invite those teachers to speak to the class about their careers.
- Search the Internet or local library for other career opportunities in music.

Progress Checkpoints

Observe students' progress in:

✓ Their ability to identify teaching careers in music.

✓ Their ability to describe the importance of the role of a music teacher.

✓ Their ability to discover other career opportunities in music.

Careers In Music

Teacher

Music teachers share their love of music with their students. To become a public school teacher, you must have a bachelor's degree in music education. That will require at least four years of college, including one semester of student teaching. High school and junior high music teachers usually specialize in one performance area such as choir, band or orchestra. They may also teach general music, music theory, music appreciation, keyboard and guitar. Elementary music teachers enjoy working with young children. Their job is varied in that they teach singing, dancing, how to play instruments, listening, world music and much more.

At the college level, a music professor must have additional training. Although the minimum requirement is to have a master's degree in music, most colleges require you to have a doctorate as well. College professors teach students how to become professional musicians and professional teachers.

Some musicians choose to teach music through their church or synagogue. Church musicians may be full-time or part-time employees. They might serve as a singer, a choir director, an organist, an instrumentalist or a **cantor** *(a person who sings and teaches music in temples or synagogues).* Some of these positions require a college degree in music.

Private studio teachers enjoy working with students on a one-on-one basis. They teach from their homes, from a private studio, or sometimes at a school. Private instructors teach voice, piano/keyboard, or any of the musical instruments. Their hours are flexible, but they often work in the evenings or weekends because that is when their students are not in school.

RESOURCES

Teacher Resource Binder

Reference 5, *Careers in Music*

National Standards

9. Understanding music in relation to history and culture. **(c)**

Choral Library

¡Aleluya, Amén!

OVERVIEW

Composer: Rafael D. Grullón
Text: Traditional Liturgy
Voicing: SATB
Key: G minor
Meter: (6/8–3/4)
Form: ABB coda
Style: Contemporary Dominican Republican Anthem
Accompaniment: Piano and Drum
Programming: Concert Closer, Multicultural Concert

Vocal Ranges:

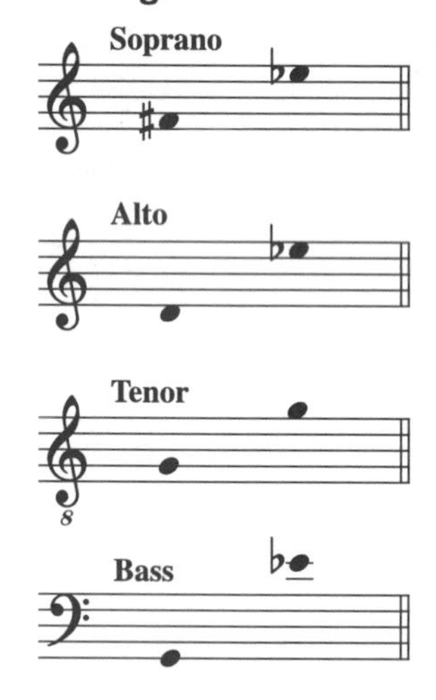

Objectives

After completing this lesson, students will be able to:

- Read and perform music in various meters, including mixed meter.
- Perform a varied repertoire of music representing styles from diverse cultures, including the Dominican Republic.

VOCABULARY

Have students review vocabulary in student lesson. Introduce terms found in the music. A complete glossary of terms is found on page 240 of the student book.

¡Aleluya, Amén!

Composer: Rafael D. Grullón
Text: Traditional Liturgy
Voicing: SATB

VOCABULARY

mangulina
mixed meter

Focus

- Perform music in mixed meter.
- Perform music representing the Dominican Republic culture.

Getting Started

What do these words have in common?

...Santa Domingo
...sugar cane
...merengue

SKILL BUILDERS

To learn more about mixed meter, see Intermediate Sight-Singing, *page 97.*

They describe three important aspects of the Dominican Republic. Santa Domingo is the capital city, sugar cane is the major agricultural crop, and the merengue is the most famous traditional dance from this Caribbean country that shares the island of Hispaniola with Haiti.

◆ History and Culture

The Dominican Republic is also known for its dynamic union of three great cultures: African, European and the indigenous culture of the island. This vibrant blend of traditions is most apparent in the food, music and religious beliefs of the population. "¡Aleluya, Amén!" could also be considered a cultural mix. Composer Rafael Grullón (b. 1933) chose a Spanish sacred text and set it to the captivating rhythms of the **mangulina,** another *traditional dance from the Dominican Republic.* This dance developed from the merging of African and European dance steps and rhythms. "¡Aleluya, Amén!" is written in **mixed meter,** or *a technique in which the time signature changes frequently within a piece.* In this song, every measure alternates between $\frac{6}{8}$ and $\frac{3}{4}$ meters. All these elements combine to make "¡Aleluya, Amén!" a song of joyful celebration—just what you would expect to hear on a beautiful tropical island.

RESOURCES

Intermediate Sight-Singing

Sight-Singing in G Minor, pages 133–136
Reading Rhythms in Mixed Meter, page 97

Teacher Resource Binder

Teaching Master 19, *Composing in Mixed Meter*
Skill Builder 18, *Major and Minor Scales*
Skill Builder 21, *Pitch and Kodály*
Skill Builder 23, *Rhythm and Kodály*
Skill Builder 30, *Solfège Hand Signs*
For additional resources, see TRB Table of Contents.

Links to Learning

◆ Vocal

Read and perform the following melodic pattern that outlines the G minor scale. A **minor scale** is *a scale that has* la *as its keynote or home tone.*

◆ Theory

To alternate between 6/8 meter and 3/4 meter, it is necessary to keep the eighth note constant. Although there are 6 eighth notes in both meters, in 6/8 meter, the dotted quarter note receives the beat (3 eighth notes). However, in 3/4 meter, the quarter note receives the beat (2 eighth notes). Read and perform the following rhythmic pattern by patting your legs with your right and left hands as indicated. Count out loud and stress the numbers 1 and 4 in 6/8 meter, and the numbers 1, 3 and 5 in 3/4 meter.

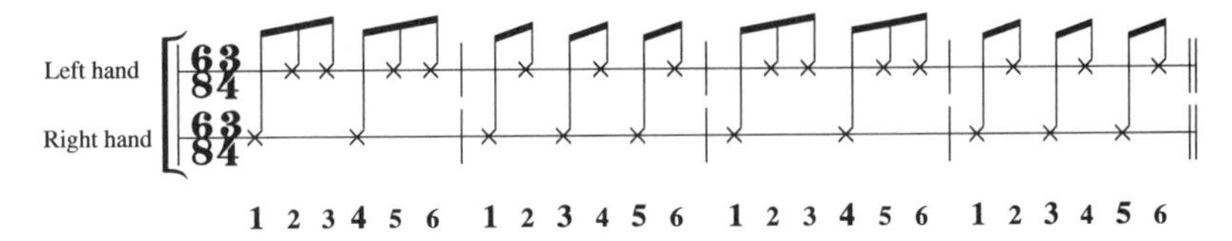

Evaluation

Demonstrate how well you have learned the skills and concepts featured in the lesson "¡Aleluya, Amén!" by completing the following:

- Chant the words in rhythm in measures 9–16, to show your ability to read music in mixed meter.
- Sing "¡Aleluya, Amén!" slowly while clapping the rhythmic pattern described in the Theory section above to feel the changing meter.

LINKS TO LEARNING

Vocal

The Vocal section is designed to prepare students to:

- Understand a minor scale.
- Sing a G minor scale.

Have students:

- Listen as you play the G minor scale on the keyboard.
- Sing the G minor scale on solfège syllables as notated.

Theory

The Theory section is designed to prepare students to:

- Read notation in mixed meter.
- Perform rhythms in mixed meter accenting the correct beats.

Have students:

- Read the directions in the Theory section.
- Perform the rhythm example in mixed meters accenting the correct beats in alternating measures.

RESOURCES

Intermediate Mixed Rehearsal/Performance CD

CD 2:1 Voices
CD 2:2 Accompaniment Only
CD 3:13 Vocal Practice Track—Soprano
CD 4:13 Vocal Practice Track—Alto
CD 5:4 Vocal Practice Track—Tenor
CD 6:13 Vocal Practice Track—Bass

National Standards

1. Singing, alone and with others, a varied repertoire of music. **(a, c, d, e)**
9. Understanding music in relation to history and culture. **(a, b)**

LESSON

Suggested Teaching Sequence and Performance Tips

1. Introduce

Direct students to:

- Read and discuss the ideas presented in the Getting Started section on student page 130.
- Practice the G minor scale in Theory section on page 131. Sing the scale as a round with one singer on each part.
- Practice the mixed-meter rhythms in the Theory section on page 131.

Progress Checkpoints

Observe students' progress in:

✓ Singing the G minor scale independently and in tune.

✓ Performing mixed meters rhythms with accuracy.

2. Rehearse

Direct students to:

- Clap or tap the rhythm in measures 9–16 while counting the constant eighth-note pulse.
- Write *Soprano, Alto, Tenor* and *Bass* on the chalkboard. Have the choir all sing measures 9–10 on solfège syllables or a neutral syllable, but point to only one voice part to continue singing measure 11–12. Repeat with measure 13–16, choosing a different voice part for measure 15–16. Repeat until all voice parts can accurately sing the skip between the unison motives and the four-part harmony.

TEACHER 2 TEACHER

Performing clean, accurate rhythm patterns when 6/8 is superimposed on 3/4 is difficult for even advanced singers. Insist on a slow and steady tempo from the beginning, and your students will find success. Bring a variety of percussion instruments to class and have one student be continually responsible for keeping a steady pulse while you sing. Let different students choose different instruments for each rehearsal.

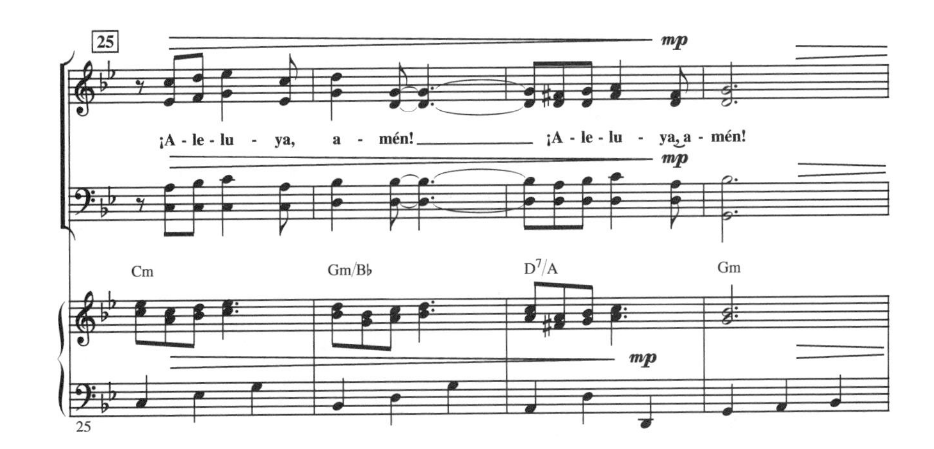

- Repeat this procedure for the remaining sections. (measures 17–24, 25–32, 33–end)

Progress Checkpoints

Observe student's progress in:

- Clapping rhythms in mixed meter.
- Their ability to independently sing in two, three and four parts.

3. Refine

Direct students to:

- Recite the Spanish text, *¡Aleluya, Amén!* in rhythm. Note the similarity of the words to the Latin spelling and pronunciation. Explain syllabic stress and its importance to vocal music. For this text, the stress is *a-le-LU-ya A-men.*
- Recite the Spanish text in rhythm with syllabic stress.
- As a choir, sing *¡Aleluya, Amén!* following the expressive markings in the score.

Progress Checkpoints

Observe students' progress in:

✓ Singing in the Spanish text.
✓ Their ability to sing with the proper syllabic stress.

EXTENSIONS

Have students:

- Find other choral pieces from any historical period or style with the same text as *¡Alleluia, Amen!* Learn a portion of one of the pieces with several classmates and perform for the choir.
- Choose a familiar song (i.e. "America The Beautiful"; "Swing Low, Sweet Chariot") and arrange it with a variety of rhythmic changes, tempo and expressive markings.
- Listen to *Concierto de Aranjuez* (Movement 1, *Allegro con spirito*) by Joaquín Rodrigo or another example of classical Spanish guitar music with a 6/8–3/4 meter feeling. How does this compare to "¡Alleluia, Amen!"?

ASSESSMENT

Informal Assessment

In this lesson, the students showed the ability to:

- Perform in mixed meter.
- Sing independently in four-parts with good intonation.
- Sing in Spanish with the correct syllabic stress.

Student Self-Assessment

Have students evaluate their individual performances based on the following:

- Posture
- Breath Management
- Foreign Language
- Accurate Rhythms
- Correct Part-Singing

Have each student rate his/her performance of this song in the areas above on a scale of 1–5, 5 being the best.

Individual and Group Performance Evaluation

To further measure growth of musical skills presented in this lesson, direct students to complete the Evaluation section on page 131.

- Ask for volunteers to come forward and chant the rhythms to measures 9–16 for the rest of the choir. The choir should evaluate that student's ability to perform in mixed meter.
- While patting the rhythmic pattern in the Theory section on page 131, sing the piece as written. Evaluate how well students keep this pattern going while singing the song.

Additional National Standards

The following National Standards are addressed through the Assessment, Extension, Enrichment and bottom-page activities:

4. Composing and arranging music within specific guidelines. **(b)**

6. Listening to, analyzing, and describing music. **(a, b, c)**

7. Evaluating music and music performances. **(b)**

8. Understanding relationships between music, the other arts, and disciplines outside the arts. **(a)**

9. Understanding music in relation to history and culture. **(a)**

Changing Voice

As we grow in size and maturity, we don't always grow at the same rate. Just look around your school or neighborhood. Some thirteen-year-olds tower over others, while some are quite small.

As the voice matures, it changes in both pitch and **timbre** *(tone quality).* Just like growing in stature, this process is not the same for every person. One person's voice might drop an octave almost overnight, while another person's might not seem to have changed at all.

The Male Voice

As a young male singer, you will face several challenges as your voice matures. Certain pitches that were once easy to sing suddenly may be out of your vocal range. While every voice change is unique, many male singers progress through several identifiable stages:

1. The voice is a treble voice with no obvious signs of changing.
2. The upper range sounds slightly breathy or hoarse.
3. The singer is able to sing lower pitches than before. Higher pitches continue to sound breathy. The speaking and singing voices are noticeably lower. There is an obvious "break" around middle C.
4. The voice "settles" into **Bass** *(the lowest-sounding male voice)* or "rises" to **Tenor** *(the highest-sounding male voice).* Higher pitches can now be sung in **falsetto,** *a register in the male voice that extends far above the natural high voice.*

With practice and attention to the principles of good singing, you can get through this transition without too much difficulty.

The Female Voice

As a young female singer, you will not face the same challenges that young male singers face. However, your voice will go through changes, too.

Between the ages of eleven and sixteen, you might notice breathiness in your vocal tone, difficulty in moving between your chest voice and head voice, and a general lack of vocal resonance.

By using the good vocal techniques of posture, breath and vowel formation, you can establish all the qualities necessary for success. You should use your full vocal range and gain experience in singing both **Alto** *(the lowest-sounding female voice)* and **Soprano** *(the highest-sounding female voice),* since your actual voice category may not be evident until you reach your middle-to-late teens.

RESOURCES

Teacher Resource Binder

Reference 7, *Checking On My Voice*

National Standards

1. Singing alone and with others. **(a, b)**

CHANGING VOICE

Objectives

- Demonstrate characteristic vocal timbre individually and in groups.

Suggested Teaching Sequence

Direct students to:

- Read Spotlight On Changing Voice on student page 135 and identify the characteristics of the male and female changing voice.
- Define *timbre.*
- Test their vocal ranges to determine their highest and lowest comfortable singing note. Check their ranges throughout the year.
- Record themselves singing "America" at the beginning of the year, the middle of the year and at the end of the year. Compare the three recordings and document changes in the voice that have occurred during the course of the year.

Progress Checkpoints

Observe students' progress in:

✓ Their ability to identify the stages of change in the male and female voice.

✓ Their ability to understand timbre.

✓ Their ability to discover the progress of change in their individual voice.

Bound For The Rio Grande

OVERVIEW

Composer: American Sea Chantey, arranged by Emily Crocker
Text: Traditional
Voicing: 3-Part Mixed
Key: C major/D major
Meter: 6/8
Form: Strophic
Style: American Folk Song
Accompaniment: Piano
Programming: Contest, Festival, Concert

Vocal Ranges:

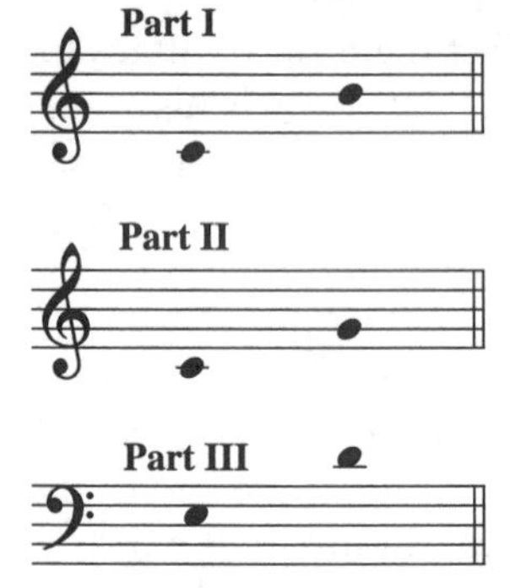

Objectives

After completing this lesson, students will be able to:

- Use standard terminology to describe in detail music notation.
- Read and perform music in various meters, including 6/8.
- Perform music representative of diverse cultures.

VOCABULARY

Have students review vocabulary in student lesson. Introduce terms found in the music. A complete glossary of terms is found on page 240 of the student book.

Bound For The Rio Grande

Composer: American Sea Chantey, arranged by Emily Crocker
Text: Traditional
Voicing: 3-Part Mixed

VOCABULARY

sea chantey
compound meter

Focus

- Identify the melody line in music.
- Read and perform music in $\frac{6}{8}$ meter.
- Perform music in the character in which it was written.

Getting Started

When it comes to cleaning your room at home, which description best fits you?

1. You love to clean and go right to work.
2. You do not enjoy cleaning, but if you play music or sing, the work gets done.

If you relate to the second statement, you have something in common with eighteenth-century English sailors. "Bound For The Rio Grande" is a **sea chantey,** or *a song sung by sailors in the rhythm of their work.* As they sang, the work was done. You might want to sing this song the next time you clean your room!

SPOTLIGHT

To learn more about changing voice, *see page 135.*

History and Culture

More specifically, "Bound For The Rio Grande" is a capstan chantey. The capstan is a mushroom-shaped object on a ship that connects to its anchor. The sailors inserted bars into holes along the top of the capstan. They would turn the capstan to raise the anchor. Capstan chanteys typically have a very steady rhythm and tell long stories because it sometimes took hours to raise the anchor.

Originally, the Rio Grande in this song may have referred to Rio Grande do Sul in Brazil. Ships would leave England and Wales and sail to Brazil for trade. Today, "Bound For The Rio Grande" is considered one of the most popular sea chanteys.

RESOURCES

Intermediate Sight-Singing

Sight-Singing in C Major, pages 7–14, 15–17, 28–30, 6–67, 110–111

Sight-Singing in D Major, pages 99–102

Reading Rhythms in 6/8 Meter, pages 114–16

Teacher Resource Binder

Teaching Master 20, *Music on the Job!*

Evaluation Master 9, *Identifying Vocal Balance*

Skill Builder 28, *Rhythm Challenge in 6/8 Meter*

Skill Builder 30, *Solfège Hand Signs*

Dalcroze 12, *Moving to the Beat and Beat Subdivisions*

For additional resources, see TRB Table of Contents.

Links to Learning

◆ Vocal

The melody to "Bound For The Rio Grande" sometimes takes on the character of the rolling sea. To feel this effect, place an accent on the syllables that fall on the beat as you read and perform the following example.

◆ Theory

$\frac{6}{8}$ meter is an example of **compound meter,** or *a meter in which the dotted quarter note receives the beat.* Read and perform the following example with the feel of two beats per measure.

◆ Artistic Expression

Pretend you are a sailor pulling a rope with the anchor attached. On the downbeat of each measure, grab the imaginary rope and pull back with resistance. On the second beat of each measure, lift one hand and reach forward as if grabbing the next section of the rope. Continue this two-beat motion as you sing the song.

Evaluation

Demonstrate how well you have learned the skills and concepts featured in the lesson "Bound For The Rio Grande" by completing the following:

- In a small group with at least one person on a part, sing measures 15–20. Raise your hand when your part has the melody. As a group, evaluate how well the melody line could be heard over the other parts.
- Chant the words in rhythm in measures 26–34 to show your ability to read music in $\frac{6}{8}$ meter.
- Stand still and sing measures 7–23 of "Bound For The Rio Grande." Then sing the passage again with the motions described in the Artistic Expression section above. Compare the two performances and decide which one you prefer and why.

RESOURCES

Intermediate Mixed Rehearsal/Performance CD

CD 2:3 Voices
CD 2:4 Accompaniment Only
CD 3:14 Vocal Practice Track—Part I
CD 4:14 Vocal Practice Track—Part II
CD 6:14 Vocal Practice Track—Part III

National Standards

1. Singing, alone and with others, a varied repertoire of music. **(a, b, c, d, e)**
5. Reading and notating music. **(a, b, c)**
6. Listening to, analyzing, and describing music. **(a, c)**
9. Understanding music in relation to history and culture. **(a, b, c)**

LINKS TO LEARNING

Vocal

The Vocal section is designed to prepare students to:

- Feel the character of the rolling sea in the music.
- Perform the music with the appropriate accents.

Have students:

- Perform the example on solfège syllables with no accents.
- Perform the example on solfège syllables with the accents as marked. Compare the difference. Which one sounds more the rolling sea?

Theory

The Theory section is designed to prepare students to:

- Understand compound meter.
- Perform rhythms in 6/8 meter.

Have students:

- Tap or clap the dotted quarter note pulse.
- Speak the rhythm example while tapping the dotted quarter note pulse.
- Speak the rhythm example while feeling the dotted quarter note pulse inside.

Artistic Expression

The Artistic Expression section is designed to prepare students to use physical movement to achieve the stress and lilt of singing in 6/8 meter, with emphasis on the downbeat of each measure.

Have students sing the song while performing the motions indicated, stressing the downbeat of each measure.

LESSON PLAN

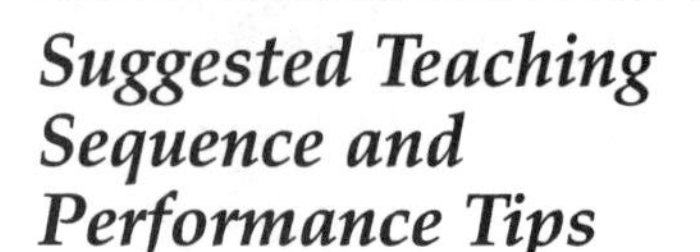

Suggested Teaching Sequence and Performance Tips

1. Introduce

Direct students to:

- Read and discuss the information found in the Getting Started section on page 136.
- Practice the exercise in the Vocal section on page 137 to feel the character of the rolling sea.
- Practice the exercise in the Theory section on page 187 to perform 6/8 meter in the feeling of two. Include some enrichment rhythmic exercises in 6/8 meter from other sources to reinforce reading accuracy. Remember to count in 6/8 and also in two.

Bound For The Rio Grande

For 3-Part Mixed and Piano

Arranged by
EMILY CROCKER

American Sea Chantey

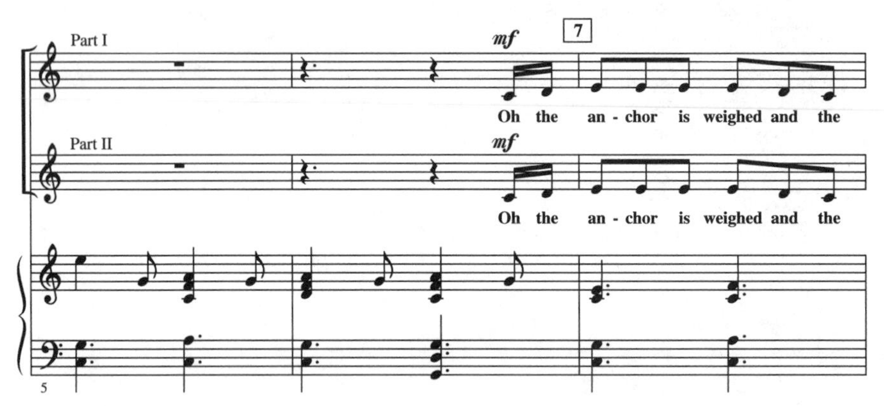

TEACHER 2 TEACHER

It would be fun to program a concert, or a section of a concert with all sea chanteys. This popular sea chantey arranged by Emily Crocker makes use of text painting as the arrangement rollicks and rolls as if mimicking the waves of the ocean.

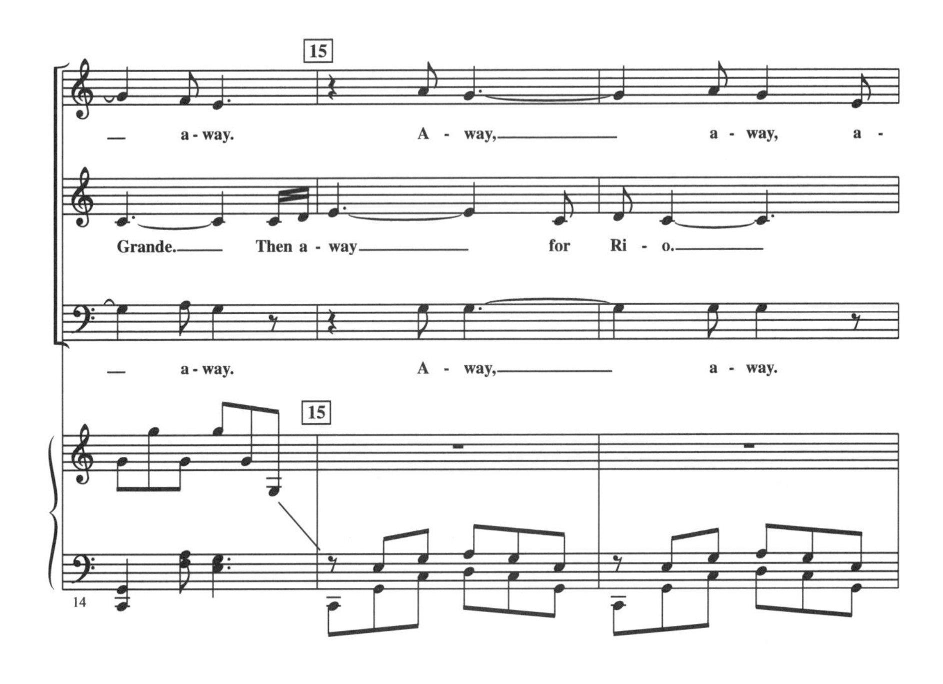

- Listen to the melody of the piece as you play it. Sing the melody on solfège. Ask students to place brackets around the melody when it occurs in their part.
- Mark breath marks in their music. Instruct them on which beat to breathe. This will help ensure accurate entrances.
- Practice singing the melodic lines from the Vocal section on page 137. Encourage breath control while singing the lines.

Progress Checkpoints

Observe students' progress in:

✓ Their accuracy in reading the rhythmic patterns both from the Theory section, and from any other source.

✓ Locating the melody line in whatever part it occurs.

✓ Applying good breath control to the melodic line.

TEACHING STRATEGY

Composing Music

For students to experience composing, direct student to:

1. Select a meter (simple meter, compound meter, asymmetric meter).
2. Write a four-measure simple or complex rhythmic pattern in that meter.
3. Select a key (major, minor, pentatonic, modal).
4. Using the newly composed rhythmic pattern, write a melody based on the selected key.
5. Exchange compositions with a classmate. Check each other's work for rhythmic and melodic accuracy.
6. Make changes and corrections as necessary, and then perform the compositions for the class.

2. Rehearse

Direct students to:

- Learn the piece by the song form for the best success. As each section is taught completely and learned without error, the teaching and learning time of the similar sections will be cut. Rhythmic accuracy is another key to the success of learning this piece. Do not move from one section to another until the students are accurately reading their parts.
- Practice the entrances in measures 14–23. Remind the students to take rhythmic breaths and only in designated places.

- Sight-sing on solfège, once they are reading rhythmically without error in the first section. Ask the students to sing the solfège using good vowel sounds. This will aid their ability to sing with good intonation during this stage of learning. Continue this style of learning throughout the entire piece.

Progress Checkpoints

Observe students' progress in:

✓ Breathing rhythmically for correct entrances.

✓ Their rhythmic accuracy when reading on the rhythm and when singing pitches.

✓ Their uniformity of vowel sounds on solfège syllables.

ENRICHMENT

The Rio Grande

Ask students to bring in one piece of information about the Rio Grande that sparked their interest. Use this to give them an idea about what they are singing, and as an extra credit project.

3. Refine

Direct students to:

- Speak the text in rhythm as you model the desired vowel sound. For a word that occurs on more than one pitch, have students write the vowel sound that you want sustained throughout the series of pitches underneath each pitch with dashes between the vowel syllable. (For example, "ah-ah-ah") This will help keep students from changing to another syllabic part of the word early.
- Underline the syllable of the word that requires stress. Practice speaking rhythmically with syllabic stress.

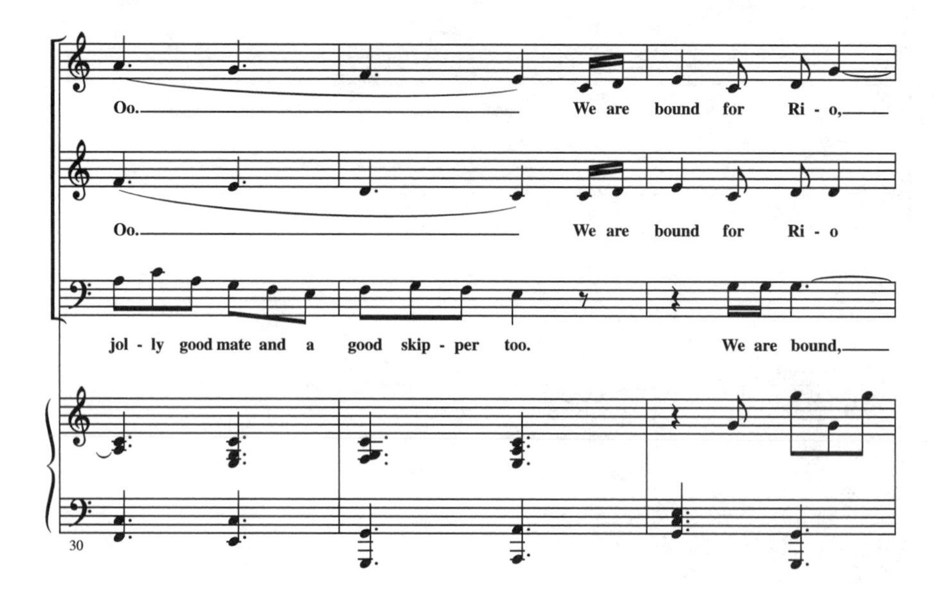

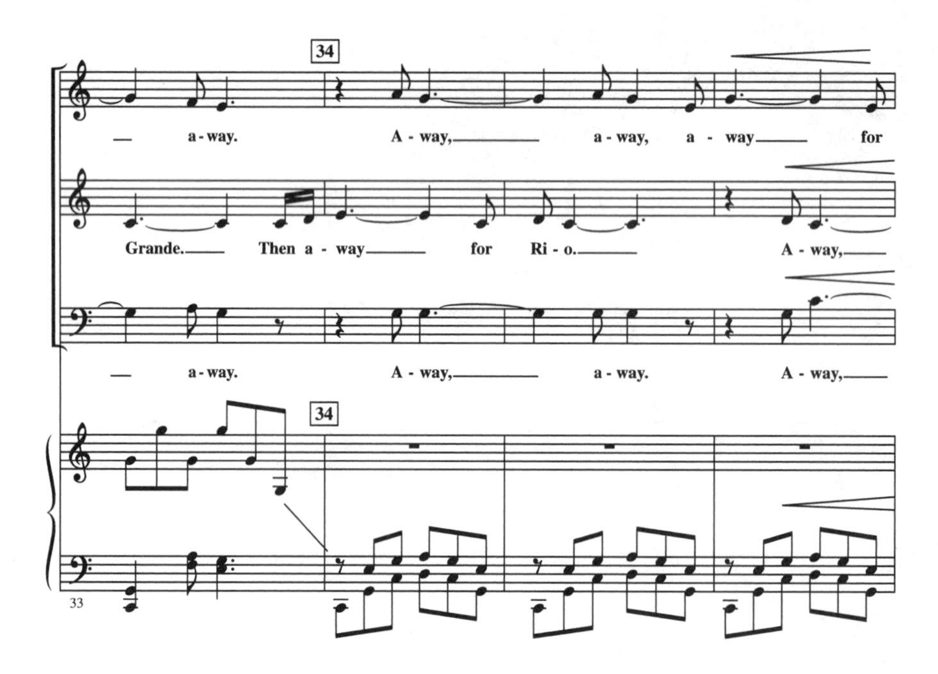

TEACHING STRATEGY

Basic Rhythms in 6/8 Meter

If students are not familiar with patterns in 6/8 meter, have them:

- Count from 1–6, with each number getting one beat.
- Count this pattern four times.
- Add hand claps on 1 and 4 as they continue to count, feeling the strong pulses in 6/8 meter.

Change the patterns to new ones they suggest. For example, clap 1, 3, 4 and 6 each time (this creates the quarter-eighth quarter-eighth pattern), and so on.

- Transfer phrase by phrase from solfège to text until all of the song is learned on text. Encourage students to sing the text with good vowel sounds and create a uniformity of sound along with singing in tune. After the pitches of each phrase are accurate, practice adding syllabic stress as marked in the music.
- Echo as you model how you would like each phrase to sound musically. Have students place musical phrasing markings in their music. Ask students to sing the phrases as modeled. Adjust as needed.
- Reinforce staggered breathing within the singing of the musical phrases.

Progress Checkpoints

Observe students' progress in:

✓ Their rhythmic accuracy during the speaking of the text and the transfer from solfège to text.

✓ Consistently singing the text with good vowels and proper syllabic stress.

✓ Singing phrases as modeled.

✓ Understanding and successfully using staggered breathing.

ASSESSMENT

Informal Assessment

In this lesson, students showed the ability to:

- Read and perform accurately in 6/8 meter.
- Sing melodic lines with good intonation in the key of C major and D major.

Student Self-Assessment

Have students evaluate their individual performances based on the following:

- Posture
- Breath Management
- Tall Vowels
- Intonation
- Correct Part-Singing

Have each student rate his/her performance of this song in the areas above on a scale of 1–5, 5 being the best.

MUSIC, SOCIETY AND CULTURE

Have students perform additional songs representing diverse cultures, including American and Texas heritage. Go to **music.glencoe.com**, the Web site for Glencoe's choral music programs, for additional music selections students can perform.

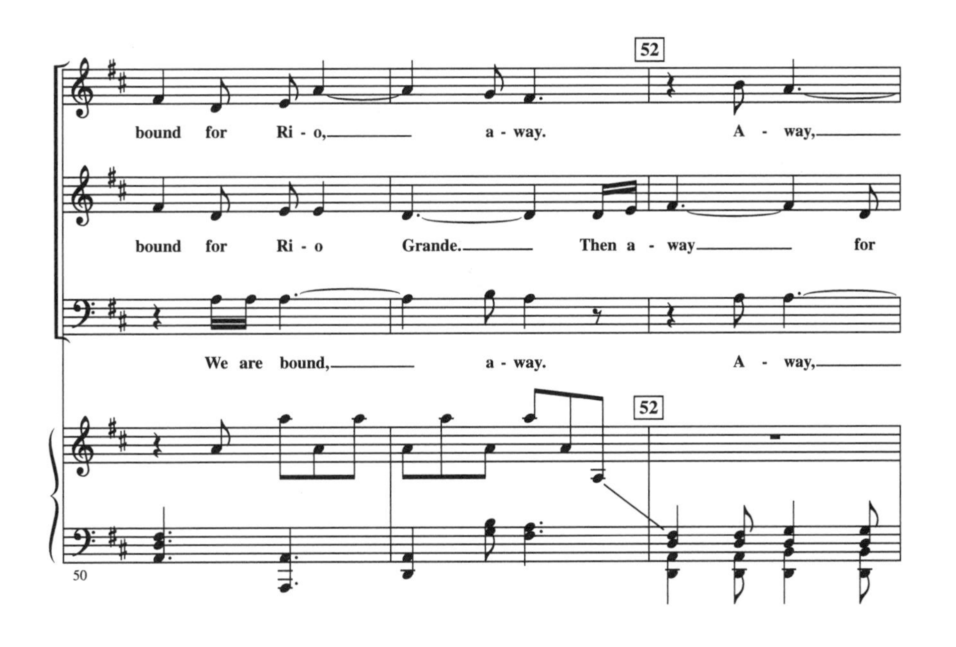

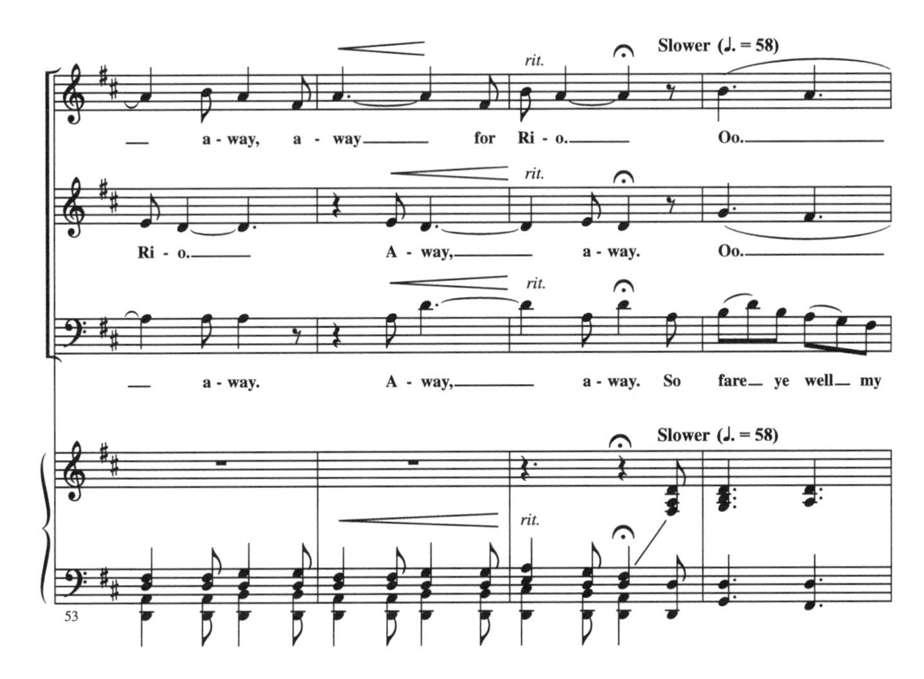

Individual and Group Performance Evaluation

To further measure growth of musical skills presented in this lesson, direct students to complete the Evaluation on page 137.

- After small groups have performed measures 15–20 and raised their hands when they were singing the melody, have that group evaluate how well the melody line could be heard over the other parts.
- Have students chant measures 26–34 and evaluate. How well did these students read rhythms in 6/8 meter?
- Have students compare singing measures 7–23 with motion and without motion. Decide which one you prefer and why.

EXTENSION

Movement to Enhance Style

Give one rope to each section (Part I, Part II, Part III). Instruct each section to tie the ends of their rope together, thus creating a circle. Have each section stand in a circle holding the rope. As students sing the song, instruct them to grab a piece of the rope in a pulling motion on the downbeat of each measure. Continue the motion hand-over-hand as they sing. Ask them if they can hear a difference in the way they sounded when pulling the rope. Repeat the same movement and ask the students to concentrate on adding the syllabic stress for each phrase. Ask students if they hear a difference. Ask students to place the rope on the floor and then sing the same way without the rope. Discuss how movement can enhance a performance.

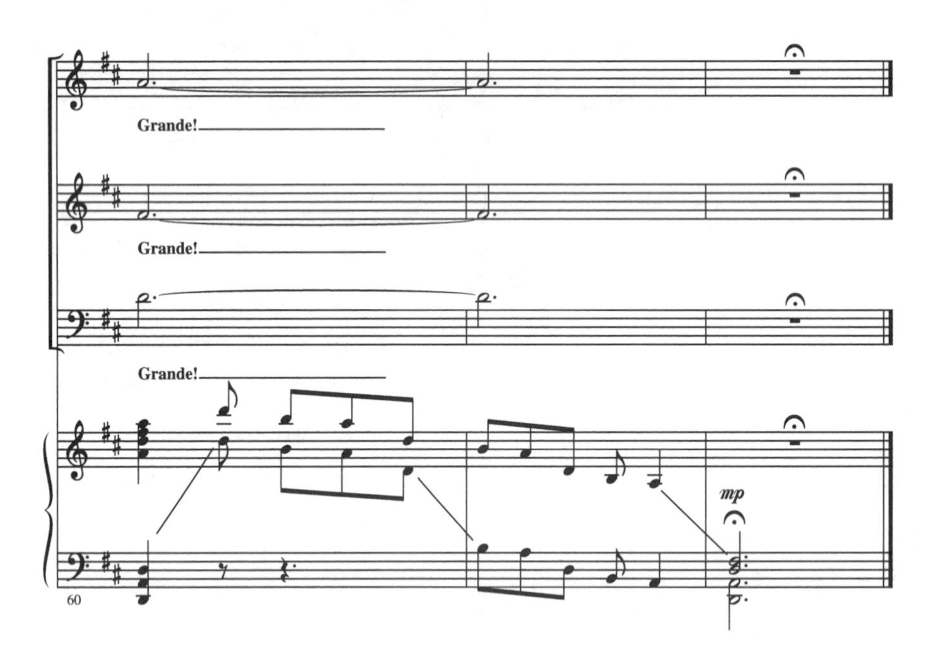

Additional National Standards

The following National Standards are addressed through the Assessment, Extension, Enrichment and bottom-page activities:

7. Evaluating music and music performances. **(a, b)**

8. Understanding relationships between music, the other arts, and disciplines outside the arts. **(a, b)**

Gospel Music

Gospel music is *religious music that originated in the African American churches of the South.* Characteristics of gospel music include improvisation, syncopation and repetition. Following the Civil War, African American churches began to form. The spirituals previously sung by the slaves served as their main source of sacred music. By the early 1900s, some sectors of the church moved to more spirited songs accompanied by tambourines, drums and piano. This new music was the beginning of the gospel style.

African American gospel music gained national recognition during the 1940s and the 1950s with the recordings and live concerts by the singing great Mahalia Jackson (1912–1972). Also of influence was composer and bandleader Thomas Andrew Dorsey (1899–1993). He published over 400 gospel songs and is known as the father of gospel music. His featured music used lively rhythms and syncopated piano accompaniments. "Precious Lord, Take My Hand" is probably his most famous song.

When asked about the correct way to sing gospel music, the contemporary composer Rollo Dilworth said that singers often debate about the appropriate use of chest and head voice registers when performing gospel style. While some believe that excessive use of the chest voice might cause vocal damage, others believe that singing in the African American idiom is not "authentic" if performed in head voice. Dilworth suggests that successful singing in most any genre requires a balanced, healthy singing tone in both head and chest registers. Vocal techniques used in gospel singing include (1) percussive singing (a style that lies between legato and staccato styles); (2) swell (an exaggerated crescendo that adds weight and breadth to an accented syllable); and (3) pitch bending (the scooping up to a pitch, often coupled with a swell or a falling off of a pitch). The rhythm is felt in an accurate yet relaxed style. Basic movements may include stepping, clapping and rocking. Improvisation of the melody is frequently heard in gospel music.

Listen to the recording of "City Called Heaven" (page 148) and identify the characteristics of gospel style singing that you hear.

RESOURCES

Teacher Resource Binder

Teaching Master 21, *Gospel Singing Style*

Reference 16, *My Music Dictionary*

National Standards

1. Singing, alone and with other, a varied repertoire of music. **(a, b, c)**

7. Evaluating music and musical performances. **(a, b)**

GOSPEL MUSIC

Objective

- Classify aurally-presented music representing diverse styles.

Suggested Teaching Sequence

Direct students to:

- Read the Spotlight On Gospel Music on student page 147 and list the characteristics.
- Make a list of familiar gospel songs or artists/composers. If possible, play an example of Thomas Dorsey's "Precious Lord, Take My Hand."
- List and demonstrate the vocal techniques used in gospel singing.
- Demonstrate movements often seen in performances of gospel music.
- Listen to the recording of "City Called Heaven" and identify the characteristics of gospel style singing that you hear.
- Share with the class any experience they may have had with gospel music, such as performing, attending a concert, and so forth.

Progress Checkpoints

Observe students' progress in:

✓ Their ability to define *gospel music.*

✓ Their ability to list the characteristics of gospel music.

✓ Their ability to list and demonstrate the vocal techniques used in gospel singing.

✓ Identifying the gospel style characteristics in the recording of "City Called Heaven."

City Called Heaven

OVERVIEW

Composer: Traditional Spiritual, arranged by Josephine Poelinitz
Text: Traditional
Voicing: SATB
Key: F minor
Meter: 9/8
Form: AA'BB'
Style: Gospel
Accompaniment: Piano
Programming: Concert, Festival, Multicultural

Vocal Ranges:

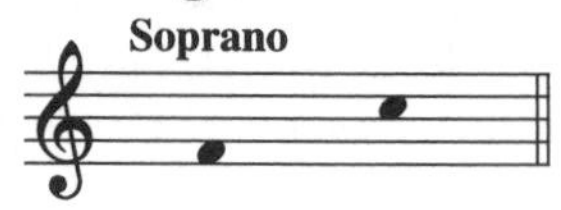

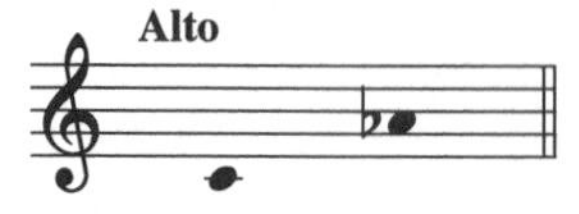

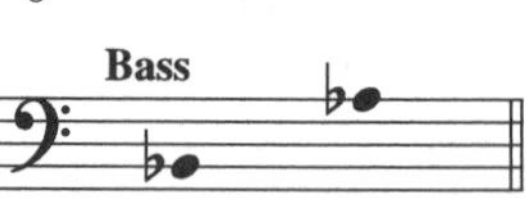

OBJECTIVES

After completing this lesson, students will be able to:

- Read and perform music in 9/8 meter.
- Identify and perform expressively based on notation symbols, such as tenuto markings.
- Perform music representative of different genres, including the gospel style.

VOCABULARY

Have students review vocabulary in student lesson. Introduce terms found in the music. A complete glossary of terms is found on page 240 of the student book.

CHORAL LIBRARY

City Called Heaven

Composer: Traditional Spiritual, arranged by Josephine Poelinitz
Text: Traditional
Voicing: SATB

VOCABULARY

gospel music
improvisation
$\frac{9}{8}$ meter
tenuto

Focus

- Read and perform music in $\frac{9}{8}$ meter.
- Identify and perform tenuto markings.
- Perform music that represents the gospel style.

SPOTLIGHT

To learn more about improvisation, see page 177.

Getting Started

Cultural traditions often pass from elders to children through storytelling. The African American spiritual "City Called Heaven" was probably first sung by slaves. It tells their story of sorrow for life here on Earth and their longing for the freedom and everlasting peace that heaven may bring.

◆ History and Culture

"City Called Heaven" has been arranged by Josephine Poelinitz, who is a choral conductor, arranger and vocal specialist in Chicago, Illinois. She has arranged this particular spiritual in a slow gospel style. **Gospel music** is *religious music that originated in the African American churches of the South and is characterized by improvisation, syncopation and the free extension or repetition of any fragment of the text.* In "City Called Heaven," the choral parts are written in a marked and detached manner consistent with traditional gospel-singing style. Sometimes the full chorus takes the lead, and at other times it performs background material that supports the soloist.

You will enjoy learning the solo line in "City Called Heaven." After you can sing the solo with confidence, try changing the solo by using **improvisation** *(the art of making it up as you sing).*

RESOURCES

Intermediate Sight-Singing

Sight-Singing in F Minor, pages 178–179
Reading Rhythms in 9/8 Meter, pages 160–162

Teacher Resource Binder

Teaching Master 22, *A Balance of Sound*
Evaluation Master 7, *Evaluating Musical Expression*
Skill Builder 1, *Building Harmony*
Skill Builder 23, *Rhythm and Kodàly*
Reference 20, *Rhythm Challenge Chart*

Links to Learning

◆ Vocal

Read and perform the following example to practice chord patterns in the key of F minor found in "City Called Heaven."

◆ Theory

"City Called Heaven" is written in $\frac{9}{8}$ **meter,** *a time signature in which there are three groups of eighth notes per measure and the dotted quarter note receives the beat.* The style markings included in this example include **tenuto** (𝅘𝅥), *a symbol used to indicate that a note should receive extra stress or be held slightly longer than its given value.* Read and perform the following rhythmic patterns, observing these markings.

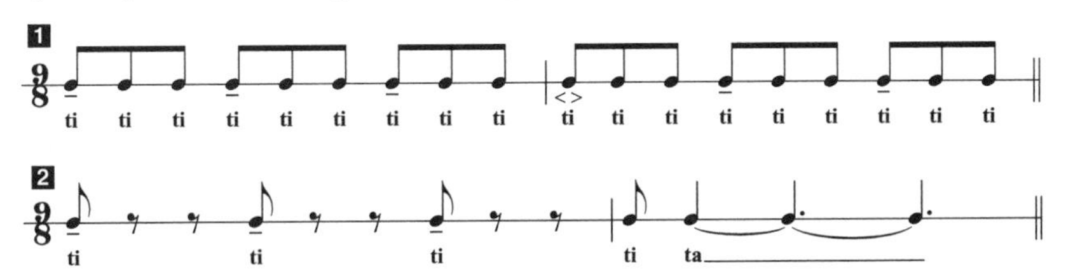

Evaluation

Demonstrate how well you have learned the skills and concepts featured in the lesson "City Called Heaven" by completing the following:

- Record yourself singing measures 5–12. Listen and evaluate how well you were able to perform the rhythms, dynamics and style markings correctly.
- Locate the passages in the music in which the choir has the lead, then locate the passages in which the choir sings background. Discuss how your singing may be different in these two instances.

LINKS TO LEARNING

Vocal

The Vocal section is designed to prepare students to sing chord progressions in the key of F minor.

Have students:

- Sing each part separately and then together.
- Listen to themselves and each other to ensure good intonation.

Theory

The Theory section is designed to prepare students to:

- Read rhythms in 9/8 meter.
- Observe articulation symbols, including tenuto markings.

Have students:

- Clap the rhythms in the examples accurately.
- Clearly stress the notes with the tenuto markings.
- Make sure they maintain a steady pulse.

RESOURCES

Intermediate Mixed Rehearsal/Performance CD

CD 2:5 Voices
CD 2:6 Accompaniment Only
CD 3:15 Vocal Practice Track—Soprano
CD 4:15 Vocal Practice Track—Alto
CD 5:5 Vocal Practice Track—Tenor
CD 6:15 Vocal Practice Track—Bass

National Standards

1. Singing alone and with others, a varied repertoire of music. **(a, b, c, d)**
5. Reading and notating music. **(a, c)**
9. Understanding music in relation to history and culture. **(a, c)**

LESSON PLAN

Suggested Teaching Sequence and Performance Tips

1. Introduce

Direct students to:

- Read and discuss the information found in the Getting Started section on student page 148.
- Practice singing the chord progressions as shown in the Vocal section on page 149.
- Practice performing the rhythmic patterns in 9/8 meter as shown in the Theory section.
- Sing measures 5–12, making sure that all rhythmic, stylistic and dynamic markings are performed with accuracy.

City Called Heaven

For SATB and Piano

Traditional Spiritual

Arranged by
JOSEPHINE POELINITZ

TEACHER 2 TEACHER

"City Called Heaven" provides the singer an opportunity to explore expressive singing in the African American spiritual and gospel styles. In addition to the tenuto markings, the crescendo-decrescendo (<>) markings will challenge the singers to "swell" certain pitches by employing a sudden and somewhat breathy tone. The vocal solo in the music offers the soloist an opportunity to develop skills in improvisation.

- Identify the passages in the piece that contain foreground choral material, or where the choir has the lead vocals. Then, identify the passages in which the choir sings in the background, or supports the soloist. *(Choir as foreground: measures 5–20, first time through, and 22–25. Choir as background: measures 5–20 on the repeat; measures 30–end of piece.)* Discuss how the choir's performance should differ when singing in the foreground versus the background.

Progress Checkpoints

Observe student's progress in:

✓ Their ability to sing in 9/8 meter.

✓ Their ability to differentiate between foreground and background material in the music.

MUSIC AND MOVEMENT

Gospel Style Movement

In the gospel choral tradition, it is common practice for a choir to sway or rock and clap during a performance. A simple, yet powerful movement pattern for this piece would be as follows (the dotted quarter note is the pulse):

1. tap right foot and lean slightly to right
2. clap
3. clap
4. tap left foot and lean slightly to left
5. clap
6. clap

(repeat this pattern throughout the piece)

2. Rehearse

Direct students to:

- Identify measures 5–20 as *Verse.*
- Identify measures 22–end as *Chorus.*
- Clap or chant the rhythms in measures 22–25.
- Add the text and chant the rhythms of the above section. Using the piano to support, challenge the Sopranos and Altos to sight-sing their parts. Next, challenge the Tenors and Basses to sight-sing their parts.
- Sing all four parts together, reviewing pitches as necessary.
- Sight-read measures 30–37 on a neutral syllable. Have students find the previous passage in the score that is similar to this one. *(measures 13–20)* Add text and secure pitches.

Progress Checkpoints

Observe students' progress in:

✓ Their ability to identify various sections of the music.

✓ Their ability to sing all pitches accurately and in tune.

EXTENSION

Improvisation

To "improvise" means to "make something up" on the spot. It is a key element in many styles of music from the African American culture, including gospel, jazz and rap music. A performer can improvise both melodic and harmonic variations, as well as changes in text.

Encourage students to sing the solo section of the piece and once comfortable, experiment with improvisation.

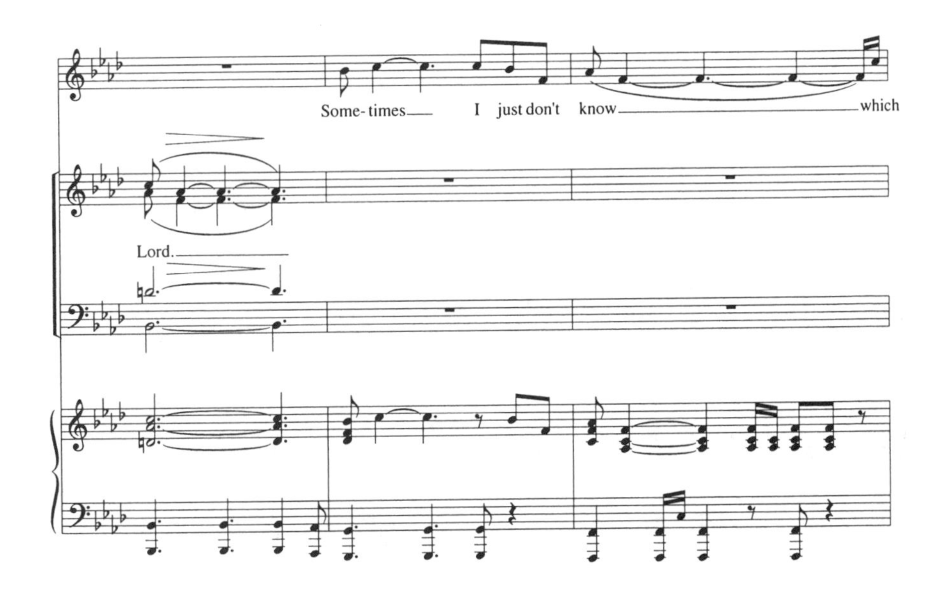

3. Refine

Direct students to:

- Return to the beginning of the piece. Identify and discuss the dynamic and stylistic symbols contained in the piece, particularly the tenuto markings.
- Observe the crescendo-decrescendo marking (<>) and to "swell" each pitch by suddenly getting louder and then softer. (The use of a dramatic and breathy singing tone is helpful here.)
- Sing through the piece with all the added markings, observing them as closely as possible.

Progress Checkpoints

Observe students' progress in:

✓ The use of audible contrasting dynamics.

✓ The use of various stylistic tools, such as tenuto and crescendo-decrescendo.

CULTURAL CONNECTIONS

Gospel Style

Gospel music is a genre of the twentieth century, originating with the sacred songs of the African American churches of the South. Gospel singers have been known to take simple melodies and vocally embellish them, such as using full falsetto voices, shouting, humming, growling, moaning, whispering, crying or screaming. Fancy melismas, syncopated rhythms, blue notes and repeated fragments of the text are musical ways of improvising a gospel song. Much of the blues and soul styles found in today's pop music can be traced to the gospel style.

ASSESSMENT

Informal Assessment

In this lesson, students showed the ability to:

- Sing rhythms in 9/8 meter with accuracy.
- Observe and perform all expression and articulation markings.
- Differentiate between foreground and background material.
- Perform music in the Gospel style.

Student Self-Assessment

Have students evaluate their individual performances based on the following:

- Diction
- Expressive Singing
- Intonation
- Accurate Rhythms
- Correct Part-Singing

Have each student rate his/her performance of this song in the areas above on a scale of 1–5, 5 being the best.

MUSIC, SOCIETY AND CULTURE

Have students perform additional songs representing diverse cultures, including American and Texas heritage. Go to **music.glencoe.com**, the Web site for Glencoe's choral music programs, for additional music selections students can perform.

Individual and Group Performance Evaluation

To further measure growth of musical skills presented in this lesson, direct students to complete the Evaluation section on page 149.

- Record either a small group or the entire choir singing measures 5–12 of "City Called Heaven." Assist students in evaluating their performance in the areas of correct rhythms, contrasting dynamics and proper use of tenuto and crescendo-decrescendo.
- Direct students to locate where they sing in the foreground and where they sing in the background. Discuss the differences in style and dynamics when singing in each of these sections.

Additional National Standards

The following National Standards are addressed through the Assessment, Extension, Enrichment and bottom-page activities:

3. Improvising melodies, variations and accompaniments. **(b, c)**
7. Evaluate music and music performances. **(b)**

Duond Akuru

OVERVIEW

Composer: Rollo A. Dilworth
Text: Rollo A. Dilworth, translation by Theodora Ayot
Voicing: SAB
Key: F major/A♭ major
Meter: 4/4
Form: AABC
Style: Gospel and African
Accompaniment: Piano and percussion
Programming: Concert, Festival, Multicultural

Vocal Ranges:

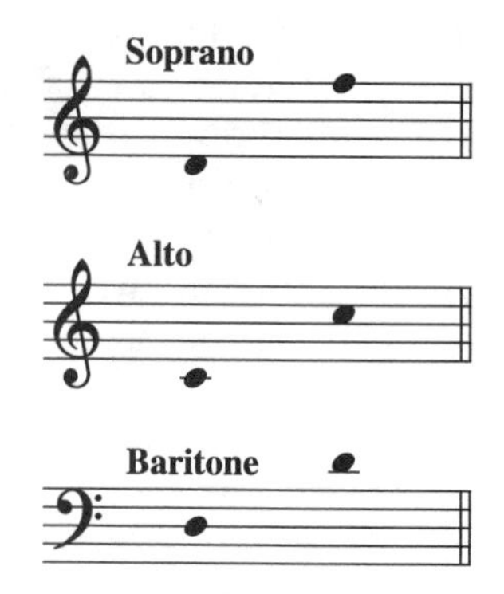

OBJECTIVES

After completing this lesson, students will be able to:

- Read and perform music that contains syncopation.
- Sing a varied repertoire of music, including music in a foreign language.
- Perform music representative of the African style.

VOCABULARY

Have students review vocabulary in student lesson. Introduce terms found in the music. A complete glossary of terms is found on page 240 of the student book.

Duond Akuru

Composer: Rollo A. Dilworth
Text: Rollo A. Dilworth, translation by Theodora Ayot
Voicing: SAB

VOCABULARY
polyrhythms
shekere

Focus

- Read and perform rhythmic patterns that contain syncopation.
- Sing in a foreign language using proper diction (Duoluo).
- Perform music written in the style of African music.

Getting Started

Do you have an inner voice that gives you guidance when you have to make a tough decision, or comfort when you are having a rough day? Do you have a pet or a favorite animal that makes you smile and brings joy to your heart? All over the world, the dove is known as a symbol of peace, joy and love. "Duond Akuru" celebrates the gentle voice, the peaceful character and the natural beauty of this bird.

SPOTLIGHT

To learn more about gospel music, see page 147.

◆ History and Culture

"Duond Akuru" literally means "the dove's voice." This piece was written by Rollo Dilworth in collaboration with Theodora Ayot, a teaching colleague at North Park University in Chicago, Illinois. "Duond Akuru" blends ideas from both African and African American cultures. In addition to English, the Duoluo language, as spoken by the Luo people of Kenya, is used throughout the piece.

Although the African American gospel style serves as a harmonic framework for this piece, "Duond Akuru" also utilizes chant techniques, **polyrhythms** *(several different rhythms performed simultaneously)*, and percussion instruments that are inherently African in their origins. To achieve an authentic effect, instruments such as a **shekere** *(an African shaker consisting of a hollow gourd surrounded by beads)*, tambourine and congas may be used. Singers are encouraged to perform this piece in a rhythmically jubilant manner.

RESOURCES

Intermediate Sight-Singing

Sight-Singing in F Major, pages 39–41, 76–77, 112–116

Sight-Singing in A♭ Major, pages 176–177

Reading Rhythms with Syncopation, page 126–129

Teacher Resource Binder

Teaching Master 23, *Pronunciation Guide for "Duond Akuru"*

Teaching Master 24, *Exploring Polyrhythms*

Reference 16, *My Music Dictionary*

Reference 29, *Zeroing in on IPA*

Links to Learning

◆ Theory

Read and perform the following rhythmic patterns found in "Duond Akuru." First clap the rhythms, then add the vowel sounds as indicated.

◆ Artistic Expression

To give "Duond Akuru" a more traditional African sound, perform the following rhythmic patterns on percussion instruments (or use body percussion). You may want to add these instruments to your performance.

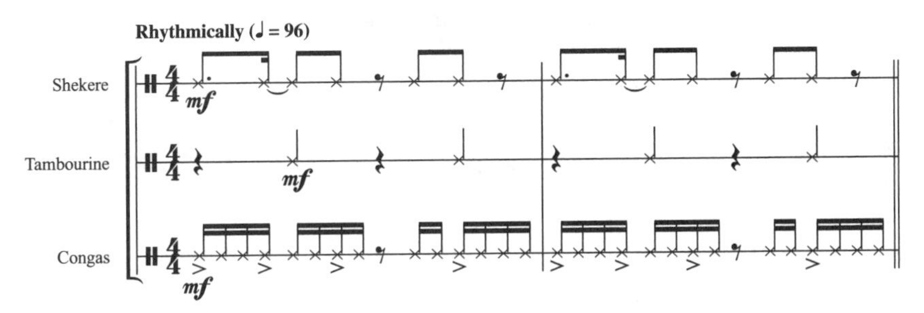

Evaluation

Demonstrate how well you have learned the skills and concepts featured in the lesson "Duond Akuru" by completing the following:

- Chant the words in rhythm to your part in measures 46–54 to show that you can read syncopated rhythms accurately. How did you do?
- Sing measures 46–54 with the Duoluo text. Sing with a smooth transition between the "ah" and "oo" vowels. Evaluate how well you were able to sing with a smooth transition between the vowels.

LINKS TO LEARNING

Theory

The Theory section is designed to prepare students to develop a smooth transition between vowel sounds.

Have students:

- Clap the rhythms in the examples.
- Chant the vowel sounds as indicated once the rhythms are secure.

Artistic Expression

The Artistic Expression section is designed to prepare students to perform syncopated ostinato patterns.

Have students:

- Clap each rhythm in the example separately and combine when secure.
- Use either body percussion or the African instruments as indicated.

RESOURCES

Intermediate Mixed Rehearsal/Performance CD

CD 2:7 Voices
CD 2:8 Accompaniment Only
CD 3:16 Vocal Practice Track—Soprano
CD 4:16 Vocal Practice Track—Alto
CD 6:16 Vocal Practice Track—Baritone

National Standards

1. Singing alone and with others, a varied repertoire of music. **(a, b, c, d)**
5. Reading and notating music. **(a, c)**
9. Understanding music in relation to history and culture. **(a)**

LESSON PLAN

Suggested Teaching Sequence and Performance Tips

1. Introduce

Direct the students to:

- Read and discuss the information found in the Getting Started section on student page 156.
- Practice performing the syncopated rhythms as shown in the Theory section on page 157.
- Identify the measures in both the flute and vocal parts that contain the same or similar rhythm patterns as shown in the first Theory exercise. *(Flute: measures 1, 3, 58; Soprano: measures 11, 15, 23–26, 35, 46–53, 56; Alto: 13, 17, 19–26, 35, 46–53, 56; Baritone: 26, 35, 47–54, 56)*

For the 2003 National ACDA Middle School/Junior High Honors Choir, Henry Leck, Conductor

Duond Akuru

(The Voice of the Dove)

For SAB and Piano with Optional Flute*

Translation by
THEODORA AYOT

Words and Music by
ROLLO A. DILWORTH

*Flute part may be found on page 167.

TEACHER 2 TEACHER

"Duond Akuru" is an original composition that blends elements of African and African American styles. Specifically, the African language and folk traditions of Kenya are fused with the gospel harmonic style pioneered by African Americans. The piece pays tribute to the dove, a universal symbol of love, peace and harmony that not only reflects the connection between humanity and nature, but the powerful bond that exists between two cultures.

- Identify the measures in the Baritone part that contain the same or similar rhythm patterns as shown in the second Theory exercise. *(measures 7–18, 20, 21, 24)*
- Practice each of the three rhythmic patterns shown in the Artistic Expression section. Use hand claps, foot stomps, patschen (hitting the lap with the hands), or percussion instruments. Divide the class into three groups and repeat as desired.

Progress Checkpoints

Observe student's progress in:

✓ Their ability to perform syncopated rhythms accurately.

✓ Their ability to identify these syncopated rhythm patterns in the music.

2. Rehearse

Direct students to:

- Identify measures 1–6 as *Introduction.*
- Identify measures 7–34 as *Section A.*
- Use the neutral syllable "doom," and sight-read and chant measures 7–26. (At this point, do not sing pitches or perform text.) Review this section until each section in the choir can perform its part with independence and proficiency.
- Use the pronunciation guide and practice speaking the words "Duond Akuru." When the pronunciation is clear, chant measures 7–26 again, this time with the text. When the text has been securely integrated with the rhythm patterns, review the section and add pitches.
- Clap the Baritone part from measure 26 (beat 4) through measure 34. Once the rhythms are secure, add pitches (using a neutral syllable) and rehearse. Meanwhile, have the Sopranos and Altos examine the similarities between the rhythmic patterns in their parts, relative to each other and to the Baritone part.

- Clap the Alto part from measures 27–34. When the part is secure, add pitches (using a neutral syllable) and rehearse the Alto and Baritone parts together.
- Clap the Alto part from measures 27–34. When the part is secure, add pitches (using a neutral syllable) and rehearse all parts together. Once all pitches are secure, add all parts and rehearse the entire A section.
- Identify measures 35–45 as *Section B.*
- Begin with the pick-up note to measure 36, and rehearse the rhythm patterns in section B using an echo activity (teacher leads, students echo). Divide the section into two- and three-bar phrases. Move to the next phrase once the current phrase becomes secure. (Notice the similarities between the patterns in measures 36–37 and 41–42, as well as the similarities between measures 38–40 and measures 43–45.) When all rhythms are secure, go back to the beginning of the section and add the pitches (using a neutral syllable) for each part.

ENRICHMENT

Self-Evaluation

Perform the piece as a class. After the performance, ask each student to create a personal list of the areas that he/she felt went well in each section of the piece, as well as a list of areas the need improvement. Allow students to get into small groups and exchange ideas for refinement.

- Use the pronunciation guide to rehearse the text. Once the pronunciation is accurate, chant the text for section B in rhythm. Review each section with pitches and rehearse the parts in various combinations until vocal lines are secure.
- Identify measures 46–58 as *Section C.*
- Sight-sing measures 46–57 with the support of the piano. Notice that the Baritone line is "imitating" the treble voices. Also notice that the flute part (beginning at measure 46) is imitating the voice parts, but the rhythms of the pitches are twice the value of the rhythms in the voice parts. This technique is called *augmentation.*
- Review pitches for individual parts as needed.

Progress Checkpoints

Observe students' progress in:

✓ Their ability to read all rhythm patterns with accuracy.

✓ Their ability to sing the text, especially the phrase "Duond Akuru" with confidence and precision.

✓ Singing all vowels in a rich and smooth manner.

CULTURAL CONNECTIONS

Blending African American and African Music Styles

Many American composers and performers have been influenced by music of African origin. For example, "The Lion Sleeps Tonight" is based on the Zulu folk tune "Mbube" (EEM-boo-beh, which is commonly misinterpreted as "Wimoweh"). Many African musicians have been influenced by the sounds of American music traditions. Listen to Paul Simon's album *Graceland* (1986) to hear how he blends American folk rock with South African rhythms, instruments and vocal sounds. Listen to Ladysmith Black Mambazo's *Shaka Zulu* (1987) album to hear a blend of both English and Zulu lyrics in the songs. Discuss what the students hear and how it relates to "Duond Akuru."

3. Refine

Direct students to:

- Return to the beginning of the piece. Discuss with students the importance of rhythm in African culture. Encourage students to chant through the piece, using a rhythmic and percussive tone. Have them imagine that their voices are drums as they chant. At this point in the rehearsal process, pay close attention to all dynamic and articulation markings.
- Sing through the piece while marching in place to the quarter note pulse (right-left-right-left, etc.). As students march in place, have them shift their weight slightly to each foot as it hits the floor.

MUSIC, SOCIETY AND CULTURE

Have students perform additional songs representing diverse cultures, including American and Texas heritage. Go to **music.glencoe.com**, the Web site for Glencoe's choral music programs, for additional music selections students can perform.

Progress Checkpoints

Observe students' progress in:

✓ Their ability to sing the piece in a rhythmic and energetic manner.

✓ Observing all dynamic and stylistic markings.

ASSESSMENT

Informal Assessment

In this lesson, students showed the ability to:

- Sing all syncopated rhythm patterns with proficiency.
- Sing all vowels in a rich, smooth, and fluid manner.
- Articulate the Duoluo (a language spoken by the Luo people of Kenya) diction with accuracy.

MORE ABOUT...

Rhythm in African Music

Rhythm is a prominent part of daily life in many African cultures. Most activities are accompanied by percussive gestures and rhythmic motion. If you were to walk into the post office in Ghana, West Africa, you may hear the repetitive and often syncopated rhythmic patterns of the postal stamps hitting the ink blotters and canceling the stamps on the mail. The postal clerks often add some excitement to their repetitive tasks by creating fun and sophisticated rhythmic patterns to accompany their labor. Knowing that rhythm is such an integral part of the African culture can help you perform an African piece vibrantly.

Student Self-Assessment

Have students evaluate their individual performances based on the following:

- Diction
- Expressive Singing
- Foreign Language
- Accurate Rhythms
- Tall Vowels

Have each student rate his/her performance of this song in the areas above on a scale of 1–5, 5 being the best.

TEACHING STRATEGY

Maintaining a Steady Tempo

Because of its complex rhythms and syncopation, this piece can get away from the conductor as singers can naturally tend to rush. To help avoid this, have students construct their own solutions to solve the problem of rushing, including conducting themselves as they sing, and watching the conductor carefully.

Individual and Group Performance Evaluation

To further measure growth of musical skills presented in this lesson, direct students to complete the Evaluation section on page 157.

- Have students chant the rhythms as directed. Students can either chant on a neutral syllable or chant the text. Assist them in developing criteria for and evaluating their performance.
- Have students perform the measures indicated, paying attention to their diction, as they sing the Duoluo text. Make sure they focus on the "ah" and "oo" vowels. Assist them in evaluating their performance.

Additional National Standards

The following National Standards are addressed through the Assessment, Extension, Enrichment and bottom-page activities:

6. Listening to, analyzing and describing music. **(b, c)**

7. Evaluate music and music performances. **(a, b)**

I Know Where I'm Goin'

OVERVIEW

Composer: Irish Folk Song, arranged by J. Chris Moore
Text: Traditional
Voicing: 2-Part Mixed
Key: E major/F major
Meter: 4/4
Form: Strophic
Style: Irish Folk Song
Accompaniment: Piano
Programming: Multicultural; Thematic Programming; Large or Small Ensemble

Vocal Ranges:

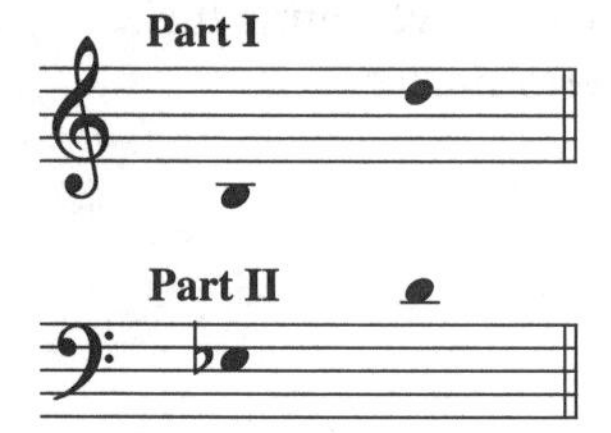

OBJECTIVES

After completing this lesson, students will be able to:

- Perform two-part music.
- Sing phrases expressively.
- Perform music representative of different genres, including the Irish culture.

VOCABULARY

Have students review vocabulary in student lesson. Introduce terms found in the music. A complete glossary of terms is found on page 240 of the student book.

CHORAL LIBRARY

I Know Where I'm Goin'

Composer: Irish Folk Song, arranged by J. Chris Moore
Text: Traditional
Voicing: 2-Part Mixed

VOCABULARY

folk song
legato
crescendo
decrescendo
phrase

Focus

- Perform two-part music.
- Sing phrases expressively.
- Perform music representing the Irish culture.

SPOTLIGHT

To learn more about arranging, see page 63.

Getting Started

Dorothy
The Scarecrow
The Tin Man
The Cowardly Lion

The characters in "The Wizard of Oz" are focused on their own individual goals. Can you describe each character's goal? Some might call this selfish or stubborn, but others would say that perseverance and focus are virtues.

The young girl in "I Know Where I'm Goin'" is focused on marrying her love, Johnny. In the lyrics, she tells us she would willingly give up many fine things in her life to marry Johnny. However, the conclusion of the story is not clear. After you learn the song, decide whether or not she marries him.

◆ History and Culture

"I Know Where I'm Goin'" is an Irish folk song. **Folk songs** are *songs that have been passed down by word of mouth from generation to generation.* Irish folk music enjoys quite a bit of popularity today and is featured on concerts, stages, radio, television and movies throughout the world. In this arrangement of "I Know Where I'm Goin'," the reflective nature of the text is complemented by an accompaniment in the style of a guitar or other folk instrument. Perhaps your focus can be to remain sensitive to the folk style of the music as you rehearse and perform.

RESOURCES

Intermediate Sight-Singing

Sight-Singing in E Major, pages 188–189
Sight-Singing in F Major, pages 39–41, 76–77, 112–116

Teacher Resource Binder

Evaluation Master 7, *Evaluating Musical Expression*
Evaluation Master 14, *Performance Evaluation: Part Singing*
Vocal Development 13, *Posture and Breathing*
Vocal Development 15, *Vowels*
Dalcroze 15, *Phrase Building*

Links to Learning

◆ Vocal

Perform the following example to practice singing **legato** *(a style of singing that is connected and sustained)*. The **crescendo** *(a dynamic marking that indicates to gradually sing louder)* and **decrescendo** *(a dynamic marking that indicates to gradually sing softer)* add expression and dynamic contrast to your performance.

Perform the following example to practice shaping the basic vowel sounds that form the basis for a good choral tone. Sing with the jaw dropped and the corners of your mouth in. Sing in two parts.

◆ Artistic Expression

A **phrase** is *a musical idea with a beginning and an end.* Sing measures 5–8 in unison while drawing an arch in the air above your head. Shape your phrase by beginning softly, then singing loudest in the middle and soft at the end.

Evaluation

Demonstrate how well you have learned the skills and concepts featured in the lesson "I Know Where I'm Goin'" by completing the following:

- In a duet with one singer on each part, perform measures 25–29. Evaluate how well you were able to sing in two parts.
- Find other phrases in the music. Select one person to come forward and serve as a "phrase leader." Sing each phrase while following the arch shown by the phrase leader. How expressively were you able to sing the phrases?

LINKS TO LEARNING

Vocal

The Vocal section is designed to prepare students to:

- Perform in a legato style when singing alone and with others.
- Shape unified vowels sounds when singing as an ensemble.

Have students:

- Sing the first example, paying special attention to the dynamic markings.
- Sing the second example, using open and tall vowels.

Artistic Expression

The Artistic Expression section is designed to prepare students to identify and shape musical phrases when singing alone and with others.

Have students:

- Sing measures 5–8 from the piece.
- Sing the selection again, but this time create a visual phrase by using arm movements. Make sure the dynamics of the students' phrase corresponds with the arm movements.

RESOURCES

Intermediate Mixed Rehearsal/Performance CD

CD 2:9 Voices
CD 2:10 Accompaniment Only
CD 3:17 Vocal Practice Track—Part I
CD 6:17 Vocal Practice Track—Part II

National Standards

1. Singing alone and with others, a varied repertoire of music. **(a, b, c, d)**
5. Reading and notating music. **(a, c)**
9. Understanding music in relation to history and culture. **(a, c)**

LESSON PLAN

Suggested Teaching Sequence and Performance Tips

1. Introduce

Direct the students to:

- Read and discuss the information found in the Getting Started section on student page 168.
- Practice the first example in the Vocal section emphasizing singing with a legato vocal line. Locate and sing examples of this passage throughout the composition. *(measures 5–8, 13–16, 25–28/24–29, 33–36, 45–48, 53–56)*

For Sally

I Know Where I'm Goin'

For 2-Part and Piano

Arranged by
J. CHRIS MOORE

Irish Folk Song

"I Know Where I'm Goin'" is an excellent selection for developing expressive singing. Emphasize well-focused, unified and sustained vowel sounds to help create a legato arching vocal line. Having students perform in small ensembles and duets will assist them in learning to develop an intimate approach toward this piece.

- Practice the second example in the Vocal section emphasizing singing legato with unified vowel sounds. Locate and sing this passage in the music. *(measures 65–70)*

Progress Checkpoints

Observe student's progress in:

✓ Singing in a legato style using pure vowels.

✓ Their ability to identify passages found in music.

MORE ABOUT...

Concert and Audience Etiquette

A member of an audience listening to "I Know Where I'm Goin'" should exhibit different concert etiquette than if the opening sounds of the Beatles' "Revolution" were being performed. Have students describe some of the appropriate audience behaviors for a performance of "I Know Where I'm Goin" if it were performed in a large concert hall, in a living room, as a solo song, or with a chorus of a thousand singers in an open-air theater. Have students identify additional performance sites and describe possible reactions and changes in audience reactions. To assess students, have them respond with appropriate posture to specific performance settings, such as concert hall, band shell in the park, and so forth.

2. Rehearse

Direct students to:

- Sing the melody found in Part II in measures 53–60. Emphasize legato, unified vowels and dynamic shaping of the phrases by following the dynamic markings when singing.
- Locate other statements of this melody in the music and have the respective section read and expressively sing the passage *(measures 5–12, 13–20, 25–32, /33–40, 45–52)*
- Describe bottom part, measures 46–52, as an imitation of the melody. Have all students read and expressively sing the imitation using a neutral vowel and text.
- Sing measures 45–52 in two parts. Emphasize expressive singing and vocal balance between melody A and the background imitation in the other vocal part.
- Identify other imitation in the music. *(Part I, measures 33–40, Part II, measures 54–60)*

TEACHING STRATEGY

Unified Vowels

Vowels are the fundamental building blocks of tone production, intonation, and blend. A pure vowel is one that does not change when sung. When pure vowels are sung identically by all singers, a musical resonance and blend can occur. The unity of vowels when sung by a choir is the key to resonance and blend. The choral instrument should sound as one voice, and even one voice singing a different sounding vowel can destroy the blend of the choral tone. Each vowel has a different shape in the mouth. Focus vocal exercises on achieving this unified shape from vowel to vowel. Have students listen carefully to each other and adjust their own vowels to blend with those around them.

- Learn and perform each section with and without accompaniment.
- Identify characteristics of legato singing, expressive singing, and phrases as studied and found in the music.
- Establish correct choral performance posture and sing the complete composition with accompaniment.

Progress Checkpoints

Observe students' progress in:

✓ Their expression as legato singing and unified vowel sounds become more evident.

✓ Their improvement of the shaping of phrases.

✓ Their musical accuracy of notes and part-singing.

3. Refine

Direct students to:

- Follow your conducting gestures as a means for helping shape individual musical phrases and sections.
- Energize and sustain vowels found on long notes.
- Stress the individual word rhythms sung on strong beats as a means for better communicating the text in an expressive manner.
- Respond to subtle changes in tempo when performing consistent with expressing the text.

Progress Checkpoints

Observe students' progress in:

✓ Their ability to sing phrases with energy from start to finish of each phrase.

✓ Proper word stress and unified vowel sounds.

✓ Their ability to perform all dynamic markings correctly.

✓ Their ability to perform all pitches and rhythms accurately.

MUSIC, SOCIETY AND CULTURE

Have students perform additional songs representing diverse cultures, including American and Texas heritage. Go to **music.glencoe.com**, the Web site for Glencoe's choral music programs, for additional music selections students can perform.

CURRICULAR CONNECTIONS

Folk Music and Art

To encourage more awareness of folk art, have students:

- Identify folk themes presented through painting, dance, movies, literature and recordings.
- Identify examples of folk music and art in their community.
- Make a list of the folk songs they know.

ASSESSMENT

Informal Assessment

In this lesson, students showed the ability to:

- Respond and adjust tempo consistent with expressing the ideas of the text.
- Perform phrases and sections expressively.
- Sing accurately in unison and two parts.
- Shape basic vowel sounds uniformly and consistently.
- Follow and perform using a musical score containing dynamic markings.

Student Self-Assessment

Have students evaluate their individual performances based on the following:

- Tall Vowels
- Expressive Singing
- Breath Management
- Posture
- Correct Part-Singing

Have each student rate his/her performance of this song in the areas above on a scale of 1–5, 5 being the best.

Individual and Group Performance Evaluation

To further measure growth of musical skills presented in this lesson, direct students to complete the Evaluation section on page 169.

- Direct students to form duets and perform the specified passage from the piece. Assist students in evaluating their performance in correct part-singing.
- Select a "phrase leader" to stand in front of the choir and use his/her arm to shape selected phrases from the piece. Help students evaluate how well they were able to follow the leader and how expressively they were able to sing phrases.

EXTENSION

Careers in Music–Arranger

An arranger is an individual who takes existing musical material and adds to or changes it in some way. For example, there are many arrangements of "The Star-Spangled Banner." Although each arrangement may be based on the same musical material, each is unique to the style of the song's arranger. Although some arrangers, like composers, are self-taught, most have a background in music theory and performance. This helps an arranger understand the individual instruments they are arranging for. In vocal music, an arranger must understand and be sensitive to the unique characteristics of voices.

176 Intermediate Mixed

Additional National Standards

The following National Standards are addressed through the Assessment, Extension, Enrichment and bottom-page activities:

7. Evaluate music and music performances. **(a)**
8. Understanding the relationships between music, the other arts and disciplines outside the arts. **(a)**

Improvisation

Improvisation is *the art of singing or playing music, making it up as you go.* **Scat singing** is *an improvisational style of singing that uses nonsense syllables instead of words.* Sometimes, these nonsense sounds can imitate the sound of an instrument. Scat singing, especially as a solo, can be the scariest part of singing jazz.

Dr. Kirby Shaw, one of the top vocal jazz composers and conductors in the world today, offers the following suggestions to help build your confidence in this fun and exciting art form.

Start your scat solo with a short melodic or rhythmic idea from the tune being performed. There is nothing wrong in having a preconceived idea before starting to sing a scat solo! By gradually developing the idea as you sing, you will have an organized solo that sounds completely improvised.

Start with scat syllables like "doo" when singing swing tunes. Try "bee," "dee," and "dn" for occasional accented eighth notes on the *and* of beats (1 *and* 2 *and* 3 *and* 4 *and*). Try "doot" or "dit" for short last notes of a musical phrase.

Be able to imitate any sound you like from the world around you, such as a soft breeze, a car horn or a musical instrument. There might be a place for that sound in one of your solos.

Listen to and imitate, note-for-note, the great jazz singers or instrumentalists. You can be inspired by musicians like Ella Fitzgerald, Jon Hendricks, Louis Armstrong or Charlie Parker.

Learn to sing the blues. You can listen to artists like B. B. King, Stevie Ray Vaughan, Buddy Guy or Luther Allison. There are many types of recordings from which to choose.

In short, learn as many different kinds of songs as you can. The best scat singers quote from such diverse sources as nursery rhymes, African chant and even opera. Above all, have fun as you develop your skills!

RESOURCES

Teacher Resource Binder

Skill Builder 16, *Improvising Melodies*

Reference 16, *My Music Dictionary*

National Standards

1. Singing, alone and with other, a varied repertoire of music. **(a, b, c)**

3. Improvising melodies, variations and accompaniments. **(a, b, c)**

IMPROVISATION

Objectives

- Create rhythmic and melodic phrases.
- Improvise melodic embellishments and simple rhythmic and melodic variations.

Suggested Teaching Sequence

Direct students to:

- Read the Spotlight On Improvisation on student page 177 and define improvisation and scat singing.
- Identify the steps to follow in learning to scat sing.
- Practice scat singing as described on page 177. Teacher may model, students imitate.
- Apply scat singing techniques to a familiar song.
- Make a list of vocal jazz singers they know and identify characteristics of their singing.

Progress Checkpoints

Observe students' progress in:

✓ Their ability to define and describe the concept of improvisation.

✓ Their ability to demonstrate scat singing.

✓ Their ability to apply improvisation techniques in the performance of a song.

Kyrie

OVERVIEW

Composer: Andrea Klouse
Text: Liturgical Latin
Voicing: SAB
Key: A minor
Meter: 3/4
Form: ABA Coda
Style: Contemporary American Anthem
Accompaniment: Piano
Programming: Contest, Festival

Vocal Ranges:

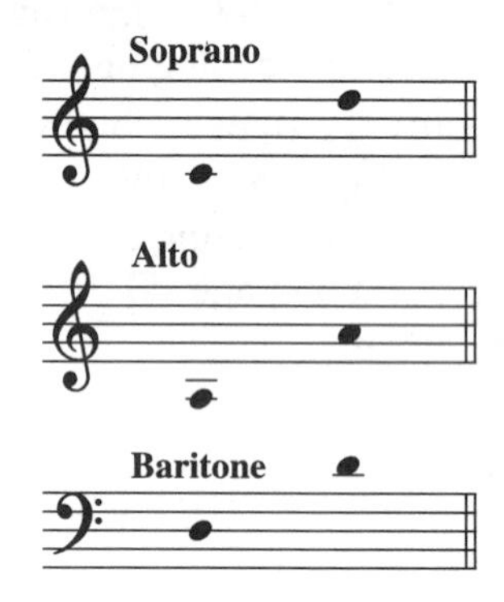

OBJECTIVES

After completing this lesson, students will be able to:

- Perform independently with accurate intonation and pitch-matching.
- Identify music form (ABA) presented through notation.
- Perform music representative of the Contemporary period.

VOCABULARY

Have students review vocabulary in student lesson. Introduce terms found in the music. A complete glossary of terms is found on page 240 of the student book.

CHORAL LIBRARY

Kyrie

Composer: Andrea Klouse
Text: Liturgical Latin
Voicing: SAB

VOCABULARY

mass
ABA form
coda
pitch matching
minor scale

Focus

- Perform music with accurate pitch matching.
- Identify ABA form and coda.
- Perform music that represents the Contemporary period.

Getting Started

One interesting benefit of singing in a choir is that you learn songs in foreign languages. Make a list of all the foreign-language choir songs you know. How many languages are on your list? Do you know songs in Spanish, French, German, Hebrew or Latin? When you learn a song in the original language, you can understand how the composer actually wanted the words to fit the music.

SPOTLIGHT

To learn more about pitch matching, *see page 77.*

◆ History and Culture

The "Kyrie" is one of the principal sections in the **mass,** *a religious service of prayers and ceremonies.* Although the traditional language of the mass is Latin, the word *Kyrie* is actually a Greek word that was adapted into the Latin mass. Composers throughout the centuries have set the words of the "Kyrie" to music. Because there are only three lines of text—

Kyrie eleison (Lord have mercy)
Christie eleison (Christ have mercy)
Kyrie eleison (Lord have mercy)

—"Kyrie" composers often use ABA form for the music. **ABA form** is *the design in which the opening phrases (section A) are followed by contrasting phrases (section B), which leads to a repetition of the opening phrases (section A).* Composer Andrea Klouse has also added a **coda,** or *a special ending to a song,* to her "Kyrie." Find these sections in the music. After you learn "Kyrie," you can add another foreign-language song to your list!

RESOURCES

Intermediate Sight-Singing

Sight-Singing in A Minor, pages 20–22, 33–35, 68–72

Reading Dotted Eighth and Sixteenth Note Combinations, pages 89–90.

Teacher Resource Binder

Teaching Master 25, *Pronunciation Guide for "Kyrie"*

Teaching Master 26, *Discovering Musical Form*

Evaluation Master 2, *Analyzing Pitch Accuracy*

For additional resources, see TRB Table of Contents.

Links to Learning

◆ Vocal

Accurate **pitch matching** *(singing on the same pitch as those around you)* requires that you hear the note in your head before you sing. Perform the following example to practice singing on pitch. Avoid unwanted scoops and slides in the vocal line.

◆ Theory

The A sections in "Kyrie" are based on the A minor scale. A **minor scale** is *a scale in which* la *is the keynote or home tone.* Sing the A minor scale below.

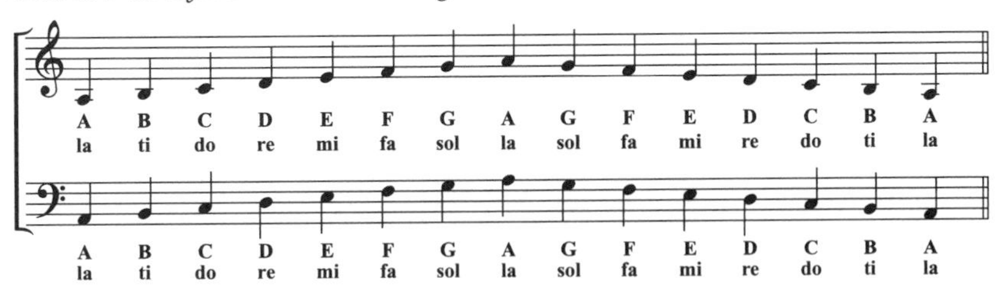

Evaluation

Demonstrate how well you have learned the skills and concepts featured in the lesson "Kyrie" by completing the following:

- Sing measures 13–21 for a classmate. Evaluate how well you were able to sing the pitches in tune without scooping or sliding.
- Describe the form of "Kyrie." Identify the measure numbers that mark the beginning of each section (ABA) and the coda. Compare your choices with those of a classmate. How did you do?

LINKS TO LEARNING

Vocal

The Vocal section is designed to prepare students to sing with accurate pitch matching.

Have students:

- Sing each part separately and then together.
- Listen to themselves and each other to ensure good intonation.
- Avoid scooping or sliding from note to note.

Theory

The Theory section is designed to prepare students to learn and sing the A minor scale.

Have students:

- Sing the pitches of the scale on a neutral syllable.
- Sing the scale using solfège syllable or note names, once pitches are secure.

RESOURCES

Intermediate Mixed Rehearsal/Performance CD

- **CD 2:11** Voices
- **CD 2:12** Accompaniment Only
- **CD 3:18** Vocal Practice Track—Soprano
- **CD 4:17** Vocal Practice Track—Alto
- **CD 6:18** Vocal Practice Track—Baritone

National Standards

1. Singing alone and with others, a varied repertoire of music. **(a, b, c, d)**

5. Reading and notating music. **(a)**

6. Listening to, analyzing and describing music. **(c)**

9. Understanding music in relation to history and culture. **(b)**

LESSON PLAN

Suggested Teaching Sequence and Performance Tips

1. Introduce

Direct students to:

- Read and discuss the information found in the Getting Started section on student page 178.
- Discuss ABA form and coda.
- Practice singing the example in the Vocal section.
- Discuss and practice singing the scale in the Theory section.
- Follow along in their music as you give them breath markings for the song.
- Locate the dynamic markings throughout the piece.

Kyrie

For SAB and Piano

Liturgical Latin

Music by
ANDREA KLOUSE

(♩ = 66-76)

Piano

mp

TEACHER 2 TEACHER

With its simple Latin text and haunting melody, "Kyrie" provides an opportunity for your students to develop a free, healthy tone. Mastering the B section of the piece will help students learn how to modulate and how to sing accidentals with accurate intonation.

*Accent the "k" in "Kyrie" gently to ensure a clean "echo" effect.

Progress Checkpoints

Observe student's progress in:

- ✓ Their ability to describe ABA form and coda.
- ✓ Their ability to sing the vocal example individually, as a section and as a choir. Isolate and take out any scoops or slides between pitches and tune.
- ✓ Their understanding of various dynamics.

MORE ABOUT...

The Latin Mass

The Kyrie is one of the principal sections of the Mass. A religious service of prayers and ceremonies, the Mass originated in the Roman Catholic Church and consists of spoken and sung sections. It consists of several sections divided into two groups: proper (text changes for every day) and ordinary (text stays the same in every Mass). Between the years 1400 and 1600 the Mass assumed its present form consisting of the Kyrie, Gloria, Credo, Sanctus, and Agnus Dei. It may include chants, hymns and psalms as well. The Mass also developed into large musical works for chorus, soloists, and even orchestra.

2. Rehearse

Direct students to:

- Read the rhythms in measures 5–12.
- Continue learning the rhythm to all parts of the music.
- Learn the Latin text by echoing the teacher.
- Read the A sections of the piece using solfège syllables. Then do the same with the B section. (Depending on the ability level of your students, you may consider learning the B section by rote.)
- Sing with the text once all Latin text, pitches and rhythms are secure.

Progress Checkpoints

Observe students' progress in:

✓ Their accuracy of rhythms and sense of an internal beat.

✓ Their ability to sing all pitches correctly, especially in the B section.

EXTENSION

Small Ensemble Performance

Divide the class into small or large ensembles. Have each ensemble sing measures 45–53. Ask the choir if they hear individual voices in each voice part or a blend of voices that sound as one. Rearrange voices to achieve a blend, and then ask the choir the same question. Have them vote on the best blended and balanced ensemble. During the next performance of the piece, consider substituting the ensemble in that section.

3. Refine

Direct students to:

- Sing the piece, observing all dynamics and expression markings.
- Isolate tempo changes in the music and rehearse them until they are natural to the students.

Progress Checkpoints

Observe students' progress in:

✓ The correct pronunciation of the Latin text. (Remind students there are no diphthongs in the Latin language.)

✓ Their ability to internalize the tempo changes by singing the changes without you conducting them.

MUSICAL LITERACY

ABA Form

Another name for ABA form is *ternary* form. By the end of this lesson, your students will have identified the form of this song as ABA and will be able to locate each section in their music. Composers frequently modify standard forms by adding introductions, interludes and codas. To help students expand their musical literacy, have them:

- List the characteristics of the A and B sections in "Kyrie."
- Compare their lists and discuss the contrast between the two sections.

ASSESSMENT

Informal Assessment

In this lesson, students showed the ability to:

- Perform music with correct pitch matching and intonation.
- Identify ABA form and coda.
- Perform music from the Contemporary period.

Student Self-Assessment

Have students evaluate their individual performances based on the following:

- Foreign Language
- Expressive Singing
- Intonation
- Breath Management
- Correct Part-Singing

Have each student rate his/her performance of this song in the areas above on a scale of 1–5, 5 being the best.

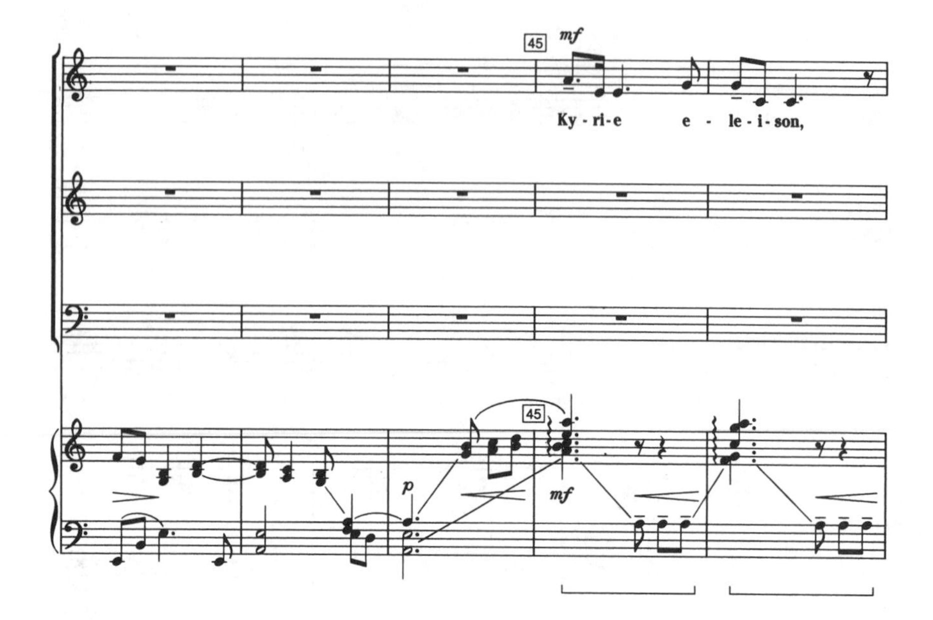

PERFORMANCE SUGGESTION:

Memorization

Due to the simple text of "Kyrie" and the repeated A section, consider having your students memorize this piece for a more polished performance. To aid students in the memorization process, have them sing the piece in small sections, each a number of times. As they repeat these sections, encourage students to use their music less and less until they have memorized that section. Repeat the process for the entire song.

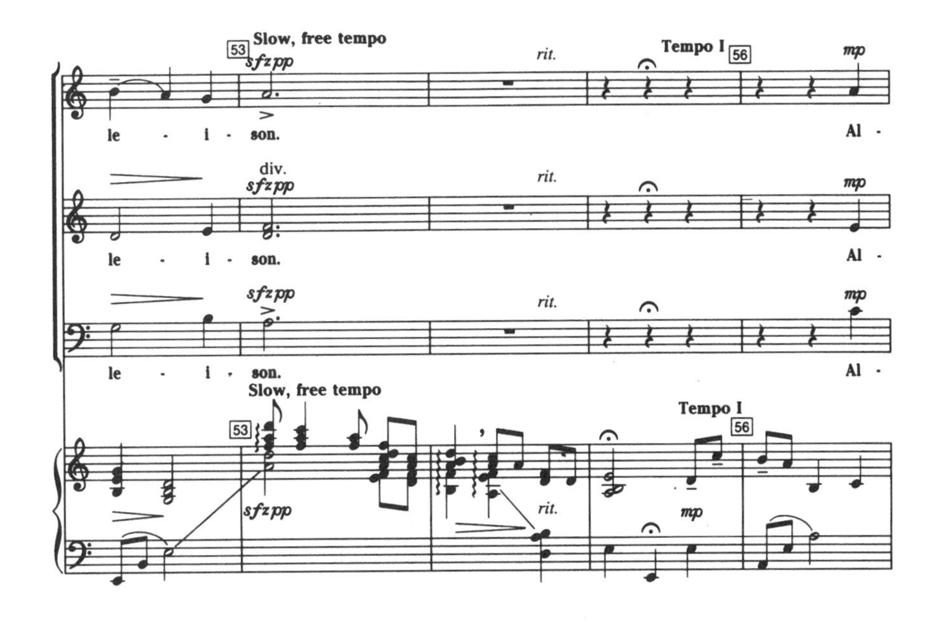

Individual and Group Performance Evaluation

To further measure growth of musical skills presented in this lesson, direct students to complete the Evaluation section on page 179.

- Direct students to form small groups and sing the passage as indicated. Remind students of the importance of not scooping and sliding from note to note. Aid them in developing criteria for evaluating their performance.
- In the same small groups, direct students to individually identify the sections and coda of "Kyrie" and have them compare their answers with the other students. *(A: measures 5–22; B: 25–39; A: 45–53; Coda: 56—61)*

Additional National Standards

The following National Standards are addressed through the Assessment, Extension, Enrichment and bottom-page activities:

7. Evaluate music and music performances. **(a, b)**

Lakota Wiyanki

OVERVIEW

Composer: Traditional Lakota Song, arranged by Judith Herrington and Gail Woodside
Text: Traditional Lakota
Voicing: SATB
Key: C Pentatonic
Meter: Multi-meter: free, 3/4, 4/4
Form: Intro A A′B Coda
Style: Native American Song
Accompaniment: Optional Percussion
Programming: Multicultural

Vocal Ranges:

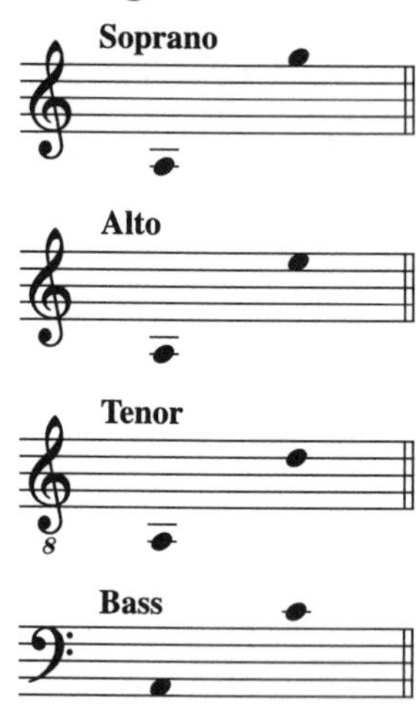

Objectives

After completing this lesson, students will be able to:

- Demonstrate fundamental skills while performing.
- Perform a varied repertoire of music representing styles from diverse cultures, including Native American.

VOCABULARY

Have students review vocabulary in student lesson. Introduce terms found in the music. A complete glossary of terms is found on page 240 of the student book.

Lakota Wiyanki

Composer: Judith Herrington and Gail Woodside
Text: Traditional Lakota
Voicing: SATB

VOCABULARY
fermata
meter
quartet

Focus

- Sing with proper vowel sounds.
- Perform music that represents the Native American culture.

Getting Started

Even though you will find shopping malls, football stadiums and fast-food restaurants across our country, the United States is still rich with cultural diversity. Many American families preserve their heritage through traditional food, customs and music. List some of your family traditions. What other cultures are represented in your school or community? Our cultural background helps define who we are.

SPOTLIGHT

To learn more about vowels, see page 55.

◆ History and Culture

"Lakota Wiyanki" is a Native American song in the Native American tradition. For the Lakota people, a song that has been "caught" belongs to the person who created it. Permission from the composer must be given before anyone else can use it. "Lakota Wiyanki," with its original Lakota words and melody, was caught by Cara Willowbrook. She then gave the song to her musician friend Gail Woodside, of the Apache Nation ancestry. When Gail received this gift, she in turn gave it to her friend Judith Herrington, who arranged and published the song for others to sing and enjoy.

The Lakota people (Teton dialect) are part of the Sioux Nation. Also included in the Sioux Nation are the Dakota people (Santee dialect) and the Nakota people (Yankton dialect). The English translation of the Lakota texts says, "Beautiful woman, standing with courage—with pride, you will go forward."

RESOURCES

Intermediate Sight-Singing

Sight-Singing in C Major, pages 7–14, 15–17, 28–30, 66–67, 110–111
Reading Rhythms in 3/4 Meter, pages 17–22
Reading Rhythms in 4/4 Meter, pages 2–6

Teacher Resource Binder

Teaching Master 27, *Pronunciation Guide for "Lakota Wiyanki"*
Teaching Master 28, *Culture and Tradition*
Evaluation Master 15, *Performance Evaluation Rubric*
Vocal Development 15, *Vowels*
Dalcroze 13, *Moving in Duple and Triple Meters*
For additional resources, see TRB Table of Contents.

Links to Learning

◆ Vocal

Perform the following example to focus on vowel placement. Keep the "ay," "ah" and "oh" vowels forward with your jaw dropped to an open, relaxed position. The **fermata** (𝄐) is *a symbol that indicates to hold a note longer than its given value.*

◆ Theory

Read and perform the following examples to establish an accent on the first beat of each measure when changing from 3/4 meter to 4/4 meter. **Meter** is *the organization of rhythm in music.*

◆ Artistic Expression

To learn more about the Lakota and other Native American cultures, divide into groups and research Native American poets and poetry. Choose your favorite poem and read it to the class.

Evaluation

Demonstrate how well you have learned the skills and concepts featured in the lesson "Lakota Wiyanki" by completing the following:

- In a **quartet** *(four singers)* with two on a part, perform measures 6–16, demonstrating the use of proper vowel sounds. Tenors, sing the part that best fits your voice. Rate your use of proper vowel sounds on a scale of 1 to 5, with 5 being the best.
- Organize a performance of "Lakota Wiyanki" that includes the Native American poetry found by your classmates. What did you learn from the poems? In what ways can the reading and studying of these Native American poems enhance your performance of "Lakota Wiyanki"?

RESOURCES

Intermediate Mixed Rehearsal/Performance CD

CD 2:13 Voices
CD 2:14 Accompaniment Only
CD 3:19 Vocal Practice Track—Soprano
CD 4:18 Vocal Practice Track—Alto
CD 5:6 Vocal Practice Track—Tenor
CD 6:19 Vocal Practice Track—Bass

National Standards

1. Singing, alone and with others, a varied repertoire of music. **(a, b, c)**
9. Understanding music in relation to history and culture. **(a, b, c)**

LINKS TO LEARNING

Vocal

The Vocal section is designed to prepare students to:

- Focus on correct vowel placement.
- Understand and perform a fermata.

Have students:

- Speak the vowels, "ay," "ah" and "oh" and concentrate on keeping the sound forward.
- Sing the exercises with an open, relaxed jaw.
- Hum first to feel the buzzing in the nasal passages before singing the exercise and keep the vowel sound in the same place as the hum.

Theory

The Theory section is designed to prepare students to:

- Understand meter.
- Establish a strong first beat in 3/4 and 4/4 meters.

Have students:

- Tap or clap the quarter note pulse.
- Speak the exercise while tapping the quarter note pulse. Accent the first beat of each measure whether it is in 3/4 or 4/4.
- Speak the exercise while watching the director conduct, emphasizing the first beat of each measure. Continue to feel the quarter note pulse inside.

Artistic Expression

The Artistic Expression section is designed to prepare students to build an understanding of the content relationship of other subjects and those of music.

Have students:

- Divide into small groups and research Native American poets and poetry.
- Choose their favorite poem and share it with the class.

LESSON PLAN

Suggested Teaching Sequence and Performance Tips

1. Introduce

Direct students to:

- Read and discuss the information found in the Getting Started section on page 186.
- Practice the exercise in the Vocal section on page 187 to reinforce forward vowel placement.
- Practice the exercise in the Theory section on page 187 to perform accurate stressed beats when moving from 3/4 to 4/4 meter.
- Speak the pitches in measures 6–11 using solfège syllables. On a solfège letter ladder, circle the pitches that will be used in this section of the melody.

Lakota Wiyanki

For SATB, a cappella with Optional Percussion

Arranged by
JUDITH HERRINGTON
and GAIL WOODSIDE

Traditional

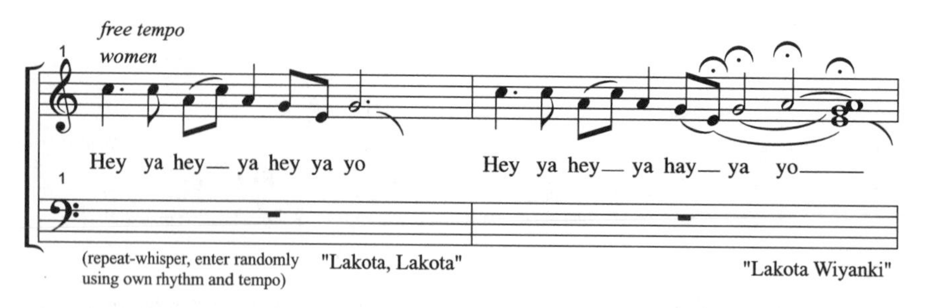

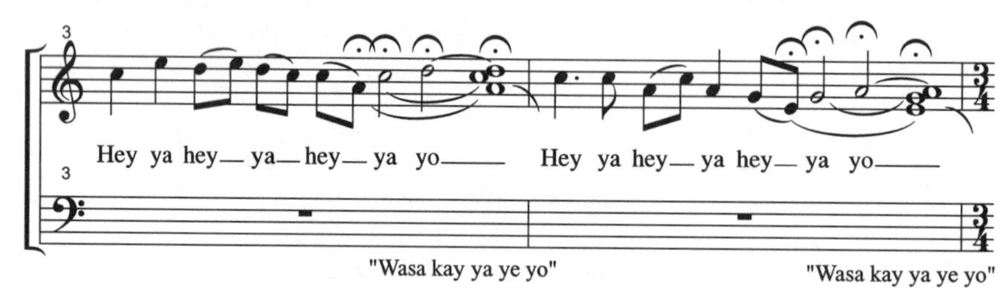

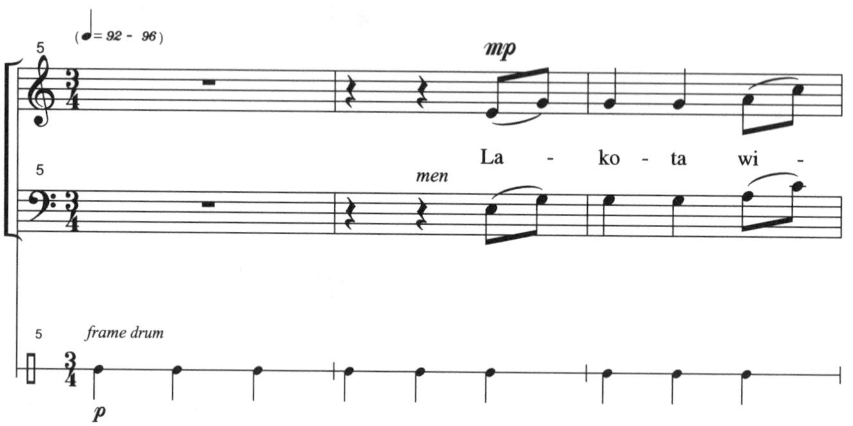

TEACHER 2 TEACHER

Sharing Native American music with students can open the door to discussion about history, cultural diversity and tolerance. "Lakota Wiyanki" can be a powerfully moving piece for both the singer and the audience.

- Define and discuss the properties of a pentatonic scale. *(a 5-tone scale using the pitches do, re, mi, fa, sol, la)*
- Echo three-beat melodic patterns in the pentatonic scale as improvised by the teacher. The conductor should tap the patterns on the letter ladder when improvising and during the echo as a visual guide.

Progress Checkpoints

Observe students' progress in:

✓ Performing the "ay," "ah" and "oh" vowels with a forward placement.

✓ Maintaining a steady pulse and clarifying 3/4 and 4/4 meters by use of an accented downbeat.

CURRICULUM CONNECTION

The Lakota People and Language

During the eighteenth century, the Dakota tribal groups of central Minnesota were moved to South Dakota. They became one of seven divisions of the Oceti Sa'kowin (Seven Council Fires). This move led to changes in their language. The Lakota dialect is one of the several dialects found among the Seven Council Fires people. It is mostly spoken in the Pine Ridge Reservation area in western South Dakota. The Lakota language is one of the few Native American languages to be well recorded in writing. This is due to the work of missionaries in the 1830s. Have students further research the history and preservation the Lakota language.

2. Rehearse

Direct students to:

- Sight-sing measures 6–11 in unison using solfège syllables and hand signs at a comfortable tempo.
- Sight-sing measures 11–16 on solfège syllables.
- Review measures 6–16 with singing rhythmic syllables.
- Learn the text in measures 6–16. A pronunciation guide can be found in the Teacher Resource Binder, Teaching Master 27.
- Sing measures 6–16 with text.
- Identify and locate which measures use 3/4 meter and which use 4/4 meter.
- Chant the text of measures 6–16 emphasizing the downbeat of each measure to demonstrate the varying meters.
- Review and sing measures 6–16.
- Sight-sing measures 17–28 using solfège syllables until secure.
- Practice measures 17–28, by first using rhythmic syllables emphasizing steady beat and meter changes, then by adding text.
- Sight-sing the Alto and Tenor/Bass parts in measures 28–39 with text.
- Sight-sing the Soprano part with text in measures 29–37.

TEACHING STRATEGY

Unified Vowels

Vowels are the fundamental building blocks of tone production, intonation and blend. A pure vowel is one that does not change when sung. When the pure vowels "ee," "ay," "ah," "oh," and "oo" are sung identically by all singers, there is a magical musical resonance and blend that can occur, seemingly an amplified sound without mechanical amplification.

Why is it important? The unity of vowels when sung by a chorus is the key to resonance and blend. The choral instrument should sound as one voice, and even one voice in a hundred singing a different sounding vowel can destroy the resonance and blend of the artistic choral tone.

- Practice all parts together in measures 28–38. Ask singers to stand when their section has the original melody.
- Locate, define and discuss tenuto markings in the Tenor/Bass line in measures 34–38. Demonstrate and practice Tenor/Bass line with and without tenuto articulation to compare and contrast building an understanding of tenuto.
- Locate and identify tenuto markings in measures 39–47.
- Locate and identify dynamic markings in measures 39–47.
- Sight-sing, with text pickup to measures 38–47 using appropriate dynamics and articulation.
- Practice and review measures 17–47. Work parts as necessary.
- Locate and identify free meter and fermatas measures 48–end.
- Sight-sing measures 48–end using solfège syllables to secure tone clusters.
- Add text to measures 48–end. Practice and review measures 39–end.

Progress Checkpoints

Observe students' progress in:

✓ Not overpowering the original melody with the harmonic parts in measures 34–end.

✓ Their dramatic and expressive use of crescendo as indicated measures 40–47.

✓ Using a tenuto to stress and lengthen pitch full value of the beat, but not as a hard-hitting accent.

TEACHING STRATEGY

Unified Vowels *(continued from page 190)*

How to Do It. Each vowel has a different shape in the mouth. Warm-ups and vocal exercises should focus on the shape and sound of each individual vowel and change from one vowel to another. The key is listening carefully to the vocal model and to the surrounding singers to adjust and blend the vowel tone. Connecting the vowel to breath support is another crucial feature of unified vowels.

Program Suggestion. Have students memorize this piece and perform it on a program or in competition. Have several Native American students or members of the community dress in costume for the performance. You could also add an authentic Native American dance.

3. Refine

Direct students to:

- Review measures 48–end, then compare to opening measures.
- Practice entire piece with heightened awareness of dynamic markings and meter changes.
- Add whispered text as indicated in the score measures 1–4 and 48–end.
- Add frame drum and hand slides as indicated throughout score. Drum must maintain a steady beat as if a "resting heart beat."

Progress Checkpoints

Observe students' progress in:

✓ Singing measures 1–4 and 48–end wistfully, with a freedom of tempo that will contrast with the obvious steady beat of the body of the piece.

✓ Whispering the text audibly and well articulated.

✓ Memorizing the piece with effective and artistic use of dynamics, good intonation and articulation.

ASSESSMENT

Informal Assessment

In this lesson, students showed the ability to:

- Sight-sing a pentatonic melody.
- Sing expressively in four parts using appropriate dynamics, accents with meter changes, articulation and intonation.
- Read and perform rhythmic patterns in 3/4 and 4/4 meter, demonstrating appropriate accented downbeats.

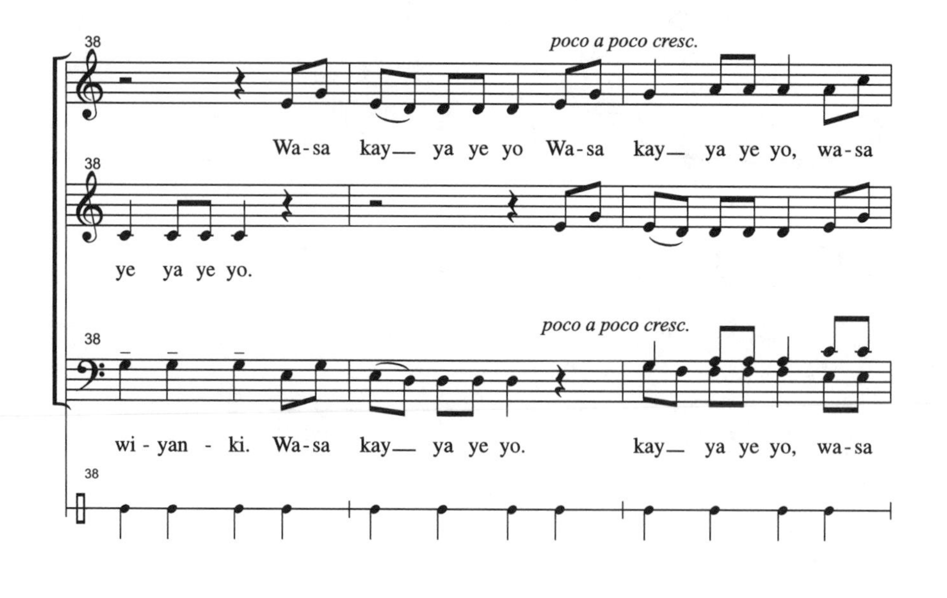

192 Intermediate Mixed

TEACHING STRATEGY

Reading Changing Meters

The only way to get comfortable with changing meters is to encounter them daily.

Have students:

- Compose short rhythm patterns for each other to read, using at least two meters.
- Use different constants, for example, try 2/4, 3/4 and 4/4 with the quarter note as the steady beat.
- Make up changing meter dances that have accents or stamps on the strong beat of each measure, so students feel the change with their whole body.

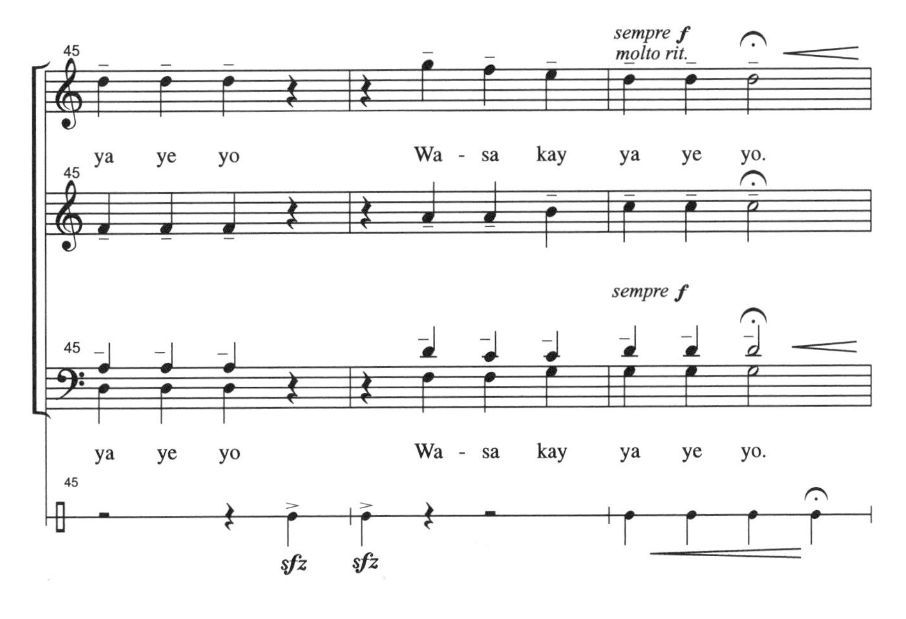

- Sing from memory music from diverse cultures and in an unfamiliar language.

Student Self-Assessment

Have students evaluate their individual performances based on the following:

- Posture
- Foreign Language
- Expressive Singing
- Accurate Rhythms
- Correct Part-Singing

Have each student rate his/her performance of this song in the areas above on a scale of 1–5, 5 being the best.

Individual and Group Performance Evaluation

To further measure growth of musical skills presented in this lesson, direct students to complete the Evaluation section on page 187.

- After each quartet has sung measures 6–16, have the students evaluate their ability to sing with forward vowels. They should rate their ability on a scale of 1 to 5, with 5 being the best.
- After completing the research project in the Artistic Expression section on page 187, open a class discussion on what the students learned from the poems. Choose a few selected poems to share with the class.

Additional National Standards

The following National Standards are addressed through the Assessment, Extension, Enrichment and bottom-page activities:

4. Composing and arranging music within specific guidelines. **(a)**

7. Evaluating music and music performances. **(a, b)**

8. Understanding relationships between music, the other arts, and disciplines outside the arts. **(b)**

9. Understanding music in relation to history and culture. **(c)**

Miserere Nobis

OVERVIEW

Composer: Victor Johnson
Text: Traditional Latin
Voicing: 3-Part Mixed
Key: C minor
Meter: 4/4
Form: ABA
Style: Contemporary American Anthem
Accompaniment: Piano
Programming: Memorial Day, Contest, Concert

Vocal Ranges:

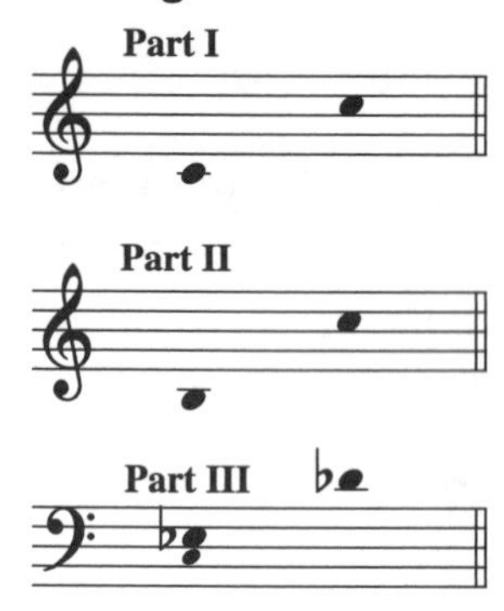

OBJECTIVES

After completing this lesson, students will be able to:

- Demonstrate fundamental skills while performing, including singing with pure Latin vowels.
- Identify the relationships between the concepts and processes of other subjects and those of music.

VOCABULARY

Have students review vocabulary in student lesson. Introduce terms found in the music. A complete glossary of terms is found on page 240 of the student book.

CHORAL LIBRARY

Miserere Nobis

Composer: Victor Johnson
Text: Traditional Latin
Voicing: 3-Part Mixed

VOCABULARY
mass
intonation

Focus

- Sing with pure Latin vowels.
- Perform music with understanding of the Latin text.

Getting Started

Composer Victor Johnson (b. 1978) graduated from the Booker T. Washington High School of Performing and Visual Arts in Dallas, Texas. He currently directs the Children's Choir of Texas at the Fort Worth Academy of Fine Arts. At the suggestion of his piano teacher, he began composing when he was in junior high. By the tenth grade, Johnson had his first piece of choral music published. He dedicated "Miserere Nobis" to the memory of his beloved piano teacher, Mrs. Carolyn Jones Campbell. Johnson knew at an early age, thanks to the encouragement of his piano teacher, that he wanted to pursue a career in music.

SPOTLIGHT

To learn more about careers in music, see page 128.

◆ History and Culture

The lyrics of "Miserere Nobis" are taken from the mass. The **mass** is *a religious service of prayers and ceremonies* that is commonly sung in Latin. The mass has many sections, some spoken and some sung. Composers traditionally set five of the sung sections to music, including the Kyrie, Gloria, Credo, Sanctus and Agnus Dei. German composer Johann Sebastian Bach's (1685–1750) *Mass in B Minor* is an example of this. A composer may also elect to set one section to music, as in American composer Samuel Barber's (1910–1981) *Agnus Dei.* Alternatively, as Victor Johnson has done, a composer may use some of the lyrics from a section. "Miserere Nobis" is from the Gloria.

RESOURCES

Intermediate Sight-Singing

Sight-Singing in C Minor, pages 147–150

Reading Rhythms in 4/4 Meter, pages 2–6

Teacher Resource Binder

Teaching Master 29, *Pronunciation Guide for "Miserere Nobis"*

Vocal Development 15, *Vowels*

Reference 5, *Careers in Music*

Reference 16, *My Music Dictionary*

Reference 29, *Zeroing in on IPA*

For additional resources, see TRB Table of Contents.

Links to Learning

◆ Vocal

Latin is a lovely language to sing, in part because the vowels are pure. Read and perform the following example to practice singing the opening phrase and its repetitions with pure vowel sounds.

◆ Theory

The example below contains chords from measures 29–32. Perform the example below to practice singing choral patterns with good **intonation** *(the art of in-tune singing).*

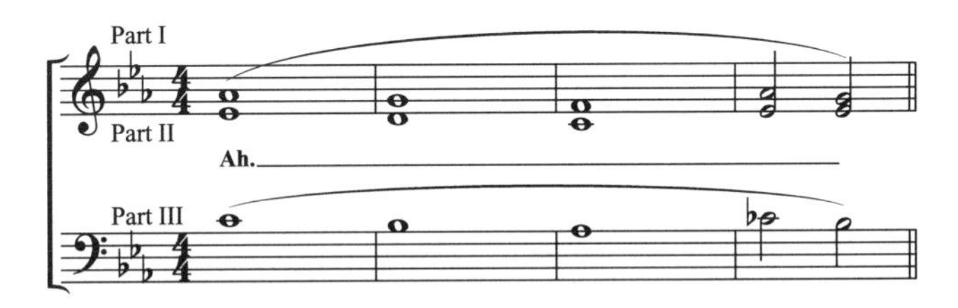

◆ Artistic Expression

To develop artistry through singing in a foreign language, memorize the phrase-by-phrase translation of the Latin text given below.

Miserere nobis.	Have mercy on us.
Qui tollis peccata mundi,	Who takes away the sins of the world,
Suscipe deprecationem nostram.	Receive our prayer.
Quoniam tu solus sanctus,	You only are holy,
Tu solus Dominus, Tu solus altissimus.	You only are Lord, You only are most high.

Evaluation

Demonstrate how well you have learned the skills and concepts featured in the lesson "Miserere Nobis" by completing the following:

- Sing your part in measures 8–12 of "Miserere Nobis" using pure Latin vowels. Evaluate how well you did.
- With a partner, take turns reciting the Latin text while the other provides the English translation. Check each other's Latin pronunciation.

LINKS TO LEARNING

Vocal

The Vocal section is designed to prepare students to sing with pure, open vowels.

Have students:

- Review the five pure vowels of the Latin language—*eh, ee, ah, oh, oo.*
- Review how each vowel in pronounced in the Latin language—*a=ah, e=eh, i=ee, o=oh, u=oh.*
- Sing the example focusing on open, pure vowels.

Theory

The Theory section is designed to prepare students to:

- Understand intonation.
- Participate in singing choral patterns with good intonation.

Have students:

- Sing each part separately, focusing on accurate intervals and pure, vowel sounds.
- Sing all parts together, listening carefully for good intonation and uniform vowels.
- Note: Nonuniform vowel sounds can cause poor intonation.

RESOURCES

Intermediate Mixed Rehearsal/Performance CD

- **CD 2:15** Voices
- **CD 2:16** Accompaniment Only
- **CD 3:20** Vocal Practice Track—Part I
- **CD 4:19** Vocal Practice Track—Part II
- **CD 6:20** Vocal Practice Track—Part III

National Standards

1. Singing, alone and with others, a varied repertoire of music. **(a, b, d)**
8. Understanding the relationships between music, the other arts, and disciplines outside the arts. **(b)**

Artistic Expression

The Artistic Expression section is designed to prepare students to memorize a phrase-by-phrase translation of the Latin text.

Have students:

- Read through each line of the Latin text, followed by the translation in English.
- Memorize the translation so that while they are singing the Latin text they are aware of the meaning of the lyrics.

LESSON PLAN

Suggested Teaching Sequence and Performance Tips

1. Introduce

Direct students to:

- Read and discuss the information found in the Getting Started section on student page 194.
- Sing the phrase shown in the Vocal section on page 195 to practice pronouncing pure Latin vowels.
- Sing the chord progression in the Theory section to practice good intonation.

TEACHER 2 TEACHER

Victor Johnson's lyrical melody and beautiful suspended harmonies create a tender setting of the text in "Miserere Nobis." Mr. Johnson suggests that choristers "internalize the text to portray its meaning."

Progress Checkpoints

Observe students' progress in:

- ✓ Their ability to pronounce Latin with pure vowels.
- ✓ Their ability to sing three-part chords in tune.

EXTENSION

Parallel Sixth Chords

Revisit the Theory section to teach the harmonic structure of parallel sixth chords. Parallel sixth chords are a succession of chords in which the interval between the lowest and highest voices is a sixth: A♭ above C; G above B♭; F above A♭. The middle voice usually sings a third above the lowest voice, but it may sing a fourth. Relate the example to measures 29–32 in the music.

2. Rehearse

Direct students to:

- Count rhythms phrase by phrase, noting where rhythms are identical and where rhythms differ between the parts.
- Chant the Latin text in rhythm. A pronunciation guide for the Latin text can be found in the Teacher Resource Binder, Teaching Master 29.
- Learn pitches part by part and then phrase by phrase, building the three-part texture.
- Give particular attention to dissonances in measures 9, 10, 12, 15, 16, 17 and 18. Also note where all three parts sing in unison or octaves in measures 25–26, 28, 43–44, measures 47–48.
- Count-sing the entire piece before singing in Latin.

ENRICHMENT

Miserere Nobis

This common text from the Mass has been used in hundreds, perhaps thousands of musical settings over the years. Have your students research this text and find various examples of settings from different time periods. Listen to different recordings and compare the characteristics and treatment of the text for each.

Progress Checkpoints

Observe students' progress in:

✓ Singing with accurate diction, with correct accentuation of the Latin syllables.
✓ Singing accurate rhythms and pitches.
✓ Tuning the dissonances.

TEACHING STRATEGY

Diaphragmatic Breathing

Have students:

- Remember that the diaphragm muscle is the major muscle of inhalation. In deep breathing, the diaphragm muscle descends approximately four inches.
- While lying on the back with legs drawn up toward the body, note the rise and fall of the abdomen during natural breathing.
- Use imagery to accomplish deep breathing, such as blowing up an inner tube or a balloon, or sipping in a thick milk shake.
- While pressing on the diaphragmatic muscle, take a surprise breath and feel the movement of the diaphragm.

3. Refine

Direct students to:

- Apply the performance markings found in the score such as the tenuto marks in measures 10, 22, 34, and 40; the dynamic marks throughout; and the tempo indications throughout.
- Sing the dissonances slightly louder than the consonances that follow.
- Breathe only where indicated by punctuation marks, such as commas and periods.

Progress Checkpoints

Observe students' progress in:

✓ Their ability to shape the phrases in the music as indicated by the composer's marks in the score.

✓ Their ability to shape musical phrases, breathing only where instructed.

200 Intermediate Mixed

TEACHING STRATEGY

Phrases

Determining phrase length is not an accurate science. Although there are guidelines for determining phrase boundaries, there are frequent disagreements among musicians, leading to very different interpretations of the same piece. Measures 5–8 of "Miserere Nobis" are a case in point. Some people contend that there are two phrases within those measures, and some say there is only one. Discuss this issue with the students, and decide together which interpretation they will use. It usually is up to the conductor to make the final call, and then everyone in the ensemble must conform for a clear performance.

ASSESSMENT

Informal Assessment

In this lesson, students showed the ability to:

- Correctly pronounce Latin with pure vowels.
- Sing chord progressions with accurate intonation
- Display knowledge of the English translation of the Latin text.

Student Self-Assessment

Have students evaluate their individual performances based on the following:

- Posture
- Tall Vowels
- Expressive Singing
- Intonation
- Correct Part-Singing

Have each student rate his/her performance of this song in the areas above on a scale of 1–5, 5 being the best.

MORE ABOUT...

Young Composers

As we learned in the Getting Started section, composer Victor Johnson began composing in junior high. Challenge your students to find a traditional text (sacred or secular) such as the one used in "Miserere Nobis," and compose a choral piece using that text for a voicing of their choice. Composing music may become a vocation or an avocation for students in your class. Encourage them to compose.

Individual and Group Performance Evaluation

To further measure growth of musical skills presented in this lesson, direct students to complete the Evaluation section on page 195.

- After students have sung measures 8–12 on their own at home or in a practice room, they should evaluate their ability to sing with pure Latin vowels.
- After students have paired up, one should speak the Latin text, while the other provides the English translation. Each student should check his/her partner's ability to pronounce the Latin correctly.

Music, Society and Culture

Have students perform additional songs representing diverse cultures, including American and Texas heritage. Go to **music.glencoe.com**, the Web site for Glencoe's choral music programs, for additional music selections students can perform.

Additional National Standards

The following National Standards are addressed through the Assessment, Extension, Enrichment and bottom-page activities:

4. Composing and arranging music within specific guidelines. **(a)**

6. Listening to, analyzing, and describing music. **(c)**

7. Evaluating music and music performances. **(a, b)**

Musical Theater

There are many ways to tell a story. You may share a story with others through storytelling, acting, drawing and even singing. When you add music and drama to the telling of a story, the storytelling becomes musical theater. **Musical theater** is *an art form that combines acting, singing and dancing to tell a story.* It also often includes staging, costumes, lighting and scenery.

The Broadway musical is an American invention. In reaction to the dramatic and often "stuffy" operas of the time, Americans invented their own version of musical theater that was less grandiose and spoke directly to the people. As New York City became a center of the arts and music, many musical theaters appeared on a street named Broadway. As a result, the word *Broadway* came to be identified with stage and music productions.

Broadway musicals blossomed during the 1920s and 1930s with the works of George Gershwin, Cole Porter and Irving Berlin. By the 1950s, the Broadway musical was well established. The composer/lyricist team of Frederick Lowe and Alan Jay Lerner wrote *My Fair Lady* (1956) and *Camelot* (1961). Some of the masterpieces created by the team of Richard Rogers and Oscar Hammerstein II include *Oklahoma!* (1943), *Carousel* (1945) and *The Sound of Music* (1959). More recently, the composers Andrew Lloyd Webber and Stephen Sondheim have contributed to the continued success of Broadway musicals. Lloyd Webber's *Cats* (1981) and *The Phantom of the Opera* (1988) are two of the longest-running musicals in Broadway history.

Many are involved in the production of a Broadway musical, but it is the performers who bring the story to life through their singing, dancing and acting. If you have seen a musical or performed in one, you know how exciting it can be. For many, musical theater is indeed storytelling at its best!

RESOURCES

Teacher Resource Binder

Teaching Master 30, *Inside the Musical Theater*

Reference 5, *Careers in Music*

Reference 16, *My Music Dictionary*

National Standards

7. Evaluating music and music performances. **(b)**

8. Understanding relationships between music, the other arts, and disciplines outside the arts. **(a)**

9. Understanding music in relation to history and culture. **(b)**

MUSICAL THEATER

Objectives

- Relate music to history.
- Identify the relationships between the content of the other fine arts and those of music.
- Evaluate a musical performance.

Suggested Teaching Sequence

Direct students to:

- Read the Spotlight On Musical Theater on student page 203 and define musical theater.
- Discuss the history of musical theater.
- Identify important musical theater composers and popular shows.
- Make a list of musical theater shows that they have either seen live, video or DVD, or on television.
- Choose one of these previously viewed shows and write a synopsis of the story line and the characters as well as an evaluation of the performance.
- Attend a live performance of a musical theater show, if possible. Encourage students to learn more about this popular musical genre and to become more involved in musical theater.

Progress Checkpoints

Observe students' progress in:

✓ Understanding musical theater and its history.

✓ Identifying important composers of musical theater and popular shows.

✓ Writing a synopsis of a familiar show and evaluating the performance.

The River Sleeps Beneath the Sky

OVERVIEW

Composer: Mary Lynn Lightfoot
Text: Paul Laurence Dunbar
Voicing: 3-Part Mixed
Key: F Major
Meter: 4/4
Form: ABAB Coda
Style: Contemporary American Anthem
Accompaniment: Piano
Programming: Festival, Contest, Concert

Vocal Ranges:

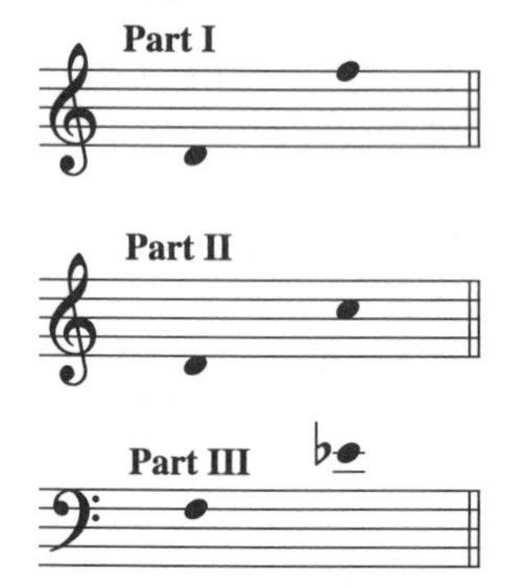

Objectives

After completing this lesson, students will be able to:

- Demonstrate musical artistry by singing expressive phrases using word stress.
- Read musical notation containing dotted patterns in 4/4 meter.
- Identify the relationships between the processes of other subjects and those of music.
- Perform a varied repertoire of music from notation.

VOCABULARY

Have students review vocabulary in student lesson. Introduce terms found in the music. A complete glossary of terms is found on page 240 of the student book.

CHORAL LIBRARY

The River Sleeps Beneath The Sky

Composer: Mary Lynn Lightfoot
Text: Paul Laurence Dunbar
Voicing: 3-Part Mixed

VOCABULARY

legato
word stress
dot
imitation

Focus

- Demonstrate musical artistry.
- Read and perform dotted rhythms.
- Relate music to poetry.

Getting Started

Have you ever heard someone say, "I'd give anything for a little peace and quiet"? In our noisy world, it is difficult to stop and find a quiet place. In addition to spending time talking to others, we must also spend time communicating with ourselves. A place so peaceful and quiet is beautifully described in "The River Sleeps Beneath The Sky." As you sing, let the **legato** *(a connected and sustained style of singing)*, musical lines and the intriguing poetry take you to a peaceful sunset at the end of a day.

SKILL BUILDERS

To learn more about dotted rhythms, see Intermediate Sight-Singing, *pages 45 and 89.*

History and Culture

Paul Laurence Dunbar (1872–1906) was the first African American poet to attain international acclaim. He wrote short stories, poems and a novel. Dunbar grew up in Dayton, Ohio. He wanted to study law, but his family was too poor to pay for his education. Poverty, however, could not suppress his love of life and the ability to express it in prose and poetry. Dunbar died from tuberculosis at the age of thirty-three. The following poem, written by Dunbar, is inscribed on the Dayton Public Library:

Because I have loved so deeply
Because I have loved so long,
God in His great compassion
Gave me the gift of song.

RESOURCES

Intermediate Sight-Singing

Sight-Singing in F Major, pages 39–41, 76–77, 112–116
Reading Rhythms in 4/4 Meter, pages 2–6
Reading Eighth Notes/Rests, pages 26–27

Teacher Resource Binder

Teaching Master 31, *Text Emphasis in "The River Sleeps Beneath the Sky"*
Teaching Master 32, *Composing Rhythmic Patterns with Dotted Note Values*
Skill Builder 23, *Rhythm and Kodály*
Kodály 6, *Music Reading: Rhythm*
For additional resources, see TRB Table of Contents.

Links to Learning

◆ Vocal

To sing expressively, it is important to create a rise and fall to the phrase by using proper word stress. Expressive **word stress** occurs when *important parts of the text are sung in a more accented style.* Perform the following example to develop expressive phrasing and word stress.

◆ Theory

Perform the following examples to develop skill in reading dotted rhythmic patterns in $\frac{4}{4}$ time. A **dot** is *a symbol that is placed to the right of a given note to increase the length of the note by half its value.*

◆ Artistic Expression

To develop artistry through expressive singing, form two groups of three to five singers. Practice performing the vocal imitation found in measures 11–14 of the song. In these measures **imitation,** or *the successive statement of a melody, theme or motive by two or more parts,* occurs both in the text and music. Follow the dynamic markings and make the music fade, just as the sun is fading away.

Evaluation

Demonstrate how well you have learned the skills and concepts featured in the lesson "The River Sleeps Beneath The Sky" by completing the following:

- Sing your part from measures 32–35, demonstrating your ability to sing in a legato style using expressive word stress. How could you sing more expressively?
- Perform the rhythmic patterns found in the Theory section above. Then, create your own dotted rhythmic pattern in $\frac{4}{4}$ meter. Check your work for rhythmic accuracy and correct notation.

RESOURCES

Intermediate Mixed Rehearsal/Performance CD

CD 2:17 Voices
CD 2:18 Accompaniment Only
CD 3:21 Vocal Practice Track—Part I
CD 4:20 Vocal Practice Track—Part II
CD 6:21 Vocal Practice Track—Part III

National Standards

1. Singing, alone and with others, a varied repertoire of music **(a, b, d)**
5. Reading and notating music. **(a, c)**
8. Understanding relationships between music, the other arts, and disciplines outside the arts. **(b)**

LINKS TO LEARNING

Vocal

The Vocal section is designed to prepare students to:

- Understand word stress.
- Create musical phrases using expressive word stress.

Have students:

- Read the definition of *word stress* and listen as you demonstrate.
- Speak the exercise in rhythm, emphasizing the words in all caps.
- Sing the exercise, creating a rise and fall to the phrase using proper word stress.

Theory

The Theory section is designed to prepare students to:

- Understand the meaning of a dot in musical notation.
- Read and perform dotted rhythms in 4/4 meter.

Have students:

- Read the definition of a dot and listen as you demonstrate examples.
- Tap or clap the quarter note pulse in 4/4 meter.
- Speak the rhythm example while tapping the quarter note pulse.
- Speak the rhythm example while the director conducts 4/4, while feeling the quarter note pulse inside.

Artistic Expression

The Artistic Expression section is designed to prepare students to identify and perform vocal imitation.

Have students:

- Define *imitation.*
- Divide into small groups and sing measures 11–14 to demonstrate imitation.

LESSON PLAN

Suggested Teaching Sequence and Performance Tips

1. Introduce

Direct students to:

- Read and discuss the information found in the Getting Started section on student page 204.
- Practice using expressive word stress as shown in the Vocal section on page 205. Practice the examples first without word stress then using the word stress as shown. Divide the poem into phrases and practice expressive word stress. Discuss how this word stress follows normal speech patterns.

For the choirs of Frontier Trail Junior High School, Olathe, Kansas, Sherri Porterfield, Director

The River Sleeps Beneath The Sky

For 3-Part Mixed and Piano

Words from "Sunset" by
PAUL LAURENCE DUNBAR (1872–1906)

Music by
MARY LYNN LIGHTFOOT

TEACHER 2 TEACHER

Students will enjoy analyzing Dunbar's expressive poetry. The composer presents an ideal opportunity to develop legato singing and use a variety of stylistic treatments while venturing into the soul of a poet!

- Discuss any words needing definition. *(lay-song, somber-serious, mantle-cloak)*
- Practice contrasting legato and marcato speaking and singing styles to determine the expressive style for this piece.
- Practice the rhythmic exercise as shown in the Theory section on page 205 to increase ability to read and perform dotted rhythms in 4/4 meter.
- Locate these patterns throughout the score.

Progress Checkpoints

Observe students' progress in:

✓ Their ability to relate to the text.

✓ Their ability to speak and sing the text using proper word stress.

✓ Their ability to contrast legato and marcato styles.

✓ Their ability to read dotted rhythms correctly and locate them in the score.

MORE ABOUT...

Poet Paul Laurence Dunbar

Paul Laurence Dunbar was the son of former slaves. His mother, Matilda, was a washerwoman in Dayton, Ohio. She worked for the family of Orville and Wilbur Wright. Matilda developed a love of prose and poetry after hearing Mrs. Wright read to her sons. She shared this love of poetry with Paul, and he wrote his first compositions at the age of six. Dunbar attended school with Orville and Wilbur. He was the only African American in his class at Dayton Central High School. After graduation, Dunbar had difficulty finding work and served as an elevator operator until he became recognized for his extraordinary literary talents.

2. Rehearse

Direct students to:

- Label measures 1–18 as Section A. Sing each part separately on solfège. Have each group listen for expressive phrasing and correct dotted rhythms as the other sections perform.
- Locate and practice the unison sections. *(measures 4–7, beat 4 and measure 15 –beat 4 measure 17)*
- Find where Section A is repeated. *(measures 32–43)* Sing these measures on solfège. Locate and perform the unison sections. *(measures 32–36 beat 2 and measure 44)* Note the change in this section beginning at measure 45 and leading to the coda. *(measures 48 to end)*
- Sing measures 20–28. Discuss the ways in which this section is different. *(new rhythms and melodies, moves faster)* Label this Section B.
- Review the form of the piece. Sing through on solfège. Indicate the form of the piece as follows: Part I—raise hand when singing Section A; Part II—raise hand when singing Section B; and Part III—raise hand when singing the coda.

Progress Checkpoints

Observe students' progress in:

✓ Understanding form.

✓ Singing correct pitches and rhythms.

✓ Singing expressively on solfège.

CURRICULUM CONNECTIONS

Creative Writing

Have the students read the text of "The River Sleeps Beneath The Sky" and discuss the meaning, or the picture, this poetry creates. The following can be done as a creative writing or journal assignment, in small group discussions, or as a whole group. Perhaps students will want to write their own "pictures" down in poetic style and then set them to melodies.

3. Refine

Direct students to:

- Read the text for Section A in rhythm, using expressive word stress and dynamic levels as indicated in the score.
- Sing the text with appropriate legato style, dynamic level and word stress.
- Work for rhythmic precision and dynamic contrasts in the imitative section in measures 11–14.
- Work the remainder of the sections in the same manner. Encourage the students to discuss ways to make the text more effective. *(clear diction, dynamic changes, phrase markings for no breath, word stress)*
- Isolate and practice measures 48 to the end. Which part has the melody? *(Alto)* Encourage the Altos to crescendo gently through the half note in measure 49 and the dotted quarter in measure 51 to create a feeling of forward motion.
- Discuss and demonstrate how the song fades away to a whisper. Rehearse with the piano accompaniment (measures 52–53) to create the natural flow from subito piano to the whisper.

Progress Checkpoints

Observe students' progress in:

✓ Singing accurate pitches and rhythms.

✓ Singing with clean diction and appropriate releases of consonant sounds.

✓ Singing with audible dynamic contrasts.

✓ Singing with legato style with appropriate word stress.

ASSESSMENT

Informal Assessment

In this lesson, students showed the ability to:

- Sing text using expressive phrasing.
- Read and perform a variety of dotted rhythms in 4/4 meter.
- Perform imitative passages and locate them in the score.

Student Self-Assessment

Have students evaluate their individual performances based on the following:

- Phrasing
- Diction
- Tall Vowels
- Expressive Singing
- Accurate Rhythms

Have each student rate his/her performance of this song in the areas above on a scale of 1–5, 5 being the best.

MUSIC LITERACY

Dynamics and Shaping Phrases

To help students expand their music literacy, have them:

- Review the parts of a phrase—beginning, peak and end.
- Discuss how to shape phrases using dynamics, with a crescendo from the beginning to the peak, and then a release to the end.

Recall that the dynamic marking at the beginning of a phrase may indicate the overall average dynamic for the entire phrase.

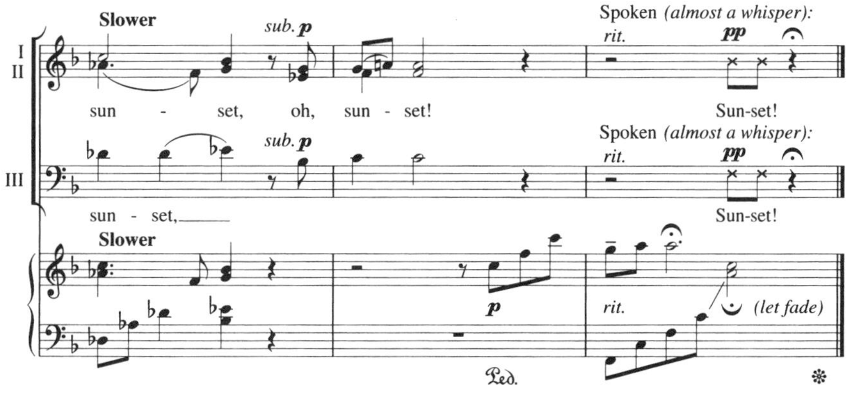

Individual and Group Performance Evaluation

To further measure growth of musical skills presented in this lesson, direct students to complete the Evaluation section on page 205.

- Have students sing measures 32–35 on their own at home or in a practice room using expressive word stress in a legato style. They should evaluate their performance and think of ways they can sing more expressively.
- After students have created their own rhythmic pattern using dotted rhythms in 4/4 meter, start at the end of the row and have students perform their pattern one after another keeping a steady beat. Evaluate for rhythmic accuracy and correct notation.

EXTENSION

Imitation

Write a descriptive phrase of 5–8 words and create a melody. Strive to make the rhythm as well as the rise and fall of the melodic line portray the text. Teach this melody to another person and practice singing it in imitation, using a variety of dynamic levels and expressive word stress. Perform your composition for the class.

Additional National Standards

The following National Standards are addressed through the Assessment, Extension, Enrichment and bottom-page activities:

4. Composing and arranging music within specific guideline. **(a)**

5. Reading and notating music. **(d)**

7. Evaluating music and music performances. **(b)**

8. Understanding relationships between music, the other arts, and disciplines outside the arts. **(b)**

Set Me As A Seal

OVERVIEW

Composer: John Leavitt
Text: Song of Solomon 8:6–7
Voicing: SATB
Key: F major
Meter: 4/4
Form: ABA
Style: Contemporary American Anthem
Accompaniment: A cappella
Programming: Contest/Festival

Vocal Ranges:

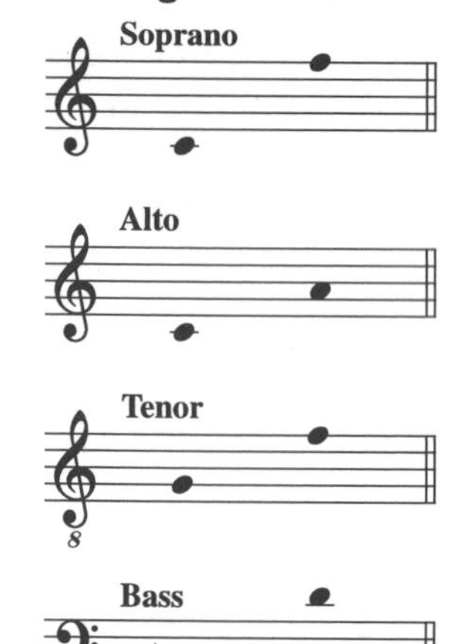

OBJECTIVES

After completing this lesson, students will be able to:

- Use standard terminology to explain compositional techniques.
- Read and write music notation in 4/4 meter.
- Demonstrate musical artistry through the use of proper breath management.

VOCABULARY

Have students review vocabulary in student lesson. Introduce terms found in the music. A complete glossary of terms is found on page 240 of the student book.

CHORAL LIBRARY

Set Me As A Seal

Composer: John Leavitt
Text: Song of Solomon 8:6–7
Voicing: SATB

VOCABULARY

staggered entrances
homophony
D.C. al Fine
$\frac{4}{4}$ meter
breath support

Focus

- Identify compositional techniques found in the music.
- Read and write music in $\frac{4}{4}$ meter.
- Demonstrate musical artistry through the use of proper breath management.

Getting Started

"Set Me As A Seal" is a song about commitment. What is commitment? It is a promise you make to someone that you will hold up your end of the bargain. If you join a soccer, baseball or football team, you have a commitment to attend practices and the games. When you join a choir, you have a commitment to do your best and to attend rehearsals and performances. "Set Me As A Seal" describes the commitment of love.

SPOTLIGHT

To learn more about breath management, page 83.

◆ History and Culture

Several musical writing techniques are found in "Set Me As A Seal." The song begins with **staggered entrances** *(a technique in which the voices enter at different times).* The Altos enter first, followed by the Basses, tenors and, finally, the Sopranos. At measure nine, **homophony,** or *music that consists of two or more voice parts with similar or identical rhythms,* is found. Then, at the very end you will find a **D.C. al Fine**. D.C. ("da capo") is *a term that indicates to go back to the beginning and repeat. The term* al fine *is a term that indicates to sing to the end or "fine."*

The text to "Set Me As A Seal" describes the "seal" as an official commitment of love. The seal upon the heart represents love, whereas the seal upon the arm represents protection and strength. What other descriptors of love can you find in this text?

RESOURCES

Intermediate Sight-Singing

Sight-Singing in F Major, pages 39–41, 76–77, 112–116

Reading Rhythms in 4/4 Meter, pages 2–6

Teacher Resource Binder

Teaching Master 33, *Composing Rhythms Patterns in 4/4 Meter*

Vocal Development 15, *Vowels*

Reference 20, *Rhythm Challenge Chart*

For additional resources, see TRB Table of Contents.

Links to Learning

◆ Vocal

The character of this piece indicates a need for warmth of choral tone. Read and perform the following example to practice singing with uniform vowel sounds to enhance the richness of tone.

◆ Theory

Perform the example below to practice reading rhythmic patterns in $\frac{4}{4}$ **meter** *(a time signature in which there are four beats per measure and the quarter note receives the beat).* Conduct the pattern as you read.

◆ Artistic Expression

"Set Me As A Seal" is written with a flowing melodic line. **Breath support** *(the constant airflow necessary to produce sound for singing)* is required to sing through the phrases without taking a breath. Sing measures 8–12 in one breath. Place your index finger to your lips as you begin to sing. Slowly move the finger away from your mouth in a slow, continuous motion. Think of the breath reaching out to your finger as you sing through the phrase.

Evaluation

Demonstrate how well you have learned the skills and concepts featured in the lesson "Set Me As A Seal" by completing the following:

- Define and locate in the music the following compositional techniques: staggered entrances, homophony and D.C. al Fine. Compare your answers with those of a classmate.
- Compose a four-measure rhythmic phrase in $\frac{4}{4}$ meter. Use the music as a guide. Check your work for rhythmic accuracy.

RESOURCES

Intermediate Mixed Rehearsal/Performance CD

CD 2:19 Voices
CD 2:20 Accompaniment Only
CD 3:22 Vocal Practice Track—Soprano
CD 4:21 Vocal Practice Track—Alto
CD 5:7 Vocal Practice Track—Tenor
CD 6:22 Vocal Practice Track—Bass

National Standards

1. Singing alone and with others, a varied repertoire of music. **(a, b, c, d)**
4. Composing and arranging music within specific guidelines. **(a)**
5. Reading and notating music. **(a, b, c, d)**

LINKS TO LEARNING

Vocal

The Vocal section is designed to prepare students to create a warm choral tone by singing uniform vowels.

Have students:

- Sing the example, listening to one another for good intonation.
- Sing the example again, focusing on the overall tone and uniform vowels.

Theory

The Theory section is designed to prepare students to read and conduct rhythms in 4/4 meter.

Have students:

- Clap or tap the rhythms in the example accurately.
- Conduct while chanting the rhythms.
- Make sure they maintain a steady pulse.

Artistic Expression

The Artistic Expression section is designed to prepare students to sing with proper breath support.

Have students:

- Sing the measures 8–12 in one breath and do the exercise as indicated.
- Work to be able to sing all four measures on one breath.

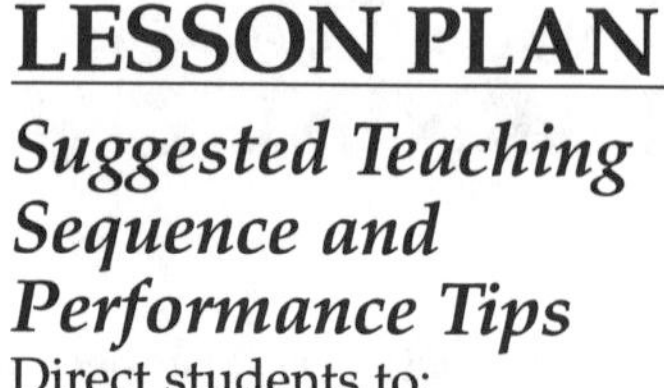

LESSON PLAN

Suggested Teaching Sequence and Performance Tips

Direct students to:

- Read and discuss the information found in the Getting Started section on student page 212.
- Break down this song into sections. Read the rhythms in each section. When secure add text and pitches. Repeat this process for all sections.
- Sing measures 1–7 to secure the accuracy of the staggered entrances. Practice with conducting to ensure accuracy of longer notes as well as tied notes.
- Practice singing the vocal lines smoothly with uniform vowel sounds.
- Observe all dynamic and expression markings.

Progress Checkpoints

Observe student's progress in:

✓ Their ability to read all rhythms and pitches.

✓ Each section's ability to sing the staggered entrances at the beginning of the song correctly.

✓ Their ability to sing with uniform vowel and an overall warm tone.

✓ Their ability to sing musically, following all dynamics and expression markings.

Set Me As A Seal

For SATB, a cappella

Text from Song of Solomon 8: 6–7

Music by JOHN LEAVITT

"Set Me As A Seal" is a great song for your students to practice singing a cappella. Upon mastering this song, they will have experienced how to sing with proper intonation and good breath support. They will be pleased with the beautiful sound they can make as a choir.

Additional National Standards

The following National Standards are addressed through the Assessment, Extension, Enrichment and bottom-page activities:

6. Listening to, analyzing, and describing music. **(c)**

ASSESSMENT

Informal Assessment

In this lesson, students showed the ability to:

- Identify and perform music with staggered entrances and homophony.
- Describe and identify *D. C. al Fine.*
- Read and write music in 4/4 meter.
- Use proper breath management and uniform vowels to produce a warm choral tone.

Student Self-Assessment

Have students evaluate their individual performances based on the following:

- Breath Management
- Expressive Singing
- Intonation
- Tall Vowels
- Correct Part-Singing

Have each student rate his/her performance of this song in the areas above on a scale of 1–5, 5 being the best.

Individual and Group Performance Evaluation

To further measure growth of musical skills presented in this lesson, direct students to complete the Evaluation section on page 213.

- Direct students to define and locate the compositional techniques listed and to compare their answers with other members of the class.
- Have students compose a four-measure rhythmic phrase in 4/4 meter. Students should check their work for accuracy.

Sing Out This Maytime

OVERVIEW

Composer: Johann Hermann Schein (1586–1630), edited by Patrick M. Liebergen
Text: Johann Hermann Schein, English text by Patrick M. Liebergen
Voicing: SAB
Key: C major
Meter: 3/4
Form: ABA
Style: German Baroque Song
Accompaniment: Piano, Optional Two Flutes
Programming: Spring Concert, Festival

Vocal Ranges:

Objectives

After completing this lesson, students will be able to:

- Identify music forms as presented through music notation.
- Perform independently with accurate rhythm.
- Interpret music terms referring to dynamics when performing.

VOCABULARY

Have students review vocabulary in student lesson. Introduce terms found in the music. A complete glossary of terms is found on page 240 of the student book.

Sing Out This Maytime

Composer: Johann Hermann Schein (1586–1630), edited by Patrick M. Liebergen
Text: Johann Hermann Schein, English text by Patrick M. Liebergen
Voicing: SAB

VOCABULARY

form
ABA form
articulation
$\frac{3}{4}$ meter
dynamics

Focus

- Identify music forms found in music (ABA).
- Perform independently with accurate rhythm.
- Perform music with varying dynamics.

Getting Started

What are some of your favorite springtime activities? Maybe you enjoy playing ball, biking or in-line skating. And if you live in a place where winters are particularly cold, then as the weather warms up you might enjoy putting away your heavy coat and boots. The words of "Sing Out This Maytime" mention events that signal the beginning of spring, such as flowers blooming and nightingales singing.

SKILL BUILDERS

To learn more about $\frac{3}{4}$ *meter, see* Intermediate Sight-Singing, *page 17.*

◆ History and Culture

Johann Hermann Schein (1586–1630) was one of three leading German composers of his generation. When he was thirteen, Schein was a Soprano in his country's best choir, which was sponsored by the Elector of Saxony in Dresden. As an adult, Schein was appointed Thomascantor in Leipzig, Germany. One hundred years later, Johann Sebastian Bach, the most famous of German Baroque composers, worked at the same church.

Form is *the structure or design of a musical composition.* "Sing Out This Maytime" is written in ABA form. **ABA form** is *the design in which the opening phrases (section A) are followed by contrasting phrases (section B), which lead to a repetition of the opening phrases (Section A).* Locate these sections in the music.

RESOURCES

Intermediate Sight-Singing

Sight-Singing in C Major, pages 7–14, 15–17, 28–30, 66–67, 110–111

Reading Rhythms in 3/4 Meter, pages 17–22

Reading Quarter and Half Notes, pages 1–9

Teacher Resource Binder

Evaluation Master 7, *Evaluating Musical Expression*

Evaluation Master 8, *Evaluating Rhythmic Accuracy*

Skill Builder 26, *Rhythm Challenge in 3/4 Meter*

For additional resources, see TRB Table of Contents.

Links to Learning

◆ Vocal

Perform the following example to practice correct articulation of quarter notes. **Articulation** is *the amount of separation or connection between notes.* In "Sing Out This Maytime," the quarter notes need to be distinct, yet also connected to the next pitch. To achieve this articulation, it is useful to imagine pressing into each tone gently, as if pressing your thumb into a sponge.

◆ Theory

3/4 meter is *a time signature in which there are three beats per measure and the quarter note receives the beat.* Sometimes at a fast tempo, 3/4 meter is conducted with one beat per measure. Read and perform the example below to practice reading rhythmic patterns in three. Begin at a slow tempo. When accurate, increase the tempo gradually until you feel only one beat in each measure.

◆ Artistic Expression

To develop artistry through expressive singing, follow the dynamic marks placed in the music by the editor. **Dynamics** are *symbols used in music to indicate how loud or soft to sing a passage.* The markings in this song include ***mf*** (medium loud), ***mp*** (medium soft) and ***f*** (loud). Be attentive to sing the repetition of each phrase softly.

Evaluation

Demonstrate how well you have learned the skills and concepts featured in the lesson "Sing Out This Maytime" by completing the following:

- Describe the form of "Sing Out This Maytime." Identify the measure number that marks the beginning of each section (ABA).
- Sing measures 59–70 to show your understanding of 3/4 meter. How did you do?
- Perform measures 29–56 to show your ability to sing the repeated phrases in this song with accurate dynamics. How well are you able to demonstrate varied dynamics while singing?

RESOURCES

Intermediate Mixed Rehearsal/Performance CD

CD 2:21 Voices

CD 2:22 Accompaniment Only

CD 3:23 Vocal Practice Track—Soprano

CD 4:22 Vocal Practice Track—Alto

CD 6:23 Vocal Practice Track—Baritone

National Standards

1. Singing, alone and with others, a varied repertoire of music. **(b)**
5. Reading and notating music. **(c)**
6. Listening to, analyzing, and describing music. **(a)**

LINKS TO LEARNING

Vocal

The Vocal section is designed to prepare students to:

- Understand articulation.
- Use proper articulation of quarter notes.

Have students:

- Read the definition of articulation and discuss who might use good articulation. *(singers, news anchors, public speakers)*
- Sing the example using good articulation.

Theory

The Theory section is designed to prepare students to:

- Understand 3/4 meter.
- Sing rhythms in 3/4 meter conducted in three and conducted in one.

Have students:

- Read the definition of 3/4 meter.
- Tap of clap the quarter note pulse.
- Speak the rhythms while tapping the quarter note pulse.
- Speak the rhythms while the director conducts in 3/4 meter, gradually increasing the tempo until the conductor moves to only one beat per measure.

Artistic Expression

The Artistic Expression section is designed to prepare students to understand and perform the dynamic marks placed in the music by the editor.

Have students:

- Locate all the dynamic marking in their choral score.
- Speak through the lyrics in rhythm using these dynamics.

LESSON PLAN

Suggested Teaching Sequence and Performance Tips

1. Introduce

Direct students to:

- Read and discuss the information found in the Getting Started section on student page 216.
- Sing the phrase shown in the Vocal section on page 217 to practice articulations.
- Practice the rhythm example shown in the Theory section on page 217 to get the feeling of 3/4 meter conducted in one.
- Read through the lyrics and discuss the ideas presented in text, the mood suggested by the lyrics, and appropriate places to breathe.

Sing Out This Maytime

(Der kühle Maien)

For SAB and Piano with Optional Flutes*

Edited with English Text by
PATRICK M. LIEBERGEN

JOHANN HERMANN SCHEIN
(1586–1630)

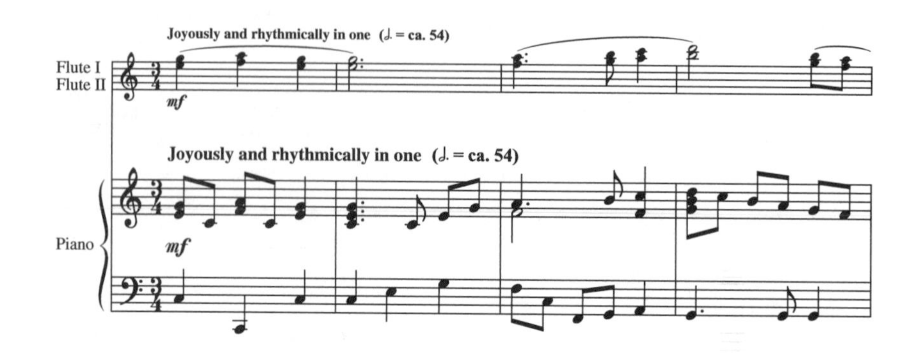

*** Flute parts may be found on pages 225 and 226**

TEACHER 2 TEACHER

Ideal for opening a spring concert, "Sing Out This Maytime" should be performed enthusiastically with a feeling of one beat per measure. Keep the rhythms energetic and the diction crisp. The harmonic progressions are basic, and, thereby, are useful for teaching young choirs to sing in three-part harmony.

- Review the lyrics to notice exact repetition of complete textual phrases. *(measures 5–16 are repeated in measures 17–28 and 59–70; measures 29–42 are repeated in measures 43–56)*

Progress Checkpoints

Observe students' progress in:

✓ Their ability to articulate quarter notes clearly.

✓ Their ability to read rhythms in 3/4 meter.

✓ Their ability to comprehend the ideas and images presented in the text.

✓ Their ability to identify repetition in the text.

2. Rehearse

Direct students to:

- Label the form of the piece. Section A begins at measure 5, Section B at measure 29, and the repetition of Section A at measure 59.
- Count the rhythms, noting that most of the time all parts sing the same rhythms. Give particular focus to the end of phrases where a half note enters on beat 2 in the measure.
- Sight-sing the vocal parts phrase by phrase, being particularly accurate with accidentals.
- Combine all parts to create three-part harmony.

- Add the lyrics, giving attention to breathing only where indicated by the punctuation in the text.
- Compare the end of Section A at measures 16 and 28 with the end of the return of Section A at measures 69–70.

Progress Checkpoints

Observe students' progress in:

✓ Listening for correct rhythms and pitches.

✓ Listening for correct intonation within all harmonies.

✓ Identifying the form of the piece.

EXTENSION

Composition

Compose a melody that models the ABA form and contrasting dynamics in "Sing Out This Maytime." Retain some of the melodic features of "Sing Out This Maytime." For example, begin the A section on *so* and end it on *do.* Compose the melody in 3/4 meter, using a suitable combination of rhythmic patterns. If time allows, find a suitable text to set. If not, choose singing syllables such as *fa la la* and focus on the creative process of writing a well-shaped melody. Add percussion accompaniment and perform for the class. Present each ABA form melody several times so that listeners can identify the formal design and the contrasting dynamics.

3. Refine

Direct students to:

- Learn the German text. A pronunciation guide can be found in the Teacher Resource Binder, Teaching Master 34. Speak until comfortable, and then sing.
- Apply the dynamic marks indicated in the score, singing an audible distinction between "mf" and "mp."
- Keep longer phrases energetic and alive by maintaining a steady airflow through longer note values, especially through syllables sustained through to the next syllable without a breath.

ENRICHMENT

May Day

The text of "Sing Out This Maytime" celebrates the beginning of May, which in colder climates is the month in which signs of spring are first visible. May Day celebrations have been traced back to ancient cultures in Egypt and India. When the Romans conquered Western Europe, they introduced an April celebration that honored their goddess of spring, Flora. Over time, Floralia merged with a Celtic spring festival celebrated on May 1. One of the strongest visual associations with May Day is of dancing around a decorative maypole while holding on to ribbons attached to the pole. May Day celebrations, though popular in Europe, were not imported to the American colonies, and, thereby, are not a traditional American holiday. Ask your students if anyone has celebrated May Day.

Progress Checkpoints

Observe students' progress in:

✓ Singing the German text with correct pronunciation.

✓ Performing the dynamic marks as indicated.

✓ Their ability to sing phrases breathing where indicated and sustaining where indicated.

ASSESSMENT

Informal Assessment

In this lesson, students showed the ability to:

- Count in 3/4 meter
- Sing dynamic marks indicated in the score.
- Identify the ABA design.

Student Self-Assessment

Have students evaluate their individual performances based on the following:

- Posture
- German Pronunciation
- Intonation
- Accurate Rhythms
- Correct Part-Singing

Have each student rate his/her performance of this song in the areas above on a scale of 1–5, 5 being the best.

Additional National Standards

The following National Standards are addressed through the Assessment, Extension, Enrichment and bottom-page activities:

4. Composing and arranging music within specific guidelines. **(a)**

5. Reading and notating music. **(d)**

6. Listening to, analyzing, and describing music. **(b)**

7. Evaluating music and music performances. **(a, b)**

9. Understanding music in relation to history and culture. **(b)**

Sing Out This Maytime

(Der kühle Maien)

FLUTE I

JOHANN HERMANN SCHEIN (1586–1630)
Edited by PATRICK M. LIEBERGEN

Individual and Group Performance Evaluation

To further measure growth of musical skills presented in this lesson, direct students to complete the Evaluation section on page 217.

- After the students have described the form of this piece, have them write the measure numbers that mark the beginning of each section. Have them exchange papers with a classmate and evaluate each other's ability to locate the form.
- Have students sing measures 59–70 on their own at home or in a practice room. They should evaluate their ability to sing in 3/4 meter.
- Have students sing measures 29–56 on their own at home or in a practice room. They should evaluate their ability to sing varied dynamics.

Music, Society and Culture

Have students perform additional songs representing diverse cultures, including American and Texas heritage. Go to **music.glencoe.com**, the Web site for Glencoe's choral music programs, for additional music selections students can perform.

Sing Out This Maytime

(Der kühle Maien)

FLUTE II

JOHANN HERMANN SCHEIN (1586–1630)
Edited by PATRICK M. LIEBERGEN

The Wells Fargo Wagon

Composer: Meredith Willson, arranged by Roger Emerson
Text: Meredith Willson
Voicing: SAB

VOCABULARY
diction
syncopation

Focus

- Demonstrate musical artistry through the use of proper diction.
- Read and perform syncopated rhythmic patterns.
- Perform music that represents the musical theater genre.

Getting Started

Have you ever waited eagerly for the mailman to arrive? Perhaps you were expecting a special card, letter or package. Although we now enjoy daily mail delivery, in the 1800s some places in America might have received mail only once a month. As people moved further west, the delivery wagons would bring not only the mail, but also the many items ordered from catalogs. The song "The Wells Fargo Wagon" describes the great excitement and anticipation of the delivery wagon coming through the area.

SPOTLIGHT

To learn more about musical theater, see page 203.

History and Culture

Wells Fargo and Company was founded in 1852 by Henry Wells and William G. Fargo. It provided express and banking between the East and California. At that time, it took fifteen days to travel by stagecoach from Nebraska to California!

"The Wells Fargo Wagon" is from the Broadway musical *The Music Man,* written by Meredith Willson in 1957. The show tells the humorous story about Professor Harold Hill, a traveling salesman and smooth-talking con artist. Hill convinces the citizens of River City, Iowa, that he can teach their children to play in a marching band if they purchase his instruments. In addition to "The Wells Fargo Wagon," *The Music Man* also features the song "Seventy-Six Trombones," among others.

RESOURCES

Intermediate Sight-Singing

Sight-Singing in G Major, pages 82–85, 89–90

Sight-Singing in A♭ Major, pages 176–177

Reading Rhythms in 4/4 Meter, pages 2–6

Reading Eighth Notes/Rests, pages 26–27

Teacher Resource Binder

Teaching Master 24, *Developing Stage Presence*

Teaching Master 35, *The Performance Context*

Evaluation Master 6, *Diction Checkup*

Skill Builder 24, *Rhythm Challenge Using Syncopation*

Vocal Development 9, *Diction*

For additional resources, see TRB Table of Contents.

Wells Fargo Wagon

OVERVIEW

Composer: Meredith Willson, arranged by Roger Emerson
Text: Meredith Willson
Voicing: SAB
Key: G major/A♭ major
Meter: 4/4
Form: ABA'ABA' Coda
Style: Broadway
Accompaniment: Piano
Programming: Broadway Concert

Vocal Ranges:

OBJECTIVES

After completing this lesson, students will be able to:

- Demonstrate fundamental skills while performing.
- Perform independently with accurate rhythm including syncopated patterns.
- Read music notation.
- Perform a varied repertoire of music representing styles from diverse genres, including musical theater.

VOCABULARY

Have students review vocabulary in student lesson. Introduce terms found in the music. A complete glossary of terms is found on page 240 of the student book.

LINKS TO LEARNING

Vocal

The Vocal section is designed to prepare students to:

- Understand diction.
- Speak the words to "The Wells Fargo Wagon" with clear diction.

Have students:

- Read the definition of diction.
- Chant the text in measures 19–29, focusing on clear diction.

Theory

The Theory section is designed to prepare students to:

- Understand syncopation.
- Perform the syncopated rhythm patterns found in "The Wells Fargo Wagon."

Have students:

- Tap or clap the quarter note pulse in 4/4 meter.
- Speak the rhythms while tapping the quarter note pulse, accenting the syncopated rhythms.
- Speak the rhythms while the director conduct a 4/4 pattern, while feeling the quarter note pulse inside.

Artistic Expression

The Artistic Expression section is designed to prepare students to relate the setting of this song to their performance.

Have students:

- Discuss the synopsis of *The Music Man* and list the characters in the show and their descriptions.
- Discuss where in the show this song occurs and what purpose it serves.

Links to Learning

◆ Vocal

Clear **diction** *(the way a singer pronounces the words while singing)* is needed to convey the many words found in "The Wells Fargo Wagon." Chant the words to the text from measures 19–29. Begin slowly and then gradually increase the tempo. Exaggerate the beginning and ending consonants of every word.

◆ Theory

Read and perform the following rhythmic patterns found in "The Wells Fargo Wagon." The rest at the beginning of the measure creates *a shift of the accent from the strong portion of the beat to the weak portion of the beat.* This is called **syncopation.**

◆ Artistic Expression

Find and read a synopsis of *The Music Man*. List the characters and write a short description for each. Where in the story do they sing "The Wells Fargo Wagon"? Discuss the plot action before and after the song.

Evaluation

Demonstrate how well you have learned the skills and concepts featured in the lesson "The Wells Fargo Wagon" by completing the following:

- With a partner, chant the words of the song one section at a time. Coach each other until you are able to pronounce the words with clear diction.
- Clap the rhythms of the Theory section above to show your understanding of syncopation. Rate your ability to clap syncopated rhythms correctly based on a scale of 1 to 5, with 5 being the best.

RESOURCES

Intermediate Tenor/Bass Rehearsal/Performance CD

- **CD 2:23** Voices
- **CD 2:24** Accompaniment Only
- **CD 3:24** Vocal Practice Track—Soprano
- **CD 4:23** Vocal Practice Track—Alto
- **CD 6:24** Vocal Practice Track—Baritone

National Standards

1. Singing, alone and with others, a varied repertoire of music. **(a, b, c, d)**
5. Reading and notating music. **(a)**

From Meredith Willson's THE MUSIC MAN

The Wells Fargo Wagon

For SAB and Piano

Arranged by
ROGER EMERSON

Words and Music by
MEREDITH WILLSON

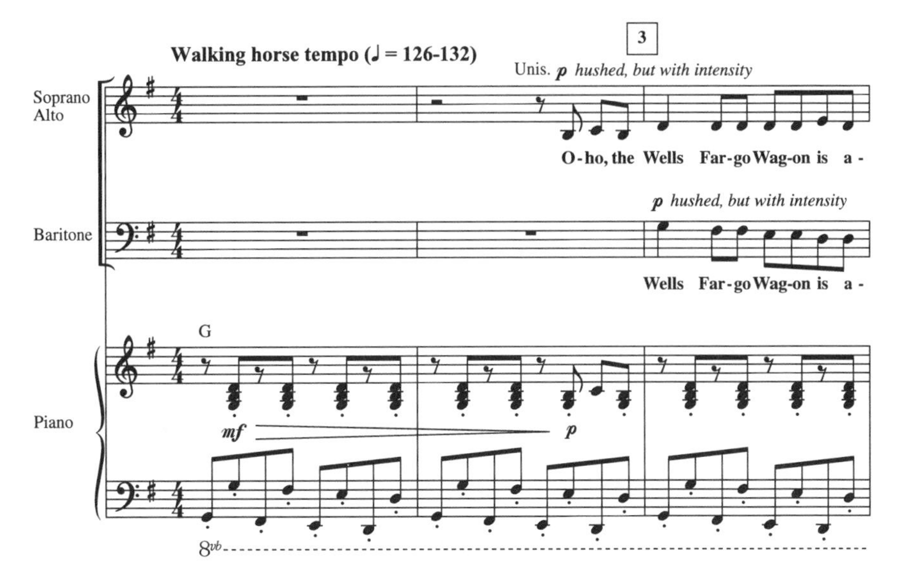

LESSON PLAN

Suggested Teaching Sequence and Performance Tips

1. Introduce

Direct students to:

- Read and discuss the information found in the Getting Started section on student page 227.
- Practice the rhythm patterns in the Theory section on page 228.
- Locate these rhythm patterns in their choral score.
- Discriminate between syncopated and nonsyncopated passages.

TEACHER 2 TEACHER

Have fun with this Broadway number from *The Music Man,* with its upbeat rhythms and clever text. It might be fun to program several numbers from this show, or fill in a section of your concert with songs from the Broadway stage.

Progress Checkpoints:

Observe students' progress in:

✓ Singing with clear diction.

✓ Performing syncopated rhythms in 4/4 meter.

✓ Locating syncopated rhythms in their choral scores.

ENRICHMENT

Performance of *The Music Man*

Locate a performance of *The Music Man* and take the choir on a field trip to see the performance. If that is not possible, encourage the students to see it on their own and award bonus points if they turn in the program with an evaluation and summary of the performance. If there is no performance in your area, show the videotape or DVD of *The Music Man* in your classroom. If time does not permit this, show only the portion showing the cast singing "The Wells Fargo Wagon." You could also encourage students to rent the video or DVD on their own to understand the entire story behind this energetic piece.

2. Rehearse

Direct students to:

- Chant the text in measures 3–10, while tapping, clapping or stepping the quarter note pulse. Emphasize syncopated rhythms.
- Continue chanting the text with clear diction through measure 29.
- Sight-sing their parts slowly in measures 3–29, gradually increasing the tempo as rhythms and pitches become secure. Make sure the Baritone is solid in their rhythms that differ from the melody.
- Sing parts separately at measures 16–18, 24–29.
- Repeat this procedure in the new key in measures 31–56. Chant text first and then sight-sing slowly at first, gradually increasing tempo.

- Sing part separately where voice parts divide.
- Chant the text (without the descant for now) in measures 59–68.
- Sight-sing their parts from measures 59–68. Work individual notes if necessary.

Progress Checkpoints

Observe students' progress in:

✓ Chanting and singing the text with clear diction.

✓ Sight-singing their parts with crisp, syncopated rhythms.

✓ Singing the pitches with accuracy.

3. Refine

Direct students to:

- Add the descant part in measures 59–63 with a small group of female voices.
- Review any difficult rhythms or pitches.
- Add dynamics throughout as marked in the score.
- Sing the entire piece while stepping the quarters in a "walking-horse tempo."
- Perform the entire piece while stepping the eighths in an "easy-jogging" tempo. For this, students can actually jog or if the proper room doesn't exist for this, shuffle their feet.

MUSIC, SOCIETY AND CULTURE

Have students perform additional songs representing diverse cultures, including American and Texas heritage. Go to **music.glencoe.com**, the Web site for Glencoe's choral music programs, for additional music selections students can perform.

- Divide the choir and try doing both simultaneously.
- Get into the character of the piece and sing as if they were on the Broadway stage.

Progress Checkpoints

Observe students' progress in:

✓ Solidifying all pitches and rhythms.

✓ Singing with the correct dynamics.

✓ Adding movement to enhance the rhythmic vitality of the piece.

✓ Portraying the character of the song.

ASSESSMENT

Informal Assessment

In this lesson, the students showed the ability to:

- Sing with clear diction in English.
- Perform syncopated rhythms in 4/4 meter.
- Add movement while continuing their part independently.
- Perform music from the Broadway stage expressively.

Student Self-Assessment

Have students evaluate their individual performances based on the following:

- Posture
- Clear Diction
- Tall Vowels
- Expressive Singing
- Accurate Rhythms

Have each student rate his/her performance of this song in the areas above on a scale of 1–5, 5 being the best.

CAREERS IN MUSIC

Music as Avocation

One school activity that helps develop students' stage presence is participation in musical theater. If your school periodically stages plays or musicals (or if there is a community theater that accepts volunteers), this might be an avocation of interest to some students. Explain that a role in the musical theater or a play can be varied. It can be as simple as being a member of the background chorus or "crowd scene" to playing the lead role and learning numerous lines and solo numbers. Have students compare and contract this avocational opportunity with others they might have already pursued.

Individual and Group Performance Evaluation

To further measure growth of musical skills presented in this lesson, direct students to complete the Evaluation section on page 228.

- Have the students pair up and chant the text of this song a section at a time. The students should coach each other on using crisp, clear diction.
- Have the students clap the rhythms of the Theory section on their own at home or in a practice room. They should rate their ability to perform syncopated rhythms on a scale of 1 to 5, with 5 being the best.

Additional National Standards

The following National Standards are addressed through the Assessment, Extension, Enrichment and bottom-page activities:

4. Composing and arranging music within specific guidelines. **(a)**

5. Reading and notating music. **(d)**

6. Listening to, analyzing, and describing music. **(c)**

7. Evaluating music and musical performance. **(b)**

8. Understanding relationships between music, the other arts, and disciplines outside the arts. **(b)**

EXTENSION

Composing Syncopation

Have students compose a four-measure pattern in 4/4 meter that incorporates syncopated patterns like those used in "The Wells Fargo Wagon." Start at the end of the row and have each student perform his/her pattern one after another keeping a steady beat. Evaluate each pattern. Did each student use syncopation in his/her pattern?

Glossary

CHORAL MUSIC TERMS

2/2 meter A time signature in which there are two beats per measure and the half note receives the beat.

2/4 meter A time signature in which there are two beats per measure and the quarter note receives the beat.

3/2 meter A time signature in which there are three beats per measure and the half note receives the beat.

3/4 meter A time signature in which there are three beats per measure and the quarter note receives the beat.

3/8 meter A time signature in which there is one group of three eighth notes per measure and the dotted quarter note receives the beat. When the tempo is very slow, this meter can be counted as having three beats per measure, with the eighth note receiving the beat.

4/4 meter A time signature in which there are four beats per measure and the quarter note receives the beat.

5/8 meter A time signature in which there are five beats per measure and the eighth note receives the beat.

6/4 meter A time signature in which there are two groups of three quarter notes per measure and the dotted half note receives the beat. When the tempo is very slow, this meter can be counted as having six beats per measure, with the quarter note receiving the beat.

6/8 meter A time signature in which there are two groups of three eighth notes per measure and the dotted quarter note receives the beat. When the tempo is very slow, this meter can be counted as having six beats per measure, with the eighth note receiving the beat.

9/8 meter A time signature in which there are three groups of three eighth notes per measure and the dotted quarter note receives the beat. When the tempo is very slow, this meter can be counted as having nine beats per measure, with the eighth note receiving the beat.

12/8 meter A time signature in which there are four groups of three eighth notes per measure and the dotted quarter note receives the beat.

A

a cappella *(ah-kah-PEH-lah)* [It.] A style of singing without instrumental accompaniment.

a tempo *(ah TEM-poh)* [It.] A tempo marking which indicates to return to the original tempo of a piece or section of music.

ABA form A form in which an opening section (A) is followed by a contrasting section (B), which leads to the repetition of the opening section (A).

accelerando *(accel.) (ah-chel-leh-RAHN-doh)* [It.] A tempo marking that indicates to gradually get faster.

accent A symbol placed above or below a given note to indicate that the note should receive extra emphasis or stress. (>)

accidental Any sharp, flat or natural that is not included in the key signature of a piece of music.

adagio *(ah-DAH-jee-oh)* [It.] Slow tempo, but not as slow as *largo*.

ad libitum *(ad. lib.)* [Lt.] An indication that the performer may vary the tempo or add or delete a vocal or instrumental part.

Aeolian scale *(ay-OH-lee-an)* [Gk.] A modal scale that starts and ends on *la*. It is made up of the same arrangement of whole and half steps as a natural minor scale.

al fine *(ahl FEE-neh)* [It.] To the end.

aleatory music *(AY-lee-uh-toh-ree)* A type of music in which certain aspects are performed randomly. Also known as chance music.

alla breve Indicates cut time; a duple meter in which there are two beats per measure, and half note receives the beat. *See* cut time.

allargando (*allarg.*) *(ahl-ahr-GAHN-doh)* [It.] To broaden, become slower.

allegro *(ah-LEH-groh)* [It.] Brisk tempo; faster than *moderato*, slower than *vivace.*

allegro non troppo *(ah-LEH-groh nohn TROH-poh)* [It.] A tempo marking that indicates not too fast. Not as fast as *allegro.*

altered pitch Another name for an accidental.

alto *(AL-toh)* The lowest-sounding female voice.

andante *(ahn-DAHN- teh)* [It.] Moderately slow; a walking tempo.

andante con moto *(ahn-DAHN- teh kohn MOH-toh)* [It.] A slightly faster tempo, "with motion."

animato Quickly, lively; "animated."

anthem A choral composition in English using a sacred text.

arpeggio *(ahr-PEH-jee-oh)* [It.] A chord in which the pitches are sounded successively, usually from lowest to highest; in broken style.

arrangement A piece of music in which a composer takes an existing melody and adds extra features or changes the melody in some way.

arranger A composer who takes an original or existing melody and adds extra features or changes the melody in some way.

art song A musical setting of a poem.

articulation The amount of separation or connection between notes.

articulators The lips, teeth, tongue and other parts of the mouth and throat that are used to produce vocal sound.

avocational Not related to a job or career.

B

barbershop A style of *a cappella* singing in which three parts harmonize with the melody. The lead sings the melody while the tenor harmonizes above and the baritone and bass harmonize below.

barcarole A Venetian boat song.

baritone The male voice between tenor and bass.

barline A vertical line placed on the musical staff that groups notes and rests together.

Baroque period *(bah-ROHK)* [Fr.] The historical period in Western civilization from 1600 to 1750.

bass The lowest-sounding male voice.

bass clef A clef that generally indicates notes that sound lower than middle C.

basso continuo *(BAH-soh cun-TIN-you-oh)* [It.] A continually moving bass line, common in music from the Baroque period.

beat The steady pulse of music.

bebop style Popular in jazz, music that features notes that are light, lively and played quickly. Often the melodic lines are complex and follow unpredictable patterns.

blues scale An altered major scale that uses flatted or lowered third, fifth and seventh notes: *ma* (lowered from *mi*), *se* (lowered from *sol*) and *te* (lowered from *ti*).

blues style An original African American art form that developed in the early twentieth century in the Mississippi Delta region of the South. The lyrics often express feelings of frustration, hardship or longing. It often contains elements such as call and response, the blues scale and swing.

body percussion The use of one's body to make a percussive sound, such as clapping, snapping or stepping.

breath mark A symbol in vocal music used to indicate where a singer should take a breath. (’)

breath support A constant airflow necessary to produce sound for singing.

C

cadence A melodic or harmonic structure that marks the end of a phrase or the completion of a song.

call and response A derivative of the field hollers used by slaves as they worked. A leader or group sings a phrase (call) followed by a response of the same phrase by another group.

calypso A style of music that originated in the West Indies and which features syncopated rhythms and comical lyrics.

canon A musical form in which one part sings a melody, and the other parts sing the same melody, but enter at different times. Canons are sometimes called rounds.

cantabile *(con-TAH-bee-leh)* [It.] In a lyrical, singing style.

cantata *(con-TAH-tah)* [It.] A large-scale musical piece made up of several movements for singers and instrumentalists. Johann Sebastian Bach was a prominent composer of cantatas.

cantor *(CAN-tor)* A person who sings and/or teaches music in a temple or synagogue.

canzona [It.] A rhythmic instrumental composition that is light and fast-moving.

chamber music Music performed by a small instrumental ensemble, generally with one instrument per part. The string quartet is a popular form of chamber music, consisting of two violins, a viola and a cello. Chamber music was popular during the Classical period.

chantey *See* sea chantey.

chanteyman A soloist who improvised and led the singing of sea chanteys.

chest voice The lower part of the singer's vocal range.

chorale *(kuh-RAL)* [Gr.] Congregational song or hymn of the German Protestant Church.

chord The combination of three or more notes played or sung together at the same time.

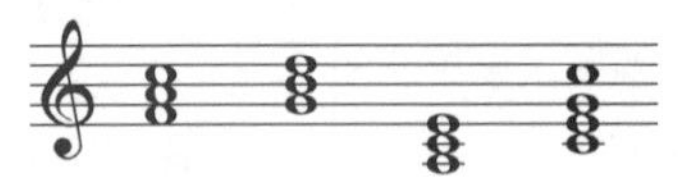

chromatic scale *(kroh-MAT-tick)* [Gk.] A scale that consists of all half steps and uses all twelve pitches in an octave.

Classical period The historical period in Western civilization from 1750 to 1820.

clef The symbol at the beginning of a staff that indicates which lines and spaces represent which notes.

coda A special ending to a song. A concluding section of a composition. (𝄌)

common time Another name for 4/4 meter. Also known as common meter. (𝄴)

composer A person who takes a musical thought and writes it out in musical notation to share it with others.

compound meter Any meter in which the dotted quarter note receives the beat, and the division of the beat is based on three eighth notes. 6/8, 9/8 and 12/8 are examples of compound meter.

con moto *(kohn MOH-toh)* [It.] With motion.

concert etiquette A term used to describe what is appropriate behavior in formal or informal musical performances.

concerto *(cun-CHAIR-toh)* [Fr., It.] A composition for a solo instrument and orchestra.

concerto grosso *(cun-CHAIR-toh GROH-soh)* [Fr., It.] A multimovement Baroque piece for a group of soloists and an orchestra.

conductor A person who uses hand and arm gestures to interpret the expressive elements of music for singers and instrumentalists.

conductus A thirteenth-century song for two, three or four voices.

consonance Harmonies in chords or music that are pleasing to the ear.

Contemporary period The historical period from 1900 to the present.

countermelody A separate melodic line that supports and/or contrasts the melody of a piece of music.

counterpoint The combination of two or more melodic lines. The parts move independently while harmony is created. Johann Sebastian Bach is considered by many to be one of the greatest composers of contrapuntal music.

contrary motion A technique in which two melodic lines move in opposite directions.

crescendo *(creh-SHEN-doh)* [It.] A dynamic marking that indicates to gradually sing or play louder.

cut time Another name for 2/2 meter. (¢)

D

da capo *(D.C.)* *(dah KAH-poh)* [It.] Go back to the beginning and repeat; *see also* dal segno *and* al fine.

dal segno *(D.S.)* *(dahl SAYN-yah)* [It.] Go back to the sign and repeat.

D. C. al Fine *(FEE-nay)* [It.] A term that indicates to go back to the beginning and repeat. The term *al fine* indicates to sing to the end, or *fine*.

decrescendo *(DAY-creh-shen-doh)* [It.] A dynamic marking that indicates to gradually sing or play softer.

descant A special part in a piece of music that is usually sung higher than the melody or other parts of the song.

diatonic scale *(die-uh-TAH-nick)* A scale that uses no altered pitches or accidentals. Both the major scale and the natural minor scale are examples of a diatonic scale.

diction The pronunciation of words while singing.

diminished chord A minor chord in which the top note is lowered one half step from *mi* to *me*.

diminuendo *(dim.)* *(duh-min-yoo-WEN-doh)* [It.] Gradually getting softer; *see also* decrescendo.

diphthong A combination of two vowel sounds.

dissonance A combination of pitches or tones that clash.

dolce *(DOHL-chay)* [It.] Sweetly.

dominant chord A chord built on the fifth note of a scale. In a major scale, this chord uses the notes *sol*, *ti* and *re*, and it may be called the **V** ("five") chord, since it is based on the fifth note of the major scale, or *sol*. In a minor scale, this chord uses the notes *mi*, *sol* and *ti* (or *mi*, *si* and *ti*), and it may be called the **v** or **V** ("five") chord, since it is based on the fifth note of the minor scale, or *mi*.

Dorian scale *(DOOR-ee-an)* [Gk.] A modal scale that starts and ends on *re*.

dot A symbol that increases the length of a given note by half its value. It is placed to the right of the note.

dotted half note A note that represents three beats of sound when the quarter note receives the beat.

double barline A set of two barlines that indicate the end of a piece or section of music.

D. S. al coda *(dahl SAYN-yoh ahl KOH-dah)* [It.] Repeat from the symbol (𝄋) and skip to the coda when you see the sign. (𝄌)

duet A group of two singers or instrumentalists.

dynamics Symbols in music that indicate how loud or soft to sing or play.

E

eighth note A note that represents one half beat of sound when the quarter note receives the beat. Two eighth notes equal one beat of sound when the quarter note receives the beat.

eighth rest A rest that represents one half beat of silence when the quarter note receives the beat. Two eighth rests equal one beat of silence when the quarter note receives the beat.

expressive singing To sing with feeling.

F

falsetto [It.] The register in the male voice that extends far above the natural voice. The light upper range.

fermata *(fur-MAH-tah)* [It.] A symbol that indicates to hold a note or rest for longer than its given value. (𝄐)

fine *(fee-NAY)* [It.] A term used to indicate the end of a piece of music.

flat A symbol that lowers the pitch of a given note by one half step.(♭)

folk music Music that passed down from generation to generation through oral tradition. Traditional music that reflects a place, event or a national feeling.

folk song A song passed down from generation to generation through oral tradition. A song that reflects a place, event or a national feeling.

form The structure or design of a musical composition.

forte *(FOR-tay)* [It.] A dynamic that indicates to sing or play loud. (*f*)

fortissimo *(for-TEE-see-moh)* [It.] A dynamic that indicates to sing or play very loud. (*ff*)

fugue *(FYOOG)* A musical form in which the same melody is performed by different instruments or voices entering at different times, thus adding layers of sound.

fusion Music that is developed by the act of combining various types and cultural influences of music into a new style.

G

gospel music Religious music that originated in the African American churches of the South. This music can be characterized by improvisation, syncopation and repetition.

grand staff A staff that is created when two staves are joined together.

grandioso [It.] Stately, majestic.

grave *(GRAH-veh)* [It.] Slow, solemn.

grazioso *(grah-tsee-OH-soh)* [It.] Graceful.

Gregorian chant A single, unaccompanied melodic line sung by male voices. Featuring a sacred text and used in the church, this style of music was developed in the medieval period.

H

half note A note that represents two beats of sound when the quarter note receives the beat. 𝅗𝅥

half rest A rest that represents two beats of silence when the quarter note receives the beat. ▬

half step The smallest distance (interval) between two notes on a keyboard; the chromatic scale is composed entirely of half steps.

harmonic minor scale A minor scale that uses a raised seventh note, *si* (raised from *sol*).

harmonics Small whistle-like tones, or overtones, that are sometimes produced over a sustained pitch.

harmony A musical sound that is formed when two or more different pitches are played or sung at the same time.

head voice The higher part of the singer's vocal range.

homophonic *(hah-muh-FAH-nik)* [Gk.] A texture where all parts sing similar rhythm in unison or harmony.

homophony *(haw-MAW-faw-nee)* [Gk.] A type of music in which there are two or more parts with similar or identical rhythms being sung or played at the same time. Also, music in which melodic interest is concentrated in one voice part and may have subordinate accompaniment.

hushed A style marking indicating a soft, whispered tone.

I

imitation The act of one part copying what another part has already played or sung.

improvisation The art of singing or playing music, making it up as you go, or composing and performing a melody at the same time.

International Phonetic Alphabet (IPA) A phonetic alphabet that provides a notational standard for all languages. Developed in Paris, France, in 1886.

interval The distance between two notes.

intonation The accuracy of pitch, in-tune singing.

Ionian scale *(eye-OWN-ee-an)* [Gk.] A modal scale that starts and ends on *do*. It is made up of the same arrangement of whole and half steps as a major scale.

J

jazz An original American style of music that features swing rhythms, syncopation and improvisation.

jongleur [Fr.] An entertainer who traveled from town to town during medieval times, often telling stories and singing songs.

K

key Determined by a song's or scale's home tone, or keynote.

key signature A symbol or set of symbols that determines the key of a piece of music.

L

ledger lines Short lines that appear above, between treble and bass clefs, or below the bass clef, used to expand the notation.

legato *(leh-GAH-toh)* [It.] A connected and sustained style of singing and playing.

lento *(LEN-toh)* [It.] Slow; a little faster than *largo*, a little slower than *adagio*.

lied *(leet)* [Ger.] A song in the German language, generally with a secular text.

liturgical text A text that has been written for the purpose of worship in a church setting.

lute An early form of the guitar.

Lydian scale *(LIH-dee-an)* [Gk.] A modal scale that starts and ends on *fa*.

lyrics The words of a song.

M

madrigal A poem that has been set to music in the language of the composer. Featuring several imitative parts, it usually has a secular text and is generally sung *a cappella*.

maestoso *(mah-eh-STOH-soh)* [It.] Perform majestically.

major chord A chord that can be based on the *do*, *mi*, and *sol* of a major scale.

major scale A scale that has *do* as its home tone, or keynote. It is made up of a specific arrangement of whole steps and half steps in the following order: W + W + H + W + W + W + H.

major tonality A song that is based on a major scale with *do* as its keynote, or home tone.

mangulina A traditional dance from the Dominican Republic.

marcato *(mar-CAH-toh)* [It.] A stressed and accented style of singing and playing.

Mass A religious service of prayers and ceremonies originating in the Roman Catholic Church consisting of spoken and sung sections. It consists of several sections divided into two groups: proper (text changes for every day) and ordinary (text stays the same in every mass). Between the years 1400 and 1600, the Mass assumed its present form consisting of the Kyrie, Gloria, Credo, Sanctus and Agnus Dei. It may include chants, hymns and psalms as well. The Mass also developed into large musical works for chorus, soloists and even orchestra.

measure The space between two barlines.

medieval period The historical period in Western civilization also known as the Middle Ages (400–1430).

medley A collection of songs musically linked together.

melisma *(muh-LIZ-mah)* [Gk.] A group of notes sung to a single syllable or word.

melismatic singing *(muh-liz-MAT-ik)* [Gk.] A style of text setting in which one syllable is sung over many notes.

melodic contour The overall shape of the melody.

melodic minor scale A minor scale that uses raised sixth and seventh notes: *fi* (raised from *fa*) and *si* (raised from *sol*). Often, these notes are raised in ascending patterns, but not in descending patterns.

melody A logical succession of musical tones.

meter A way of organizing rhythm.

meter signature *See* time signature.

metronome marking A sign that appears over the top line of the staff at the beginning of a piece or section of music that indicates the tempo. It shows the kind of note that will receive the beat and the number of beats per minute as measured by a metronome.

mezzo forte *(MEH-tsoh FOR tay)* [It.] A dynamic that indicates to sing or play medium loud. (***mf***)

mezzo piano *(MEH-tsoh pee-AH-noh)* [It.] A dynamic that indicates to sing or play medium soft. (***mp***)

mezzo voce *(MEH-tsoh VOH-cheh)* [It.] With half voice; reduced volume and tone.

minor chord A chord that can be based on the *la, do,* and *mi* of a minor scale.

minor scale A scale that has *la* as its home tone, or keynote. It is made up of a specific arrangement of whole steps and half steps in the following order: W + H +W + W + H + W + W.

minor tonality A song that is based on a minor scale with *la* as its keynote, or home tone.

mixed meter A technique in which the time signature or meter changes frequently within a piece of music.

Mixolydian scale *(mix-oh-LIH-dee-an)* [Gr.] A modal scale that starts and ends on *sol*.

modal scale A scale based on a mode. Like major and minor scales, each modal scale is made up of a specific arrangement of whole steps and half steps, with the half steps occurring between *mi* and *fa*, and *ti* and *do*.

mode An early system of pitch organization that was used before major and minor scales and keys were developed.

modulation A change in the key or tonal center of a piece of music within the same song.

molto [It.] Very or much; for example, *molto rit.* means "much slower."

motet *(moh-teht)* Originating as a medieval and Renaissance polyphonic song, this choral form of composition became an unaccompanied work, often in contrapuntal style. Also, a short, sacred choral piece with a Latin text that is used in religious services but is not a part of the regular Mass.

motive A shortened expression, sometimes contained within a phrase.

music critic A writer who gives an evaluation of a musical performance.

music notation Any means of writing down music, including the use of notes, rests and symbols.

musical A play or film whose action and dialogue are combined with singing and dancing.

musical theater An art form that combines acting, singing, and dancing to tell a story. It often includes staging, costumes, lighting and scenery.

mysterioso [It.] Perform in a mysterious or haunting way; to create a haunting mood.

N

narrative song A song that tells a story.

national anthem A patriotic song adopted by nations through tradition or decree.

nationalism Patriotism; pride of country. This feeling influenced many Romantic composers such as Wagner, Tchaikovsky, Dvorák, Chopin and Brahms.

natural A symbol that cancels a previous sharp or flat, or a sharp or flat in a key signature. (♮)

natural minor scale A minor scale that uses no altered pitches or accidentals.

no breath mark A direction not to take a breath at a specific place in the composition. (N.B.)

non troppo *(nahn TROH-poh)* [It.] Not too much; for example, *allegro non troppo*, "not too fast."

notation Written notes, symbols and directions used to represent music within a composition.

O

octave An interval of two pitches that are eight notes apart on a staff.

ode A poem written in honor of a special person or occasion. These poems were generally dedicated to a member of a royal family. In music, an ode usually includes several sections for choir, soloists and orchestra.

opera A combination of singing, instrumental music, dancing and drama that tells a story.

optional divisi (*opt.div.*) Indicating a split in the music into optional harmony, shown by a smaller cued note.

oral tradition Music that is learned through rote or by ear and is interpreted by its performer(s).

oratorio *(or-uh-TOR-ee-oh)* [It.] A dramatic work for solo voices, chorus and orchestra presented without theatrical action. Usually, oratorios are based on a literary or religious theme.

ostinato *(ahs-tuh-NAH-toh)* [It.] A rhythmic or melodic passage that is repeated continuosly.

overture A piece for orchestra that serves as an introduction to an opera or other dramatic work.

P

palate The roof of the mouth; the hard palate is at the front, the soft palate is at the back.

parallel motion A technique in which two or more melodic lines move in the same direction.

parallel sixths A group of intervals that are a sixth apart and which move at the same time and in the same direction.

parallel thirds A group of intervals that are a third apart and which move at the same time and in the same direction.

part-singing Two or more parts singing an independent melodic line at the same time.

patsch The act of slapping one's hands on one's thighs.

pentatonic scale A five-tone scale using the pitches *do, re, mi, sol* and *la.*

perfect fifth An interval of two pitches that are five notes apart on a staff.

perfect fourth An interval of two pitches that are four notes apart on a staff.

phrase A musical idea with a beginning and an end.

Phrygian scale *(FRIH-gee-an)* [Gk.] A modal scale that starts and ends on *mi.*

pianissimo *(pee-ah-NEE-see-moh)* [It.] A dynamic that indicates to sing or play very soft. (*pp*)

piano *(pee-AH-noh)* [It.] A dynamic that indicates to sing or play soft. (*p*)

pitch Sound, the result of vibration; the highness or lowness of a tone, determined by the number of vibrations per second.

pitch matching In a choral ensemble, the ability to sing the same notes as those around you.

piu *(pew)* [It.] More; for example, *piu forte* means "more loudly."

poco *(POH-koh)* [It.] Little; for example *poco dim.* means "a little softer."

poco a poco *(POH-koh ah POH-koh)* [It.] Little by little; for example, *poco a poco cresc.* means "little by little increase in volume."

polyphony *(pah-LIH-fun-nee)* [Gk.] Literally, "many sounding." A type of music in which there are two or more different melodic lines being sung or played at the same time. Polyphony was refined during the Renaissance, and this period is sometimes called "golden age of polyphony."

polyrhythms A technique in which several different rhythms are performed at the same time.

presto *(PREH-stoh)* [It.] Very fast.

program music A descriptive style of music composed to relate or illustrate a specific incident, situation or drama; the form of the piece is often dictated or influenced by the nonmusical program. This style commonly occurs in music composed during the Romantic period.

Q

quarter note A note that represents one beat of sound when the quarter note receives the beat. ♩

quarter rest A rest that represents one beat of silence when the quarter note receives the beat. 𝄽

quartet A group of four singers or instrumentalists.

R

rallentando (*rall.*) *(rahl-en-TAHN-doh)* [It.] Meaning to "perform more and more slowly." *See also* ritard.

refrain A repeated section at the end of each phrase or verse in a song. Also known as a chorus.

register, vocal A term used for different parts of the singer's range, such as head register, or head voice (high notes); and chest register, or chest voice (low notes).

relative minor scale A minor scale that shares the same key signature as its corresponding major scale. Both scales share the same half steps, between *mi* and *fa,* and *ti* and *do.*

Renaissance period The historical period in Western civilization from 1430 to 1600.

repeat sign A symbol that indicates that a section of music should be repeated. (:‖)

repetition The restatement of a musical idea; repeated pitches; repeated "A" section in ABA form.

requiem *(REK-wee-ehm)* [Lt.] Literally, "rest." A mass written and performed to honor the dead and comfort the living.

resonance Reinforcement and intensification of sound by vibration.

rest A symbol used in music notation to indicate silence.

rhythm The combination of long and short notes and rests in music. These may move with the beat, faster than the beat or slower than the beat.

ritard *(rit.) (ree-TAHRD)* [It.] A tempo marking that indicates to gradually get slower.

Romantic period The historical period in Western civilization from 1820 to 1900.

rondo form A form in which a repeated section is separated by several contrasting sections.

rote The act of learning a song by hearing it over and over again.

round *See* canon.

rubato *(roo-BAH-toh)* [It.] The freedom to slow down and/or speed up the tempo without changing the overall pulse of a piece of music.

S

sacred music Music associated with religious services or themes.

scale A group of pitches that are sung or played in succession and are based on a particular home tone, or keynote.

scat singing An improvisational style of singing that uses nonsense syllables instead of words. It was made popular by jazz trumpeter Louis Armstrong.

sea chantey A song sung by sailors, usually in rhythm with their work.

secular music Music not associated with religious services or themes.

sempre *(SEHM-preh)* [It.] Always, continually.

sempre accelerando *(sempre accel.) (SEHM-preh ahk-chel)* [It.] A term that indicates to gradually increase the tempo of a piece or section of music.

sequence A successive musical pattern that begins on a higher or lower pitch each time it is repeated.

serenata [It.] A large-scale musical work written in honor of a special occasion. Generally performed in the evening or outside, it is often based on a mythological theme.

sforzando *(sfohr-TSAHN-doh)* [It.] A sudden strong accent on a note or chord. (*sfz*)

sharp A symbol that raises the pitch of a given note one half step. (♯)

shekere An African shaker consisting of a hollow gourd surrounded by beads.

sight-sing Reading and singing music at first sight.

simile (*sim.*) *(SIM-ee-leh)* [It.] To continue the same way.

simple meter Any meter in which the quarter note receives the beat, and the division of the beat is based on two eighth notes. 2/4, 3/4 and 4/4 are examples of simple meter.

singing posture The way one sits or stands while singing.

sixteenth note A note that represents one quarter beat of sound when the quarter note receives the beat. Four sixteenth notes equal one beat of sound when the quarter note receives the beat.

sixteenth rest A rest that represents one quarter beat of silence when the quarter note receives the beat. Four sixteenth rests equal one beat of silence when the quarter note receives the beat.

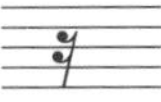

skip-wise motion The movement from a given note to another note that is two or more notes above or below it on the staff.

slur A curved line placed over or under a group of notes to indicate that they are to be performed without a break.

solfège syllables Pitch names using *do, re, mi, fa, sol, la, ti, do*, etc.

solo One person singing or playing an instrument alone.

sonata-allegro form A large ABA form consisting of three sections: exposition, development and recapitulation. This form was made popular during the Classical period.

soprano The highest-sounding female voice.

sostenuto *(SAHS-tuh-noot-oh)* [It.] The sustaining of a tone or the slackening of tempo.

sotto voce In a quiet, subdued manner; "under" the voice.

spirito *(SPEE-ree-toh)* [It.] Spirited; for example, *con spirito* ("with spirit").

spiritual Songs that were first sung by African American slaves, usually based on biblical themes or stories.

staccato *(stah-KAH-toh)* [It.] A short and detached style of singing or playing.

staff A series of five horizontal lines and four spaces on which notes are written. A staff is like a ladder. Notes placed higher on the staff sound higher than notes placed lower on the staff.

5 4 3 2 1 / 1 2 3 4

stage presence A performer's overall appearance on stage, including enthusiasm, facial expression and posture.

staggered breathing In ensemble singing, the practice of planning breaths so that no two singers take a breath at the same time, thus creating the overall effect of continuous singing.

staggered entrances A technique in which different parts and voices enter at different times.

stanza A section in a song in which the words change on each repeat. Also known as a verse.

step-wise motion The movement from a given note to another note that is directly above or below it on the staff.

strophe A verse or stanza in a song.

strophic A form in which the melody repeats while the words change from verse to verse.

style The particular character of a musical work; often indicated by words at the beginning of a composition, telling the performer the general manner in which the piece is to be performed.

subdominant chord A chord built on the fourth note of a scale. In a major scale, this chord uses the notes *fa, la* and *do*, and it may be called the **IV** ("four") chord, since it is based on the fourth note of the major scale, or *fa*. In a minor scale, this chord uses the notes *re, fa* and *la*, and it may be called the **iv** ("four") chord, since it is based on the fourth note of the minor scale, or *re*.

subito (sub.) *(SOO-bee-toh)* [It.] Suddenly.

suspension The holding over of one or more musical tones in a chord into the following chord, producing a momentary discord.

swing rhythms Rhythms in which the second eighth note of each beat is played or sung like the last third of triplet, creating an uneven, "swing" feel. A style often found in jazz and blues. Swing rhythms are usually indicated at the beginning of a song or section. (♫ = ♩ ♪ with triplet 3)

syllabic *See* syllabic singing.

syllabic singing A style of text setting in which one syllable is sung on each note.

syllabic stress The stressing of one syllable over another.

symphonic poem A single-movement work for orchestra, inspired by a painting, play or other literary or visual work. Franz Liszt was a prominent composer of symphonic poems. Also known as a tone poem.

symphony A large-scale work for orchestra.

syncopation The placement of accents on a weak beat or a weak portion of the beat, or on a note or notes that normally do not receive extra emphasis.

synthesizer A musical instrument that produces sounds electronically, rather than by the physical vibrations of an acoustic instrument.

T

tempo Terms in music that indicate how fast or slow to sing or play.

tempo I or tempo primo *See a tempo.*

tenor The highest-sounding male voice.

tenuto *(teh-NOO-toh)* [It.] A symbol placed above or below a given note indicating that the note should receive stress and/or that its value should be slightly extended.

text Words, usually set in a poetic style, that express a central thought, idea or narrative.

texture The thickness of the different layers of horizontal and vertical sounds.

theme A musical idea, usually a melody.

theme and variation form A musical form in which variations of the basic theme make up the composition.

third An interval of two pitches that are three notes apart on a staff.

tie A curved line used to connect two or more notes of the same pitch together in order to make one longer note.

tied notes Two or more notes of the same pitch connected together with a tie in order to make one longer note.

timbre The tone quality of a person's voice or musical instrument.

time signature The set of numbers at the beginning of a piece of music. The top number indicates the number of beats per measure. The bottom number indicates the kind of note that receives the beat. Time signature is sometimes called meter signature.

to coda Skip to (⊕) or CODA.

tone color That which distinguishes the voice or tone of one singer or instrument from another; for example, a soprano from an alto, or a flute from a clarinet. *See also timbre.*

tonic chord A chord built on the home tone, or keynote of a scale. In a major scale, this chord uses the notes *do, mi* and *sol*, and it may be called the **I** ("one") chord, since it is based on the first note of the major scale, or *do*. In a minor scale, this chord uses the notes *la, do* and *mi*, and it may be called the **i** ("one") chord, since it is based on the first note of the minor scale, or *la*.

treble clef A clef that generally indicates notes that sound higher than middle C.

trio A group of three singers or instrumentalists with usually one on a part.

triplet A group of notes in which three notes of equal duration are sung in the time normally given to two notes of equal duration.

troppo *(TROHP-oh)* [It.] Too much; for example, *allegro non troppo* ("not too fast").

tutti *(TOO-tee)* [It.] Meaning "all" or "together."

twelve-tone music A type of music that uses all twelve tones of the scale equally. Developed in the early twentieth century, Arnold Schoenberg is considered to be the pioneer of this style of music.

two-part music A type of music in which two different parts are sung or played.

U

unison All parts singing or playing the same notes at the same time.

V

variation A modification of a musical idea, usually after its initial appearance in a piece.

vivace *(vee-VAH-chay)* [It.] Very fast; lively.

vocal jazz A popular style of music characterized by strong prominent meter, improvisation and dotted or syncopated patterns. Sometimes sung *a cappella.*

W

whole note A note that represents four beats of sound when the quarter note receives the beat. 𝅝

whole rest A rest that represents four beats of silence when the quarter note receives the beat. ▬

whole step The combination of two successive half steps.

word painting A technique in which the music reflects the meaning of the words.

word stress The act of singing important parts of the text in a more accented style than the other parts.

Y

yoik A vocal tradition of the Sámi people of the Arctic region of Sampi that features short melodic phrases that are repeated with slight variations.

Classified Index

Music & History

Poetry

Seasonal, Patriotic

Listening Selections

Index of Songs and Spotlights

Spotlights